NetObjects Fusion™ 3 For Dummies®

COMPUTER
BOOK SERIES
FROM IDG

GW01080931

Interface basics

- Picture tool
- Text tool
- Zoom tool
- Selection tool
- Style view
- Page view
- Assets view
- Site view
- Publish view
- Go to last page
- Go to page
- Preview site/page
- Properties palette
- New page

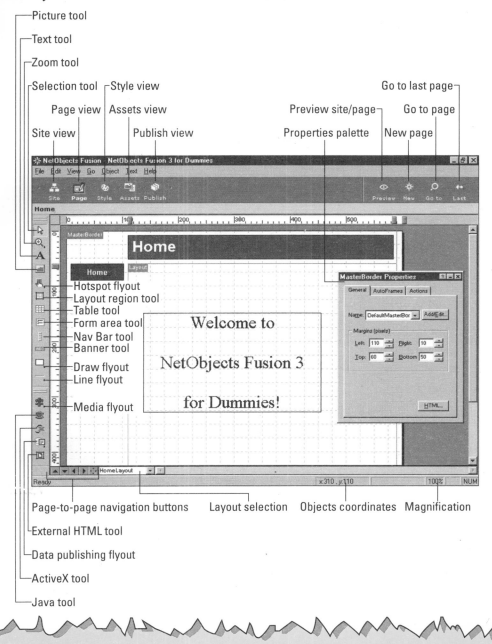

- Hotspot flyout
- Layout region tool
- Table tool
- Form area tool
- Nav Bar tool
- Banner tool
- Draw flyout
- Line flyout
- Media flyout

- Page-to-page navigation buttons
- Layout selection
- Objects coordinates
- Magnification

- External HTML tool
- Data publishing flyout
- ActiveX tool
- Java tool

...For Dummies: #1 Computer Book Series for Beginners

NetObjects Fusion™ 3 For Dummies®

Cheat Sheet

The Keyboard Shortcut Zone

Changing your view

To Do This	Press This
Go to Site view	Ctrl+1
Go to Page view	Ctrl+2
Go to Style view	Ctrl+3
Go to Assets view	Ctrl+4
Go to Publish view	Ctrl+5
Preview your site	Alt+P
Preview the current page	Ctrl+Alt+P

Site manipulation

To Do This	Press This
Open a site	Ctrl+O
Save your site	Ctrl+S
Save your site as	Ctrl+Shift+S
Create a new blank site	Ctrl+Shift+N
Exit the program	Alt+F4

Going from page to page in Page view

To Do This	Press This
Next page	Ctrl+right arrow
Previous page	Ctrl+left arrow
Parent page	Ctrl+up arrow
First child page	Ctrl+down arrow
Follow a link	Ctrl+Shift+K

Selecting this and that

To Do This	Press This
Select all	Ctrl+A
Select Layout properties	F9
Select MasterBorder properties	F10
Select Page properties	F11
Select next object	Tab
Select previous object	Shift+Tab

Grids and rulers

To Do This	Press This
Show rulers and guides	Ctrl+U
Snap to guides	Ctrl+Shift+U
Show grid	Ctrl+D
Snap to grids	Ctrl+Shift+D

Manipulating objects

To Do This	Press This
Hide an object	Ctrl+H
Show all objects	Ctrl+Shift+A
Size Layout to objects	Ctrl+Shift+L
Size MasterBorder to objects	Ctrl+Shift+M
Nudge an object	(any arrow key)

Miscellaneous

To Do This	Press This
Undo an action	Ctrl+Z
Redo an action	Ctrl+Y

...For Dummies: #1 Computer Book Series for Beginners

TM

References for the Rest of Us!®

BESTSELLING BOOK SERIES FROM IDG

Are you intimidated and confused by computers? Do you find that traditional manuals are overloaded with technical details you'll never use? Do your friends and family always call you to fix simple problems on their PCs? Then the *...For Dummies*® computer book series from IDG Books Worldwide is for you.

...For Dummies books are written for those frustrated computer users who know they aren't really dumb but find that PC hardware, software, and indeed the unique vocabulary of computing make them feel helpless. *...For Dummies* books use a lighthearted approach, a down-to-earth style, and even cartoons and humorous icons to diffuse computer novices' fears and build their confidence. Lighthearted but not lightweight, these books are a perfect survival guide for anyone forced to use a computer.

Already, millions of satisfied readers agree. They have made *...For Dummies* books the #1 introductory level computer book series and have written asking for more. So, if you're looking for the most fun and easy way to learn about computers, look to *...For Dummies* books to give you a helping hand.

TM

IDG BOOKS
WORLDWIDE

4/98

NETOBJECTS FUSION™ 3
FOR
DUMMIES®

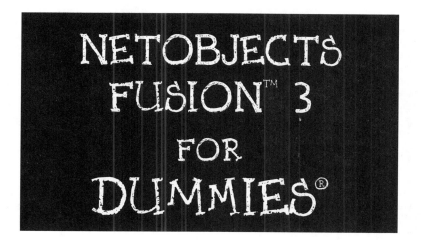

NETOBJECTS FUSION™ 3 FOR DUMMIES®

by John San Filippo

IDG
BOOKS
WORLDWIDE

IDG Books Worldwide, Inc.
An International Data Group Company

Foster City, CA ◆ Chicago, IL ◆ Indianapolis, IN ◆ New York, NY

NetObjects Fusion™ 3 For Dummies®

Published by
IDG Books Worldwide, Inc.
An International Data Group Company
919 E. Hillsdale Blvd.
Suite 400
Foster City, CA 94404
www.idgbooks.com (IDG Books Worldwide Web site)
www.dummies.com (Dummies Press Web site)

Library of Congress Catalog Card No.: 98-84660

ISBN: 0-7645-0236-0

Printed in the United States of America

10 9 8 7 6 5 4 3 2 1

1O/SZ/QV/ZY/IN

Distributed in the United States by IDG Books Worldwide, Inc.

Distributed by Macmillan Canada for Canada; by Transworld Publishers Limited in the United Kingdom; by IDG Norge Books for Norway; by IDG Sweden Books for Sweden; by Woodslane Pty. Ltd. for Australia; by Woodslane Enterprises Ltd. for New Zealand; by Longman Singapore Publishers Ltd. for Singapore, Malaysia, Thailand, and Indonesia; by Simron Pty. Ltd. for South Africa; by Toppan Company Ltd. for Japan; by Distribuidora Cuspide for Argentina; by Livraria Cultura for Brazil; by Ediciencia S.A. for Ecuador; by Addison-Wesley Publishing Company for Korea; by Ediciones ZETA S.C.R. Ltda. for Peru; by WS Computer Publishing Corporation, Inc., for the Philippines; by Unalis Corporation for Taiwan; by Contemporanea de Ediciones for Venezuela; by Computer Book & Magazine Store for Puerto Rico; by Express Computer Distributors for the Caribbean and West Indies. Authorized Sales Agent: Anthony Rudkin Associates for the Middle East and North Africa.

For general information on IDG Books Worldwide's books in the U.S., please call our Consumer Customer Service department at 800-762-2974. For reseller information, including discounts and premium sales, please call our Reseller Customer Service department at 800-434-3422.

For information on where to purchase IDG Books Worldwide's books outside the U.S., please contact our International Sales department at 650-655-3200 or fax 650-655-3295.

For information on foreign language translations, please contact our Foreign & Subsidiary Rights department at 650-655-3021 or fax 650-655-3281.

For sales inquiries and special prices for bulk quantities, please contact our Sales department at 650-655-3200 or write to the address above.

For information on using IDG Books Worldwide's books in the classroom or for ordering examination copies, please contact our Educational Sales department at 800-434-2086 or fax 817-251-8174.

For press review copies, author interviews, or other publicity information, please contact our Public Relations department at 650-655-3000 or fax 650-655-3299.

For authorization to photocopy items for corporate, personal, or educational use, please contact Copyright Clearance Center, 222 Rosewood Drive, Danvers, MA 01923, or fax 978-750-4470.

About the Author

John San Filippo first got the urge to be a writer in second grade. It wasn't until sixth grade that he became interested in computers — back when Bill Gates's biggest concern was still finding a Clearisil fix. John's been able to merge these interests into a hectic yet enjoyable career. When he's not writing computer books, he's busy as editor of *ComputorEdge* magazine, development editor for FileMaker Pro Advisor, and technology correspondent for The Credit Union Journal. In between, he still finds time to serve as president of the local Pop Warner youth football league. And against all reason, he still expects to fit in a crime novel some time in 1998. (Whether the book's ever actually published anywhere besides his Web site is another matter.)

ABOUT IDG BOOKS WORLDWIDE

Welcome to the world of IDG Books Worldwide.

IDG Books Worldwide, Inc., is a subsidiary of International Data Group, the world's largest publisher of computer-related information and the leading global provider of information services on information technology. IDG was founded more than 25 years ago and now employs more than 8,500 people worldwide. IDG publishes more than 275 computer publications in over 75 countries (see listing below). More than 90 million people read one or more IDG publications each month.

Launched in 1990, IDG Books Worldwide is today the #1 publisher of best-selling computer books in the United States. We are proud to have received eight awards from the Computer Press Association in recognition of editorial excellence and three from *Computer Currents'* First Annual Readers' Choice Awards. Our best-selling ...*For Dummies*® series has more than 50 million copies in print with translations in 38 languages. IDG Books Worldwide, through a joint venture with IDG's Hi-Tech Beijing, became the first U.S. publisher to publish a computer book in the People's Republic of China. In record time, IDG Books Worldwide has become the first choice for millions of readers around the world who want to learn how to better manage their businesses.

Our mission is simple: Every one of our books is designed to bring extra value and skill-building instructions to the reader. Our books are written by experts who understand and care about our readers. The knowledge base of our editorial staff comes from years of experience in publishing, education, and journalism — experience we use to produce books for the '90s. In short, we care about books, so we attract the best people. We devote special attention to details such as audience, interior design, use of icons, and illustrations. And because we use an efficient process of authoring, editing, and desktop publishing our books electronically, we can spend more time ensuring superior content and spend less time on the technicalities of making books.

You can count on our commitment to deliver high-quality books at competitive prices on topics you want to read about. At IDG Books Worldwide, we continue in the IDG tradition of delivering quality for more than 25 years. You'll find no better book on a subject than one from IDG Books Worldwide.

John Kilcullen
John Kilcullen
CEO
IDG Books Worldwide, Inc.

Steven Berkowitz
Steven Berkowitz
President and Publisher
IDG Books Worldwide, Inc.

Eighth Annual Computer Press Awards ≥ 1992

Ninth Annual Computer Press Awards ≥ 1993

Tenth Annual Computer Press Awards ≥ 1994

Eleventh Annual Computer Press Awards ≥ 1995

IDG Books Worldwide, Inc., is a subsidiary of International Data Group, the world's largest publisher of computer-related information and the leading global provider of information services on information technology. International Data Group publishes over 275 computer publications in over 75 countries. More than 90 million people read one or more International Data Group publications each month. International Data Group's publications include: **ARGENTINA:** Buyer's Guide, Computerworld Argentina, PC World Argentina; **AUSTRALIA:** Australian Macworld, Australian PC World, Australian Reseller News, Computerworld, IT Casebook, Network World, Publish, Webmaster; **AUSTRIA:** Computerwelt Österreich, Networks Austria, PC Tip Austria; **BANGLADESH:** PC World Bangladesh; **BELARUS:** PC World Belarus; **BELGIUM:** Data News; **BRAZIL:** Anuário de Informática, Computerworld, Connections, Macworld, PC Player, PC World, Publish, Reseller News, Supergamepower; **BULGARIA:** Computerworld Bulgaria, Network World Bulgaria, PC & MacWorld Bulgaria; **CANADA:** CIO Canada, Client/Server World, ComputerWorld Canada, InfoWorld Canada, NetworkWorld Canada, WebWorld; **CHILE:** Computerworld Chile, PC World Chile; **COLOMBIA:** Computerworld Colombia, PC World Colombia; **COSTA RICA:** PC World Centro America; **THE CZECH AND SLOVAK REPUBLICS:** Computerworld Czechoslovakia, Macworld Czech Republic, PC World Czechoslovakia; **DENMARK:** Communications World Danmark, Computerworld Danmark, Macworld Danmark, PC World Danmark, Techworld Denmark; **DOMINICAN REPUBLIC:** PC World Republica Dominicana; **ECUADOR:** PC World Ecuador; **EGYPT:** Computerworld Middle East, PC World Middle East; **EL SALVADOR:** PC World Centro America; **FINLAND:** MikroPC, Tietoverkko, Tietoviikko; **FRANCE:** Distributique, Hebdo, Info PC, Le Monde Informatique, Macworld, Reseaux & Telecoms, WebMaster France; **GERMANY:** Computer Partner, Computerwoche, Computerwoche Extra, Computerwoche FOCUS, Global Online, Macwelt, PC Welt; **GREECE:** Amiga Computing, GamePro Greece, Multimedia World; **GUATEMALA:** PC World Centro America; **HONDURAS:** PC World Centro America; **HONG KONG:** Computerworld Hong Kong, PC World Hong Kong, Publish in Asia; **HUNGARY:** ABCD CD-ROM, Computerworld Szamitastechnika, Internetto online Magazine, PC World Hungary, PC-X Magazin Hungary; **ICELAND:** Tolvuheimur PC World Island; **INDIA:** Information Communications World, Information Systems Computerworld, PC World India, Publish in Asia; **INDONESIA:** InfoKomputer PC World, Komputek Computerworld, Publish in Asia; **IRELAND:** ComputerScope, PC Live!; **ISRAEL:** Macworld Israel, People & Computers/Computerworld; **ITALY:** Computerworld Italia, Macworld Italia, Networking Italia, PC World Italia; **JAPAN:** DTP World, Macworld Japan, Nikkei Personal Computing, OS/2 World Japan, SunWorld Japan, Windows NT World, Windows World Japan; **KENYA:** PC World East African; **KOREA:** Hi-Tech Information, Macworld Korea, PC World Korea; **MACEDONIA:** PC World Macedonia; **MALAYSIA:** Computerworld Malaysia, PC World Malaysia, Publish in Asia; **MALTA:** PC World Malta; **MEXICO:** Computerworld Mexico, PC World Mexico; **MYANMAR:** PC World Myanmar; **NETHERLANDS:** Computer! Totaal, LAN Internetworking Magazine, LAN World Buyers Guide, Macworld Netherlands, Net, WebWereld; **NEW ZEALAND:** Absolute Beginners Guide and Plain & Simple Series, Computer Buyer, Computer Industry Directory, Computerworld New Zealand, MTB, Network World, PC World New Zealand; **NICARAGUA:** PC World Centro America; **NORWAY:** Computerworld Norge, CW Rapport, Datamagasinet, Financial Rapport, Kursguide Norge, Macworld Norge, Multimediaworld Norge, PC World Ekspress Norge, PC World Nettverk, PC World Norge, PC World ProduktGuide Norge; **PAKISTAN:** Computerworld Pakistan; **PANAMA:** PC World Panama; **PEOPLE'S REPUBLIC OF CHINA:** China Computer Users, China Computerworld, China Telecom World Weekly, Computer & Communication, Electronic Design China, Electronics Today, Electronics Weekly, Game Software, PC World China, Popular Computer Week, Software Weekly, Software World, Telecom World; **PERU:** Computerworld Peru, PC World Profesional Peru, PC World SoHo Peru; **PHILIPPINES:** Click!, Computerworld Philippines, PC World Philippines, Publish in Asia; **POLAND:** Computerworld Poland, Computerworld Special Report Poland, Cyber, Macworld Poland, Networld Poland, PC World Komputer; **PORTUGAL:** Cerebro/PC World, Computerworld/Correio Informático, Dealer World Portugal, Mac*In/PC*In Portugal, Multimedia World; **PUERTO RICO:** PC World Puerto Rico; **ROMANIA:** Computerworld Romania, PC World Romania, Telecom Romania; **RUSSIA:** Computerworld Russia, Mir PK, Publish, Seti; **SINGAPORE:** Computerworld Singapore, PC World Singapore, Publish in Asia; **SLOVENIA:** Monitor; **SOUTH AFRICA:** Computing SA, Network World SA, Software World SA; **SPAIN:** Communicaciones World España, Computerworld España, Dealer World España, Macworld España, PC World España; **SRI LANKA:** Infolink PC World; **SWEDEN:** CAP&Design, Computer Sweden, Corporate Computing Sweden, Internetworld Sweden, it.branschen, Macworld Sweden, MaxiData Sweden, MikroDatorn, Nätverk & Kommunikation, PC World Sweden, PCaktiv, Windows World Sweden; **SWITZERLAND:** Computerworld Schweiz, Macworld Schweiz, PCtip; **TAIWAN:** Computerworld Taiwan, Macworld Taiwan, NEW ViSiON/Publish, PC World Taiwan, Windows World Taiwan; **THAILAND:** Publish in Asia, Thai Computerworld; **TURKEY:** Computerworld Turkiye, Macworld Turkiye, Network World Turkiye, PC World Turkiye; **UKRAINE:** Computerworld Kiev, Multimedia World Ukraine, PC World Ukraine; **UNITED KINGDOM:** Acorn User UK, Amiga Action UK, Amiga Computing UK, Apple Talk UK, Computing, Macworld, Parents and Computers UK, PC Advisor, PC Home, PSX Pro, The WEB; **UNITED STATES:** Cable in the Classroom, CIO Magazine, Computerworld, DOS World, Federal Computer Week, GamePro Magazine, InfoWorld, I-Way, Macworld, Network World, PC Games, PC World, Publish, Video Event, THE WEB Magazine, and WebMaster; online webzines: JavaWorld, NetscapeWorld, and SunWorld Online; **URUGUAY:** InfoWorld Uruguay; **VENEZUELA:** Computerworld Venezuela, PC World Venezuela; and **VIETNAM:** PC World Vietnam. 5/7/98

Dedication

To Mom, who never experienced the joy and misery of publication in her own life, but who laid the foundation for me to do so in mine.

Author's Acknowledgments

I don't want to sound like some dork who just got his first Oscar, but in many ways, my entire career has led up to the publishing of this book. As such, many people have helped me out along the way, all of whom deserve a small bit of thanks.

Among them, in somewhat chronological order, are: Mike Corum, my PC mentor when I bought my first computer, a Tandy 1000HX; Jack Dunning and the other folks at *ComputorEdge,* who were kind enough to publish my first freelance article, and even kinder years later when they hired me as editor; Kim Komando, a good friend and fellow IDG author who has been a continual source of encouragement; my agent David Fugate, who said, "Yeah, I can help" when I said I wanted to write computer books; Nan Borreson, my NetObjects contact whose continued assistance helped keep the ball rolling on this project; Kyle Looper, my editor at IDG, who managed to keep his cool even when things didn't go exactly as planned; my good friend Mike Lowery (a.k.a., Partner A — or is it Partner B?) who did the tech edit on this book; and most of all, my wife Shelley and sons Vinnie and Derek, who tolerated (for the most part without complaint) the long hours I spent huddled in front of my computer to get this project out the door. To all of you, and to anyone I may have inadvertantly missed, I offer my sincerest thanks.

Publisher's Acknowledgments

We're proud of this book; please register your comments through our IDG Books Worldwide Online Registration Form located at http://my2cents.dummies.com.

Some of the people who helped bring this book to market include the following:

Acquisitions, Editorial, and Media Development

Project Editors: Kyle Looper, Colleen Williams

Senior Acquisitions Editor: Jill Pisoni

Copy Editor: Felicity O'Meara

Technical Editor: Mike Lowery

Media Development Technical Editor: Joell Smith

Associate Permissions Editor: Carmen Krikorian

Editorial Manager: Leah P. Cameron

Media Development Manager: Heather Heath Dismore

Editorial Assistant: Donna Love

Production

Associate Project Coordinator: Tom Missler

Layout and Graphics: Lou Boudreau, Maridee V. Ennis, Angela F. Hunckler, Jane E. Martin, Drew R. Moore, Brent Savage, Janet Seib, and Michael A. Sullivan

Proofreaders: Kelli Botta, Sally Burton, Michelle Croninger, Nancy Price, Rebecca Senninger, Janet M. Withers

Indexer: Sherry Massey

General and Administrative

IDG Books Worldwide, Inc.: John Kilcullen, CEO; Steven Berkowitz, President and Publisher

IDG Books Technology Publishing: Brenda McLaughlin, Senior Vice President and Group Publisher

Dummies Technology Press and Dummies Editorial: Diane Graves Steele, Vice President and Associate Publisher; Mary Bednarek, Director of Acquisitions and Product Development; Kristin A. Cocks, Editorial Director

Dummies Trade Press: Kathleen A. Welton, Vice President and Publisher; Kevin Thornton, Acquisitions Manager

IDG Books Production for Dummies Press: Michael R. Britton, Vice President of Production; Beth Jenkins Roberts, Production Director; Cindy L. Phipps, Manager of Project Coordination, Production Proofreading, and Indexing; Kathie S. Schutte, Supervisor of Page Layout; Shelley Lea, Supervisor of Graphics and Design; Debbie J. Gates, Production Systems Specialist; Robert Springer, Supervisor of Proofreading; Debbie Stailey, Special Projects Coordinator; Tony Augsburger, Supervisor of Reprints and Bluelines; Leslie Popplewell, Media Archive Coordinator

Dummies Packaging and Book Design: Robin Seaman, Creative Director; Jocelyn Kelaita, Product Packaging Coordinator; Kavish + Kavish, Cover Design

◆

The publisher would like to give special thanks to Patrick J. McGovern, without whom this book would not have been possible.

◆

Contents at a Glance

Cartoons at a Glance

By Rich Tennant

"Hold your horses. It takes time to build a home page for someone your size."

page 63

page 245

"What do you mean you're updating our Web Homepage?"

page 153

"YOU KNOW KIDS — YOU CAN'T BUY THEM JUST ANY WEB AUTHORING SOFTWARE."

page 7

"He found a dog site over an hour ago and has been in a staring contest ever since."

page 319

page 297

Fax: 978-546-7747 • **E-mail:** the5wave@tiac.net

Table of Contents

Introduction

*I*t wasn't too many years ago that I began hearing about this great, new "thing" called the Internet. Everyone who used it raved about it. But quite frankly, none of these people — at least the ones I talked to — could ever quite put their finger on *why* they thought it was so great. I'd had accounts at America Online and CompuServe and could understand how anything else, especially something so uncontrolled, could be significantly better.

Then people started talking about this new "sub-thing" called the World Wide Web. How great could that be? Whoever invented it didn't even know how to spell. Everybody knows that *worldwide* is one word, right?

Well, curiosity finally got the best of me, and I opened my first Internet account with a local service provider. Wow! Suddenly I was the one who couldn't quite convey my excitement to my uninitiated friends. Suddenly I was the one who wondered how I'd ever gotten along without the Internet. And that World Wide Web! Who cares about the spelling? It was extremely cool, even back then when you only had text and still graphics.

I've never been a code geek, so the thought of tediously scripting an HTML page didn't hold much appeal for me. But before I knew it, shareware programs designed to simplify Web authoring started popping up left and right. I latched onto one of them and shortly thereafter became one of the code geeks my parents warned me about.

Still, in my previous life as the manager of a marketing communications department, I was used to programs like PageMaker. In short, I was used to WYSIWYG (what you see is what you get). Handy as my shareware Web tool was, it couldn't compare with the ease of creating a page in PageMaker. Then along came PageMill, which was to the best of my knowledge the world's first mass-market WYSIWYG Web authoring package. I was hooked again (and I even ended up co-authoring *PageMill 2 For Dummies*).

I loved PageMill for its simplicity (and in fact, I still do), but for better or worse, the Web is no longer a simple place. It's gone from simple to sophisticated, clean to complex, and miniature to monstrous in record time. These days, that simple little Web page you created with PageMill doesn't always cut it.

Just as I was beginning to feel the need for something more in Web authoring tools, I read about a program called NetObjects Fusion. At the time, version 2 had just shown up on store shelves. When I got my copy, I was in for another *wow*. Not only could NetObjects Fusion 2 do more than any program I'd tried before; it made incredibly easy work of it.

But times change, and on the Web, they change much faster than elsewhere. The 4.*x* browsers (the collective term for both Microsoft Internet Explorer 4.*x* and Netscape Navigator 4.*x*) brought with them many new capabilities that older Web authoring tools simply weren't designed to take advantage of.

That brings me to NetObjects Fusion 3, a dynamite package that quite honestly in my opinion deserves a spot in the best-of-class category. And believe me, I should know. I've probably tried a couple of dozen Web authoring tools since I first set cyber foot on the Web. If you can think of it, Fusion 3 can probably do it — and easily at that.

Why the history lesson? I want to make a couple of points up front. First of all, I want you to realize that I've been around long enough and used enough Web programs to offer a well informed opinion. Second, I want to make it clear that I didn't take on this project just because I had a chance to write another book. Fusion 3 is a product I believe in. For the money, I don't think you'll find a better, more flexible, more powerful, more easy to use program anywhere.

If you still have your doubts about investing in NetObjects Fusion, at least invest the small amount that this book will cost you. The CD at the back of the book includes a fully functioning time-limited trial version of NetObjects Fusion 3. Take the book home, give NetObjects Fusion a try, and see for yourself that this program is really the Big Kahuna of Web authoring that I claim it is.

About This Book

You're probably a pretty busy individual. You want to cut to the chase and get your Web pages up and running in the shortest amount of time. If so, you're in luck. NetObjects Fusion is the program for you, and this book is the guide for you.

NetObjects Fusion 3 For Dummies is different because it's a reference unlike any other. You don't necessarily need to read all the chapters to understand what's going on. Say you've already figured out the basics of how to get stuff onto your Web page and now need to know how to create links. No problemo. Just look it up, read all about it, and start creating those links! It's that easy!

Foolish Assumptions

Let's face it. If you got this far, you obviously didn't buy your computer yesterday. I have to believe that you've had at least a modicum of experience at least browsing the Web. (Web creation experience is definitely *not* a prerequisite.) And I also can't help but assume that you know how to do a few basic tasks in Windows, like click the Start button or open a file from within an application. If you meet these minimum requirements, you're ready for some Web action with NetObjects Fusion.

What's in This Book?

There's no doubt about it. NetObjects Fusion 3 is very easy to use. Yet, the results it produces can be quite sophisticated. And that's where a little confusion may creep in. Don't worry. My singular goal in writing this book has been to create a resource that walks you through the wonderful world of NetObjects Fusion. If you don't fully understand something at first, just follow the steps I provide. Somewhere along the way, I guarantee you'll stop and say, "Gee, now I get it."

To help make sense of it all, I've divided the chapters into what I believe are logical chunks. Although I've attempted to create a resource that allows you to jump in at any point you feel comfortable, you quite understandably need to know the basics before you can use some of the advanced features of NetObjects Fusion. With that said, here's a brief description of each of these chunks.

Part I: Getting Going on Your First Web Site

Unless your goal is to become a shark trainer or cliff diver, the best way to figure out anything is to jump right in. Because NetObjects Fusion looks at your Web site as a whole (versus other pages that focus on a collection of separate Web pages), the easiest way to get going is to create a site and then worry about what goes in it later. In this first part of the book, I explain the various options you have for creating a new NetObjects Fusion site — or a fusionized version of any old site you may having lurking around your hard drive.

Part II: The Site Is the Castle, but the Page Is King

NetObjects Fusion makes it easy to develop a complex site with a minimum effort. Yet, it's the individual pages that visitors to your site will encounter. And it's the content of those pages upon which those visitors are likely to judge both you and your site. With that thought in mind, Part II covers how to get some common HTML stuff — text, graphics, links, and so on — onto your pages. If you have anything more than a little experience creating Web pages, you may be able to figure a lot of this out for yourself.

Part III: Advanced Goodies to Put on Your Page

In all honesty, putting text and graphics on a Web page is not a phenomenal task for even the most meager of Web authoring tools. It's the more complex page elements that really separate the big dogs from the pups. This is an area where NetObjects Fusion really shines. The two most exciting things that fall into this category are NetObjects Components (mini applications that you can add right to your Web pages to jazz them up) and data publishing (its ability to quickly and easy publish an entire database of information with just a few mouse clicks). You'll find some powerful stuff in this part.

Part IV: Other Views You Can Use

When you're working in NetObjects Fusion, you work in different *views*, depending on what you're doing at the time. For example, most of the things I cover in Part I take place in the Site view. Parts II and III primarily address the Page view. Part IV address the remaining views: the Style view, where you can customize the look of your site; the Assets view, where you can manage the various elements that make up your site; and the Publish view, where you prepare your site for publishing on the Web — and then publish right from within NetObjects Fusion.

Part V: The Part of Tens

This section represents my personal top-ten lists for NetObjects Fusion users, and often for Web designers in general. I'll admit, mine aren't as funny as Letterman's, but I assure you they're much more useful.

Part VI: Appendixes

NetObjects Fusion makes managing your Web site a breeze, but it can't give you a Web presence by itself. You also have to deal with an Internet Service Provider (ISP) before you can publish your Web pages. Appendix A gives you the scoop on finding an ISP, registering your domain name, and other nuts-and-bolts issues.

Appendix B outlines the content of the amazing, spectacular, wonderful, never-before-seen-on-the-face-of-this-planet CD that comes with the book.

Icons Used in This Book

 This icon indicates the technical stuff you can skip if you want to stick to the basics.

 Tips provide helpful hints on saving time and effort.

 When you see this, remember what it says. It's pretty important.

 Definitely look at this icon when you come across one. It'll save you lots of time and heartache.

 Watch for valuable content you can find on the *NetObjects Fusion 3 For Dummies* CD-ROM.

Where to Go from Here

It would be impossible to include in this book everything you could possibly do with NetObjects Fusion. That's actually good news, because the reason is that with NetObjects Fusion, the possibilities are infinite. I'd like to close this introduction with one final bit of advice.

NetObjects is tops at creating great software. And the company's also tops at taking care of their customers. If you finish this book and still want to know more, I urge you to visit the NetObjects Web site at www.netobjects.com. This Web site has one of the best customer support centers I've seen anywhere, and it's constantly updated, meaning that you'll be able to turn there for current information long after the pages of this book have yellowed.

Part I
Getting Going on
Your First Web Site

The 5th Wave   By Rich Tennant

"YOU KNOW KIDS — YOU CAN'T BUY THEM JUST ANY WEB AUTHORING SOFTWARE."

In this part . . .

*N*etObjects Fusion is different from most other Web authoring tools in that it concentrates on your site as a whole. In most other programs, you start a site by creating a page, adding content, and then moving on to another page to repeat the process. However, in NetObjects Fusion, you start a site by, well . . . starting the site. You decide the basic structure of the site — which you can easily change later — and create the pages you think you'll need at the same time. Then you can direct your attention to the content of each page. I think this "big picture" approach gives you a much better grasp on exactly what you're doing and how to design an effective site.

This part opens with an overview of the capabilities of NetObjects Fusion just to make sure everyone is on the same page, so to speak. Then it moves on to the various ways you can create a site in NetObjects Fusion. You have three options: You can create a site completely from scratch, you can create a site using one of the templates provided with NetObjects Fusion, or you can import a site that you or someone else has created in some other program. A separate chapter is devoted to each of these techniques.

Chapter 1

Why NetObjects Fusion Packs the Knockout Punch

* *

In This Chapter

▶ Simplifying Web site management with NetObjects Fusion

▶ Controlling object placement precisely

▶ An overview of MasterBorders

▶ Auto-creating navigational aids

▶ Updating sites and links automatically

▶ Uploading a site to a Web server

* *

*W*hile the World Wide Web will never bite your ear off, it can be one tough contender. The last thing you want to do is go into the Web ring unprepared or with the wrong equipment. With NetObjects Fusion in your corner, you have everything you need to be the heavyweight champion of the Web.

NetObjects Fusion gives you unmatched muscle in three key areas: precision layout, automation, and total site management. That combination gives you the power to create exactly the Web site you want in as short a time as possible.

NetObjects is poised to deliver the knock-out punch to the other Web authoring programs on the market. In this chapter, I give you a peek at some of the secret moves that will help the program on its quest for ultimate victory.

Flexing Site Management Muscle

Visit the Web site for any major high tech company, say Microsoft (www.microsoft.com) or Apple (www.apple.com) and you can't help but be amazed at how many volumes of information are presented to you in a neat, orderly fashion. The information on these sites changes daily and using the Web authoring tools of the old days (say a year or two ago), it would be literally impossible to maintain such a site.

Thanks to NetObjects Fusion (and your wise decision to invest in it), you have at your fingertips the tools you need to automate the vast majority of site management tasks so that you can devote your time and efforts to what's really important: creating a great Web site.

Taking a look at your site

Figure 1-1 shows a sample of the NetObjects Fusion Site view, a way of looking at your Web site as a whole so you can see exactly how it's laid out and make changes accordingly.

The *NetObjects Fusion 3 For Dummies* CD-ROM comes with a 30-day trial version of NetObjects Fusion 3. So even if you don't own the most current version of NetObjects Fusion, you can still follow along with all the steps in this book!

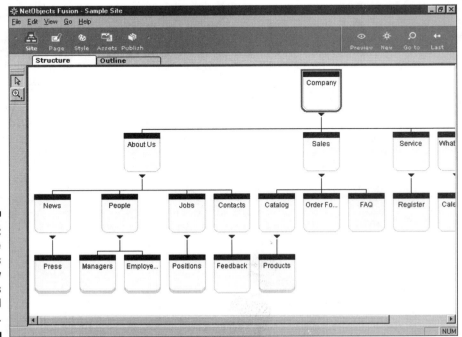

Figure 1-1:
The Site
view lets
you view
your site's
hierarchical
structure.

If you don't like what you see, you can just drag pages around and put them wherever you want. You'll find out all the ins and outs in Chapter 2, but take a moment now to get a sneak peek.

1. Turn on your computer and start NetObjects Fusion.

If you did a normal installation of NetObjects Fusion, you have the option of going through the Start menu or simply double-clicking on the NetObjects Fusion 3.0 shortcut that appears on your Windows desktop. The choice is yours.

Assuming that this is the first time you've used NetObjects Fusion, the program gives you the option to create a new site or open an existing one, as shown in Figure 1-2. If you've already fiddled around in NetObjects Fusion, the program automatically opens whatever site you already created. If that's the case, you can skip to Step 4.

Figure 1-2:
This is
where it all
begins.

2. Click the Blank Site radio button and then click OK.

Actually, you don't need to click; the Blank Site button is selected by default.

Now it's time to name your site, as you can see from Figure 1-3.

Figure 1-3:
You can
give your
site any
name you
want.

3. **Type** My First Fusion Site **or some other name that you like in the field provided and then click Open.**

   You're now in the Site view with your lone home page displayed.

4. **Click the New Page button in the taskbar at the top of your screen.**

   This creates a new, untitled page below your home page.

5. **Click the word** Untitled **in the icon that represents your new page.**

   The word becomes highlighted, giving you the opportunity to change the page's name.

6. **Type in** One.

7. **Now click the New Page button again.**

   Another new page appears below your One page. It too is untitled.

8. **Click the word** Untitled **again and name this page** Two.

   Now you've created a Web site with three levels in its hierarchy. You have your home page; below that is page One and below that page is page Two. But suppose you don't like that page order. Suppose, for example, that what you really wanted to do was have pages One and Two on the same level in the hierarchy.

9. **Click and hold your left mouse button on the page** Two **icon and drag it over the page** One **icon.**

   As you do, notice the red line that appears around the page One icon. If you drag to the left of the icon, a red arrow pops out of the left side; as you drag to the right, the red arrow pops out of the right side. Check Figure 1-5 to see what I mean.

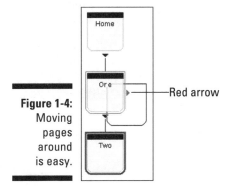

Figure 1-4:
Moving
pages
around
is easy.

10. When you see the red arrow popping out of the right side, release your mouse button.

Before you can say *pepperoni*, page Two has changed its relative position. That's what I call easy.

And if you prefer to view your site in an outline format, you can do that, too. Just click the Outline tab at the top of the window, as shown in Figure 1-5. Outline view gives you a different way to look at essentially the same information. You're free to use whichever Site view option you find easiest to work with.

The amazing thing is that as you drag pages here and there, NetObjects Fusion automatically modifies any links you made to those pages. You never have to worry about going through your pages one-by-one to make sure all your links are still intact.

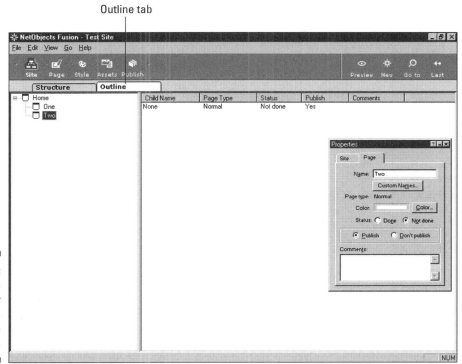

Figure 1-5: Click here to see your site in Outline mode.

Linking the easy way

Of course, there's more to your Web site than just the individual pages. Within those pages are graphics, links, multimedia elements, and what-not. Just keeping track of all those elements could prove to be an impossible task if you had to do it yourself. As you may have guessed, you don't have to, thanks to your trusty assistant, NetObjects Fusion.

Consider links, for example. I cover these thoroughly in Chapter 8, but I want to take a moment here just to show you how easy they are.

In most Web authoring programs, if you want to link to another page within your site, you at least have to know the name of the HTML file that contains that page. Furthermore, if that file happens to reside in a different folder than the file you're linking from, you need to know the path from one file to another. If you don't understand exactly what I mean, don't worry. The whole point here is that when you're using NetObjects Fusion, you don't have to know any of this stuff.

Take a look at Figure 1-6. This is the dialog box you see when you create a link.

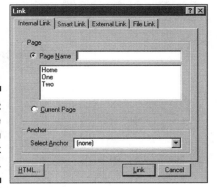

Figure 1-6:
You create
links from
this Link
dialog box.

As you can see, this dialog box displays a list of the names of all the pages on your Web site. Instead of wondering about filenames and paths, all you have to do is click on the page you want to link to. NetObjects Fusion does the rest.

Also take note of the Smart Link and External Link tabs on this dialog box. In Chapter 8, I explain how to use these two options to create relative links (for example, to the next page up from the current page) and links to pages on other Web sites, all with minimum effort. The File Link option allows you to create links to Web pages that you've created with programs other than NetObjects Fusion.

Asset management that puts your broker to shame

In NetObjects Fusion, graphics, links, multimedia objects, and other such elements are collectively called *assets*. And the bigger and more complicated your site becomes, the harder it gets to keep track of these various assets. Once again, it's NetObjects Fusion to the rescue — this time with its Assets view, which I cover in detail in Chapter 17.

Figure 1-7 shows an example of the Assets view. In this particular instance, I've elected to display the Files list; you can also display Links, DataObjects (covered in Chapter 15) and Variables (covered in Chapter 6). If you still have your little test site displayed on your computer, you can click on the Assets button and see for yourself (although you won't see all that much).

Why is this such a big deal? Well, suppose you've had your company Web site up for a couple of months when the new marketing director decides that the company logo needs a make-over. If you have a few dozen pages on your site with the company logo strategically placed on each, this new logo could mean trouble in the hands of a lesser software package. In a fusionless world, you'd have to go to each page and manually replace each old logo with the new one. On the other hand, using the Assets view, you can tell

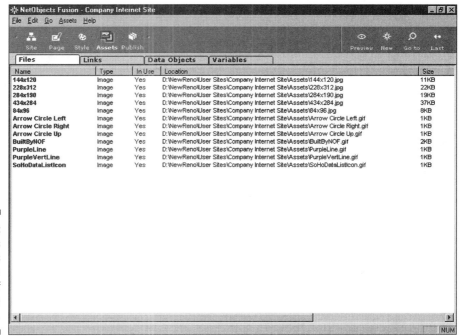

Figure 1-7: The Assets view lets you see a list of all site elements.

NetObjects Fusion to replace every old logo with the new logo throughout the entire site. In short, this can mean the difference between a few seconds' work and a few hours' work.

The Quark XPress of Web Authoring

From a design standpoint, one of the greatest shortcomings of HTML is that it doesn't offer much in terms of the precise placement of objects on a page. If you have desktop publishing experience with programs like Quark XPress or Adobe PageMaker, you're likely to find this aspect of Web authoring quite frustrating — that is, at least until you get going with NetObjects Fusion.

You see, HTML code is all just a series of text characters that your Web browser (for example, Microsoft Internet Explorer or Netscape Navigator) knows how to interpret and display in a graphical format. Most Web authoring programs generate HTML code on the fly, so that when you insert a particular element on a page, the HTML code for that element just gets plopped in the middle of whatever elements are already there. While the current version of HTML does offer some control over the relative alignment and placement of elements, it can hardly be described as precise.

Creating Web pages with NetObjects Fusion gives you much better control over the placement of each element than any program I've seen. Instead of creating HTML code on the fly, the Web pages you initially create in NetObjects Fusion are saved in a proprietary format and aren't converted to HTML until you *publish* your site, which I cover in Chapter 18. This means that as you're working on any given Web page, NetObjects Fusion lets you position various elements (graphics, text blocks, etc.) independent of each other. In other words, NetObjects Fusion provides for the very precise placement of each element.

In NetObjects Fusion, you can move or alter any object or element on your page without affecting any of the other elements. In a typical Web authoring program, moving an element causes any element that comes after it to shift its position.

Wait a second here! Something's wrong. If the pages you create in NetObjects Fusion are ultimately converted to HTML code, any page layout you create in NetObjects Fusion must be able to be duplicated with standard HTML code, right? In fact, that's absolutely correct. Here's where I let you in on the secret trick used by NetObjects Fusion.

A couple of years ago, Web developers became dismayed by the fact that HTML offered no provision for formatting tabular data. The only way to create a table of information was to use a monospaced typeface and separate the "cells" of data with spaces. Pretty low-tech, eh? There had to be a better way.

Mama-mia! It's web pizza!

I've been on the Internet and fiddling around with Web pages for a few years now. Given that the Web itself isn't all that old, I suppose that makes me something of a Web veteran. Considering my Italian last name, *San Filippo,* it probably comes as no great surprise that I'm also a veteran of eating pizza. In fact, I've been doing that for just about as long as I can remember. My earliest memories of family get-togethers include an extra-large pizza with the works from the Grapevine, a restaurant a couple of blocks from our home in Jamestown, New York.

With veteran status in both of these thoroughly enjoyable activities, I can't help but notice how similar Web sites are to pizza. Think I'm nuts? Just give me a chance here.

Just like pizzas, all Web sites are built from the same basic ingredients. The difference from one Web site to the next (and one pizza to the next) is exactly how those ingredients are combined to create the finished product.

Over the years, I've come to realize that one pizza parlor can combine relatively few ingredients to create a truly delicious masterpiece, while another pizza parlor may pile the works to the ceiling and end up with a pizza I wouldn't feed to my dachshund, JJ. The reverse is also true: You can combine just a few ingredients and come up with a pizza that can only be described as boring. Or, you may have a knack for adding everything but the kitchen sink and creating a remarkable culinary delight.

If you've spent any time at all on the Web, you've undoubtedly come across Web sites that equate with the different kinds of pizzas I just described. Some of them are lean and mean; others are lean and lame. Some are packed with so much great stuff, you can hardly believe your luck in finding the site; others are packed with so much stuff, your eyeballs and your modem explode simultaneously.

Thus was born a new component of HTML called *tables.* By using the appropriate code for HTML tables, which I discuss in Chapter 10, you can format data into neat, little rows and columns with no problem.

Well, some time between then and now, Web developers realized that they could exercise greater control over element placement by putting those elements within the cells of invisible tables. (By *invisible tables,* I mean tables with no visible borders.) They further realized that placement could be even more precise by creating *nested tables,* that is, tables within other tables.

The folks at NetObjects have taken this approach to its ultimate implementation. When you lay out a complicated Web page in NetObjects Fusion and then publish it, NetObjects Fusion automatically converts your layout to whatever combination of HTML tables are necessary to preserve your original layout.

Furthermore, with NetObjects Fusion 3.0, the folks at NetObjects have also given you Cascading Style Sheets (CSS) as an alternative to nested tables. CSS is a new Web standard incorporated into 4.*x* and later browsers from Netscape and Microsoft. Among other things, CSS allows for precise element placement by specifying exact pixel coordinates in the HTML.

So, sure, you could create the same pages you create in NetObjects Fusion in any other Web authoring program. However, it would probably take weeks of fiddling and diddling to achieve the same results that NetObjects Fusion does in a few minutes. Why bother?

Versions 4.*x* and later of both Internet Explorer and Navigator provide support for Cascading Style Sheets (CSS). Using CSS is fine for, say, a corporate intranet where you're sure everyone is using the same browser. However, given the newness of CSS and its incompatibility with older browsers, I currently recommend using the standard "table" approach for sites you plan to publish for a global audience. I explain more about this in Chapter 2.

You're the Master of the Border

Let me jump back to my pizza metaphor for a moment. If you have any taste at all for pizza, you probably have your favorite pizza parlor (even if it's some huge chain like Pizza Hut). The reason you go back to that same pizza parlor time after time is because they make pizza the way you like it and they do it consistently. You don't have to worry about getting too many mushrooms this time and not enough cheese the next time. In other words, you're assured of a pizza with the same look and feel each time you place an order.

Web surfers expect consistency in your Web site just like you expect consistent pizzas from your favorite pizza parlor. For the novice Web designer, there's a real temptation to make every page look different just because it's so easy to do. It's an opportunity to show some real creative flair. It's also an opportunity to look like a rookie.

If people visit your site and discover a different look and feel on every page, I can guarantee that most of the time, the awe you hope to inspire will be confusion instead. Your visitors will feel lost, as if they took a wrong turn somewhere, and chances are they'll opt for a quick U-turn right out of your Web site.

The point I'm trying to make is that it's very important to give your entire site a consistent look and feel. Naturally, I wouldn't bring that up now if NetObjects Fusion didn't make doing so a snap. Of course, it does.

One of the most useful means by which NetObjects Fusion enables you to maintain that consistent look and feel is with MasterBorders, which I cover thoroughly in Chapter 5. If you've worked with a page layout program, or even a word processor, you've most certainly encountered margins, headers, and footers. A margin is the empty space on either side of the document body, while headers and footers give you the opportunity to place text and objects uniformly on the top and bottom of every page in the document.

A MasterBorder is like a header, a footer, and the margins all rolled into one. The big difference between a Master Border and, for example, a word processor, is that you can freely place elements anywhere in a MasterBorder, including the side areas, which would normally be considered to be in the margin.

Creating Graphical Links on the Fly

Your site can include the most amazing content on the World Wide Web, but if visitors find it difficult to navigate from one page to another, they're likely to look elsewhere on the Internet for the information they need. That means that a first-rate site provides convenient navigational aids on each and every page within the site. Maybe I sound like a broken record by now, but this is another area where NetObjects Fusion excels.

NavBars to the rescue

One of the most common navigational aids you'll find on the Web is what NetObjects Fusion calls a NavBar (see Chapter 8). As shown in Figure 1-8, a NavBar is a grouping of buttons, each of which provides a link to a different page. The links usually lead to other pages on the same hierarchical level.

Figure 1-8:
A NavBar helps you find your way around.

One of the most amazing things about NavBars is that NetObjects Fusion automatically adjusts them as you add and delete pages. Go back to the test site you created earlier in this chapter. When you left off, you were still in Site view. Now double-click on the icon for the home page. This automatically pops you into Page view for the home page.

Take a look at the NavBar on the left side of the page. It includes the two pages you created, plus the home page. Wow! You didn't have to do anything to make that happen.

However, the NavBar can also help you know where you currently are. Notice that the dot above the word *Company* in the previous figure appears in a different shade than the others. (In color, this dot is red, where the rest are black.) This lets you know that this is the current page; click on this button in the NavBar and nothing happens.

I think you can imagine how difficult it is to create a new NavBar from scratch for each page on your site. Fortunately, NetObjects Fusion lets you create one in just a few seconds and a couple of mouse clicks. Once you create the NavBar, you can control it as a single element.

Map to the stars

Another handy navigational aid is what's commonly called a site map. This is a separate page on your site that shows its complete layout in a graphical format.

If you place a link to your site map on alternating pages, that means that no two pages are more than two mouse clicks away from each other, regardless of their relative locations in the structure of your site. No matter where you are, you click once to get to the site map and once more to get to the page you want.

Creating a single site map from scratch can be a big enough pain, but suppose your site changes frequently. You could end up spending all your valuable time just making sure your site map is current.

Luckily, one of the NetObjects Components (which are all covered in Chapter 13) is called the SiteMapper. When you add this Component to your site, it automatically handles the creation and updating of your site map. No matter how many changes you make, SiteMapper knows and makes all the appropriate adjustments.

No Fuss, No Muss When You Make Changes

I've already mentioned a few of the ways that NetObjects Fusion makes changing your site easy, but I really want to drive the point home. Most successful sites (not necessarily financially, but at least in terms of user activity) are the ones that are continually updated. Typical Web surfers don't want stale information; they want up-to-the-minute information and they want it now.

The more complicated your Web site, the bigger the challenge to keep the whole shebang current. The premise of NetObjects Fusion in respect to site modification and maintenance is that you should only have to make changes once.

That means that if you happen to change the name of a particular page, NetObjects Fusion automatically changes the page's name in all of the NavBars that link to that page. If the Web address for some external link changes, you change it once and the address is updated on every page that offers a link to that site.

I could go on and on with examples like this, but I think you get the picture. No matter how many changes you need to make and how complicated they are, I personally guarantee that NetObjects Fusion will help you implement those changes in the absolute least number of steps possible.

FTP This!

After you've finished working on your cyber masterpiece (*finished* being a relative term, because a good Web site is never really finished), you have to get it from your computer to a Web server. The *Web server* is the computer that serves as the gateway between your Web site and the rest of the online world. This transfer is normally accomplished using an Internet feature known as File Transfer Protocol, or ftp. This is the same technique that you use to download files from various sites around the Internet.

Many Web authoring programs leave you on your own when it comes to uploading your site to its new home, requiring you to supply your own ftp program and identify which files actually need to be uploaded. Such is not the case with NetObjects Fusion. Instead, NetObjects Fusion automates the entire process with its built-in ftp-upload capabilities.

You tell NetObjects Fusion some basic information about how to find your intended Web server. Then during the publishing stage (see Chapter 18), NetObjects Fusion figures out exactly which files are needed, connects to your Web server, and puts all of the files where they belong.

The instant that this process is complete, your Web site is ready for the entire world to see.

Okay. You have the tools (definitely). You have the talent (hopefully). The bell for the first round is about to ring. Just come out swinging and show 'em your stuff.

Chapter 2

The Basics of Site Creation

In This Chapter

▶ Creating a simple Web site

▶ Getting around in the NetObjects Fusion Site view

▶ Adding and deleting pages

▶ Renaming pages

▶ Adding some finishing touches

*W*ith most Web publishing programs, you start your Web site project by sitting down with a paper and pencil and mapping out a flow chart of exactly how you want your site to be organized. With NetObjects Fusion, however, you can keep all those pencils stashed securely in your desk! NetObjects Fusion provides you with all the tools you need to do every inch of your design work right on your computer, including that preliminary planning.

NetObjects Fusion comes with all sorts of goodies that make Web-site creation easier and your Web site more visually pleasing. Before you jump into all those extras, however, you need to know the basics of creating and modifying a Web site in NetObjects Fusion. That's what this chapter delivers!

Creating a Web Site

Chances are you've already created some sort of Web site in NetObjects Fusion, but I'll walk you through the steps just to make sure that you and I are on the same page (excuse the lame pun).

1. **Turn on your computer and start NetObjects Fusion.**

   If you did a normal installation of NetObjects Fusion, you have the option of going through the Start menu or simply double-clicking the NetObjects Fusion 3.0 shortcut that appears on your Windows desktop.

If you've created a site previously, NetObjects Fusion opens that site at whatever point you left it. If you've never created a Web site, NetObjects Fusion brings up the Welcome to NetObjects Fusion dialog box, which asks you to create or open a new site.

2. **Choose File➪New Site➪Blank Site.**

   You can also use Ctrl+N to create a new blank site.

   NetObjects Fusion displays a New Blank Site dialog box, as shown in Figure 2-1, and prompts you to type in a file name for your new site. You can use just about any name you want; you're allowed to use spaces, punctuation, and so on.

Figure 2-1:
Give your
site a name.

You also have the opportunity at this point to specify the exact location on your hard drive where you want to store the files for your new site. The default location is a NetObjects subfolder called User Sites. Although you can specify any location you want, I believe the User Sites folder is a good choice.

3. **Type in a name for your new site and click the Save button in the lower-right corner of the dialog box.**

   NetObjects Fusion displays your new site with its lone home page in the Site view. If your new site doesn't appear in Site view, click the Site view button at the top of the page to switch over.

Note that you can only have one site open at a time. Any time you open or create a new site while another site is already open, NetObjects Fusion takes a few seconds to close and compact (clean up unnecessary stuff) the open site. Exactly how long this takes depends on the speed of your computer, so just be patient.

Take special notice of the Properties palette that most likely appeared somewhere on the right side of the screen. If you don't see the Properties palette, choose Window➪Properties Palette, or simply press Ctrl+U.

This little palette is destined to become one of your closest allies as you create Web sites in NetObjects Fusion. Depending on exactly what view you're in and what you're doing, you can access almost all of your options from the Properties palette.

Adding Pages — Moving and Deleting Too!

Every Web site starts with a *home page,* the first page that people encounter when they visit your Web site. The rest of your site is arranged in a hierarchy (which rhymes with malarkey). *Hierarchy* is a word that Web nerds and computer geeks use to impress each other (and bore everyone else). It basically means that something is grouped in ranks, with some things above others and some things below others. If you've ever bothered to look at your company's org chart, you know what I'm talking about. In the case of your Web site, you can have one or more pages directly below your home page in this hierarchy, one or more pages below each of those pages, and so on.

For example, if you were to visit my personal Web site (www.info-wave.com/js) today, you'd see a little information about me on my home page, as shown in Figure 2-2.

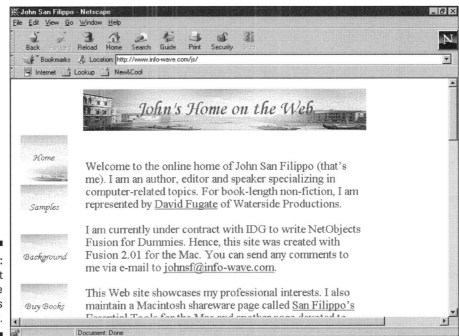

Figure 2-2:
This is what my home page looks like today.

At my Web site, after viewing my home page, you have the option to visit three other pages that are below my home page in the site's hierarchy. One page leads to samples of my writing, one leads to more detailed background information about me, and one allows you to buy copies of books I have written.

The Samples button on my Web page leads to another page where you can drill down even further into the hierarchy, choosing among samples of my magazine articles, my technical writing, my copy writing, or my creative writing. Those options give you the opportunity to choose actual samples of my work, which reside at the following level in the hierarchy. Confused? Well, Figure 2-3 shows what this whole thing looks like in the previous version of NetObjects Fusion (which I used to create this site).

Adding pages to your site

In this set of steps, I assume that you've already started the NetObjects Fusion program and created a new blank site, as I explain in the preceding section "Creating a Web Site." Adding more pages to your site is easy.

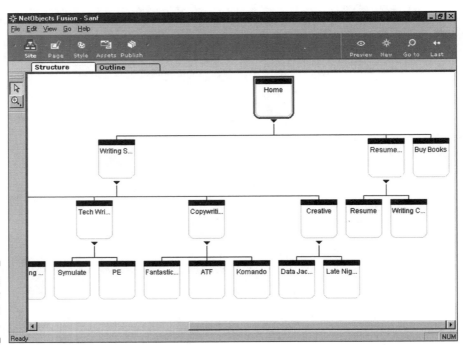

Figure 2-3:
This is my site in Site view.

1. **Click the New button in the tool bar, or what NetObjects Fusion calls the control bar, at the top of the screen.**

   A new untitled page appears directly below your home page.

   You can also press the Insert key or choose Edit⇨New Page to create a new page.

   Notice the blue border around the home page. The blue border indicates the page that is currently selected. Any time you create a new page, NetObjects Fusion places that page one level down in the hierarchy from the currently selected page.

2. **To create another page at the same level as the previous new page, click the New Page button again.**

   A third page appears next to the second one.

3. **To create another new page below one of the existing new pages, click that page to select it; then click the New Page button.**

   This time around, the new page appears below the one you selected.

You can now add all the pages you want using this same basic technique.

Take a look at the small arrow pointing out of the bottom of the home page (assuming you've created other pages below it). This arrow, as shown in Figure 2-4, appears below any page that has pages below it. If you click that arrow, all the pages below that page are hidden. This can help save a little room when you're working in Site view. To see them again, just click the little circle with the plus sign in it.

Figure 2-4:
You can
hide extra
pages.

Moving pages around

Suppose you create a new page and then decide you created it in the wrong place. Moving a page around in the Site view is as easy as dragging and dropping. Just follow these steps.

1. **Click and hold the mouse pointer on the page that you want to move.**

2. **Drag the mouse pointer over another page.**

   An outline of the icon for the page you're moving moves along with the mouse pointer as you drag.

As you drag the mouse pointer over the icon for another page, a little red arrow appears along one of the borders of the other page's icon. The border on which the red arrow appears depends on where you drag the mouse pointer. For example, if you drag the mouse pointer along the right side, the red arrow appears on the right border. The position of the red arrow tells you where, in relation to the other page, NetObjects Fusion will place the page you're moving after you release the mouse button. Figure 2-5 shows one example with the red arrow on the right side of the other page. Releasing the mouse button moves the page to its new position, as indicated by the little, red arrow.

3. Release the mouse button to complete the move.

You can use this same basic technique to move pages anywhere you want within your site's hierarchy.

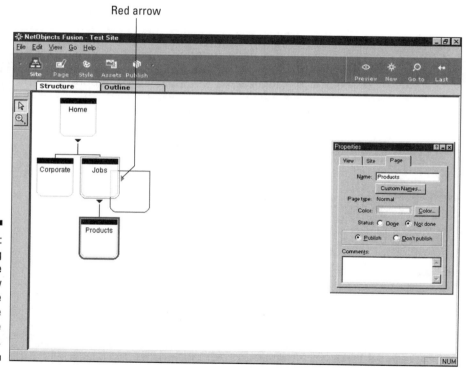

Figure 2-5: Releasing the mouse button now places the page to the right of the Jobs page.

Deleting a page

To delete a page, follow these steps.

1. Click the page you want to delete.

As you probably remember, when you're in the Site view, the currently selected page is indicated by a blue border.

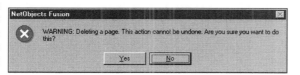

2. Press the Delete key on your keyboard, or choose Edit⇨Delete Page.

Once you delete a page, there's no turning back, so make sure this is what you really want to do.

NetObjects Fusion displays a warning message like the one shown in Figure 2-6.

Figure 2-6:
Once you delete a page, it's deleted for good.

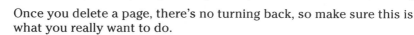

3. To complete the deletion, click the Yes button in the warning box.

The next page up in the hierarchy becomes the selected page.

Playing the Name Game

Maybe you've already noticed that each time you create a new page, it's simply named *Untitled* — kind of like, "This is my brother Darryl, and this is my other brother Darryl." As you're planning the structure of your Web site, having a bunch of pages named *Untitled* is sure to confuse the matter. Imagine if you stopped by to pick up a pizza at your favorite pizza parlor and they had five different pizzas named *The Special*. How could you possibly know which one you were ordering?

To make your life as a Web author as easy as possible, you want to give each page on your site a unique name. That way, you keep any name confusion to an absolute minimum. To change a page's name, make sure you're in Site view and follow these brief steps.

1. **Move your mouse pointer over the name of the page you want to change.**

   As you do this, a light box appears around the name and the current name changes color.

2. **Click the mouse pointer on the current name.**

   The current name becomes highlighted.

3. **Type in the desired name for the page.**

   The old name is automatically replaced with the new name. Press the Enter key and you're done.

NetObjects Fusion automatically fills in the name you entered into the Properties palette. Make sure that the page you just named is still selected (if not, click it), and take a look over at the Properties palette on the right side of your screen. (If you can't see the Properties palette, press Ctrl+U.) NetObjects Fusion displays the Page tab and, among other things, you can see the new name you gave the page in the Name text box. For Figure 2-7, I changed the page name to Jobs.

Page name

Figure 2-7: The Properties palette shows the page name.

Give each page a name that's easy for you to identify and work with.

NetObjects Fusion fills in a page name for you at other times, too. Because the name that is easy for you to work with may not necessarily be the name you want other people to see, however, NetObjects Fusion allows you to specify other names for it to use. That's where the Custom Names button comes in.

The Custom Names button enables you to specify different page names for NetObjects Fusion to use in different situations. You can find the Custom Names button below the page name in the Properties palette.

Custom Names... To see what you can do with the Custom Names button, look again at my current home page, as shown in Figure 2-8.

Notice that NetObjects Fusion displays different variations of the page name in three different places. The title bar at the top of the browser window shows the actual HTML name of the page, John San Filippo. In the banner at the top of the page, the page is called John's Home on the Web. Then over in the NavBar (which I cover in Chapter 8), the icon for this page is simply called Home.

Here's how to change the custom names for any given page.

1. **Click the desired page to select it.**

   The selected page is the one with the blue border.

2. **Click the Custom Names button in the Properties palette.**

   A Custom Names dialog box appears on your screen, as shown in Figure 2-9.

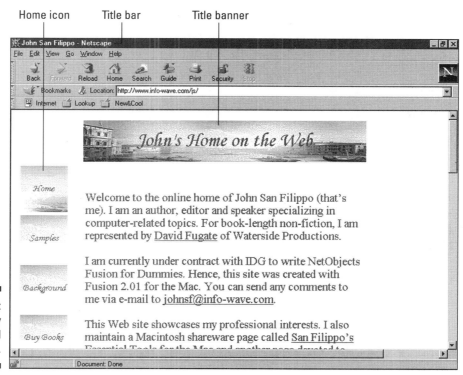

Figure 2-8: Here's my virtual home again.

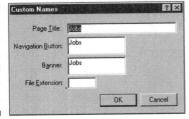

Figure 2-9:
This is where you specify custom names.

3. **Type in the page name in the Page Title field as you want it to appear across the top of the browser window when people visit this page; then press Tab.**

   The next field in the dialog box becomes highlighted.

4. **Type in the page name in the Navigation Button field as you want it to appear on buttons that NetObjects Fusion creates for you; then press Tab.**

   Because buttons have limited space for text, you should keep the name brief. For example, on my site, the button name for the page that links to my writing samples is simply Samples.

5. **Type in the page name in the Banner field as you want it to appear in the banner across the top of the page.**

   If you want your banner to have more than one line of text, you can press the Enter key to move down to a new line.

   If you're creating a page for some specialized application that requires pages to have some extension other than the standard *.html,* you can change that here on a page-by-page basis. However, that's outside the scope of this book.

6. **When you're done specifying the various names, click the OK button to close this dialog box.**

Fine-Tuning Your Site

NetObjects Fusion offers several other options to help you make sure your site turns out just the way you want. You control some options by using the Properties palette and some by using other buttons.

More fun with the Properties palette

When you're in the NetObjects Fusion Site view, the Properties palette usually displays three different tabs: Page, Site, and View. The only exception is that when you display your site in Outline View, there is no View tab. For more on this, check out the following section, "Structure view versus Outline view," in this chapter.

The Page tab

In addition to Custom Names, these are the things you can control from the Page tab, which is shown in Figure 2-10:

Figure 2-10:
The Page
tab is
always
available in
Site view.

✔ **The Color button** allows you to change the color of the icon used to represent any given page in Site view. When you click this button, NetObjects Fusion displays a typical Windows-style color-selection dialog box. You may find this feature handy if, for example, you want all pages that relate to a particular topic to be readily visible when you're in Site view.

✔ **Status** offers two radio buttons, Done and Not Done. The default is Not Done. When you select the Done button, a small check mark appears in the upper-right corner of the selected page's icon, as shown in Figure 2-11. The check mark gives you visual notice that this particular page no longer requires your attention.

Figure 2-11:
This page is
ready to go.

✔ **Publish** and **Don't Publish** offer you the choice of whether to publish your page on the Web. Why would you want to not publish a page? Suppose you're working on a big site and you need to get part of it online before the whole project is complete. You can choose to not publish the pages that are only partially complete, and NetObjects Fusion temporarily leaves them out.

> ✔ **The Comments text box** is simply a place where you can type in any notes or reminders that may help you out later.

The Site tab

As you can see in Figure 2-12, the Site tab tells you the name of the site you're working on, the date and time it was created, the date and time it was last modified, and the total number of pages in the site. It also provides a field where you can type in your name as author of the site.

Figure 2-12:
The Site tab provides a summary of your site.

After you type in your name, NetObjects Fusion generates HTML code for your site, including meta tags on each page. A *meta tag* is a segment of HTML code that is included on a Web page but is not visible in any way when the page is viewed through a Web browser like Netscape Navigator or Microsoft Internet Explorer.

Meta tags can

> ✔ **Cause an action to occur.** For example, if you were coding all your HTML manually (versus using a program like NetObjects Fusion), you could add a meta tag that automatically advances the user to a different page after a specified period of time.
>
> ✔ **Provide information to people or programs that examine the HTML code that makes up your pages.** For example, when NetObjects Fusion generates the HTML code for your site, it automatically adds a meta tag to each page that tells the name of the author of the Web page and that the site was created using NetObjects Fusion.

The View tab

The View tab gives you two options for how to display your site when you're looking at it in Structure view (versus Outline view, the difference of which I explain in the section "Structure view versus Outline view"). You can look at your site in what I call the normal view, or what I call the sideways view, as shown in Figure 2-13.

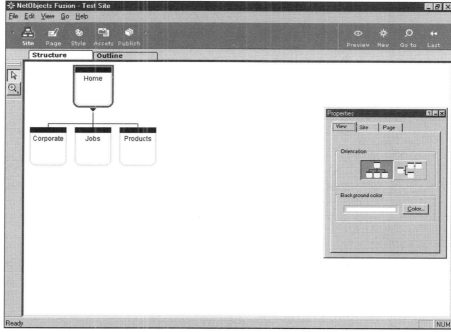

Figure 2-13:
If you want,
you can
look at
your site
sideways or
in normal
view.

This tab also gives you the option to change the background color that you see when you're in Site view. When you click the Colors button, NetObjects Fusion displays a typical Windows-style color-selection dialog box that allows you to choose any color you want.

Other tools and buttons that put you in control

The Site view also provides a couple of other options to help you control how your site appears on the screen.

The Standard Tools palette

When you're in Site view, the Standard Tools palette that appears along the left side of the screen holds only two tools, a pointer and a magnifying glass. Most of the time, you're going to be using the pointer tool. However, if you ever want to zoom in to see something better, you can click the magnifying glass and then click the portion of the site you want to magnify.

You can create a little more working room by hiding the Standard Tools palette completely. To do so choose View➪Toolbars➪Standard Tools. You can later use the same procedure to bring the palette back.

Structure view versus Outline view

When you're in Site view, just below the control bar, you find two tabs: *Structure* and *Outline*. Structure view, the default, shows your site as a flow chart. When you click the Outline tab, NetObjects Fusion switches over to — you guessed it — a view that looks like an outline, as shown in Figure 2-14.

You can't find any new information here but, depending on your personal preference, you may find the Outline view easier to work with. One interesting column that you see on the right side of the screen is called Child Name. In Web authoring lingo, any page that sits below another page in the hierarchy is called a *child*. Likewise, the page directly above any given page in the hierarchy is called its *parent*.

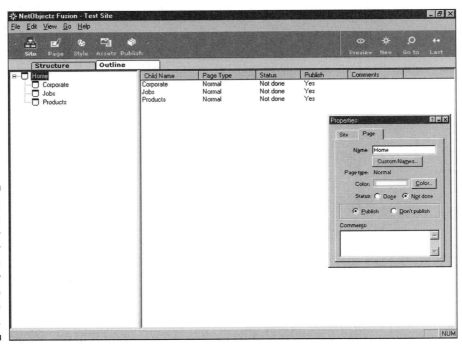

Figure 2-14:
Here's the
Site view
with your
perspective
already
changed to
an outline
view.

Chapter 3

Take the Easy Way Out with Templates and Styles

● ●

● ●

*I*n a way, building your Web site in NetObjects Fusion is like building a bookshelf. If you want to build a bookshelf, you can go down to the local lumber store, buy a pile of wood, bring it back home, spend hours cutting the wood, get ticked when you screw up, start over . . . (you may actually be handier with wood than I am). The option that seems to work better for a novice woodworker like me is to make a trip to the department store, buy a kit that has everything cut to the rights sizes, bring it home, and promptly assemble it (now if I could just figure out what language those instructions are in).

When you use NetObjects Fusion to create your Web site, you can certainly start from scratch, but you may not want to go to all the trouble. Before you get too far down the build-it-from-scratch road, you should take a look at two of NetObjects Fusion's most useful features: AutoTemplates and Styles.

An *AutoTemplate* is a predesigned, fill-in-the-blank site that you can use as a model for your own site and modify wherever you see fit. NetObjects Fusion comes with three AutoTemplates (or just templates for short): Business Presentation, Company Internet, and Department Intranet. A *SiteStyle,* or simply *Style,* is a collection of coordinated elements that NetObjects Fusion uses to create your site. Every site you create in NetObjects Fusion also employs a Style. NetObjects Fusion comes with more than 50 Styles to choose from. Plus, as I explain in Chapter 16, you can also create your own Styles.

Using AutoTemplates

No, AutoTemplates aren't molds used by the big-three auto makers, but they can save you as much time as driving a car saves you over, say, riding a bullock. What's more, they're easy to use. To create a Web site using an AutoTemplate, just follow these steps:

1. **Choose File⇨New Site⇨From Template.**

   NetObjects Fusion displays a Select a Template File dialog box, as Figure 3-1 shows, which includes the contents of the Templates folder in NetObjects Fusion. In addition to full site templates, the program also includes templates for various types of forms (see Chapter 11), some specialized Web pages (see Chapter 5), and data publishing examples (see Chapter 14).

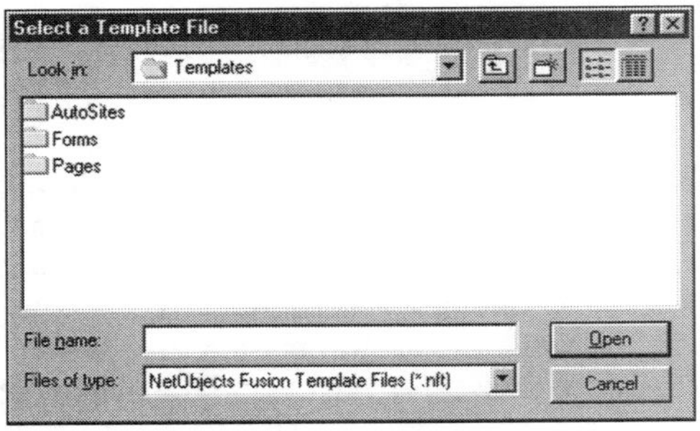

Figure 3-1: The NetObjects Fusion templates are divided into three categories.

2. **Double-click the AutoSites folder.**

   The dialog box displays five folders:

   - *Blank Site:* The template that NetObjects Fusion uses when you choose File⇨New Site⇨Blank Site or press Ctrl+Shift+N. This is the default site template. For more information, check out Chapter 1.

   - *Business Presentation:* This template enables you to put a presentation on the Internet similar to a Microsoft PowerPoint presentation, complete with animated effects. I explain the Business Presentation template in the section "Facts and figures" later in this chapter.

   - *Corporate Internet:* This template gives you a big head start if you are trying to put your corporation on the Internet for the first time. The template also contains methods of publishing database information on the Web such as open positions at your company. I explain the Corporate Internet template in the section "Your corporate presence" later in this chapter.

- *Department Intranet:* This template is the structure for sharing information within the same department of a company. I explain the Department Intranet template in the section "An online compartment for your department" later in this chapter.

- *Import:* NetObjects Fusion uses this template when you choose File⇨New Site⇨From Local Import. Check out Chapter 4 for information on importing.

3. **Double-click the folder for the template you want to use.**

   The dialog box displays the Assets folder for that template, as well as the template file.

4. **Click the template file and then the Open button in the lower right corner of the dialog box.**

   NetObjects Fusion switches to a Save Site As dialog box, giving you the opportunity to name your new site.

5. **Type in a name for your new site and click the Save button in the lower right corner of the dialog box.**

   NetObjects Fusion creates a new site based on the template you selected. This may take a minute or two, depending on the speed of your computer. Once you see the site displayed in Site view, you're ready to get to work customizing the template to your specific needs.

Contemplating Templates

Previous versions of NetObjects Fusion shipped with about a dozen different templates, but none of them were really anything special. This time around, my friends at NetObjects focus more on quality than quantity. NetObjects Fusion 3.0 ships with only three templates, but each represents a very common use of a Web site (and each showcases a different aspect of the program). You can use one template as a model for a business presentation, one for your company's Web site, and one for a department site on a company intranet. Use a template as a starting point, and then customize it to meet your specific needs.

Facts and figures

To be perfectly honest, the Business Presentation template doesn't offer that much in the "fill in the blank" department as you might hope for. You can customize some of the pages, but others use graphics (for example, a pie chart) that are specific to the fictional company represented in this template. What this template does do, however, is provide a fine example of what's possible with a NetObjects Fusion feature called *Actions* (described in detail in Chapter 15). A little background info is in order here.

Version 4.*x* browsers (the term commonly used to refer collectively to both Microsoft Internet Explorer 4.*x* and Netscape Navigator 4.*x*) and later support a new HTML feature called Cascading Style Sheets (CSS). One component of CSS is the precise positioning of elements on a Web page. On one of these Web pages, the position of each element is specified using exact coordinates in relation to the upper left corner of the page.

Using a combination of CSS positioning and JavaScript, Actions enable you to control the animation of objects on your Web pages. Figure 3-2 shows one of the Business Presentation pages as it loads.

The reason the pieces of the pie chart are scattered all around is that as the page loads, you see those pieces fly in from opposite corners of the page and assemble before your eyes. With all the pieces in place, the page looks like the one Figure 3-3 shows.

As of this writing, millions of people out there haven't upgraded to a 4.*x* browser. Unless you're sure that the bulk of your audience is using a 4.*x* browser, you may want to think twice about using this template, or any other page that uses Actions.

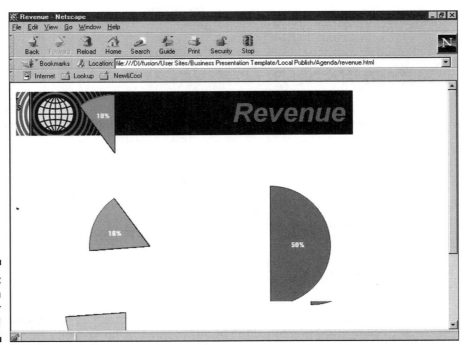

Figure 3-2:
You can make your pie fly!

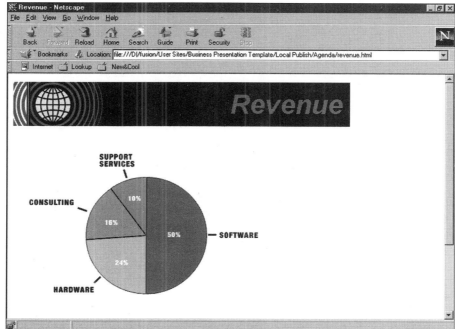

Figure 3-3:
Your 4.*x*
Web
browser
puts the
pie back
together.

Your corporate presence

If you're building your company's Web site from scratch, one of the big questions is what information to put in and what information to leave out. You probably won't be faulted for putting in too much, but leave out something the CEO thinks is critical (even if it really isn't — you know those pesky CEOs) and you could find yourself in hot water. The Corporate Internet template may not include everything you need for your Web site, but it's a great start.

As you can see from the Site view displayed in Figure 3-4, the Corporate Internet template provides the basic framework for a corporate Web site.

Just as with any template, you can add, delete, and modify as you see fit.

One extremely useful NetObjects Fusion feature that this template showcases is the program's awesome data publishing capabilities. In the previous figure, take special note of the page icons marked Press, Managers, Employ, Positions, and Products. If you look carefully, you see that there appear to be additional pages behind them. This indicates that these are *stacked pages*, which you use to publish data. Each page in a group of stacked pages contains the data from a single record in your database.

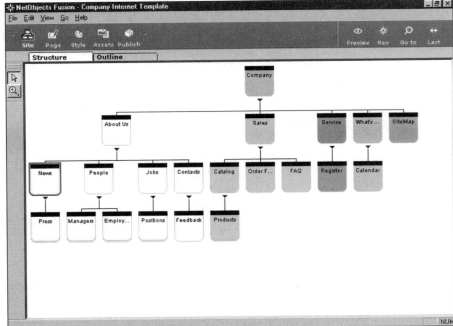

Figure 3-4:
Use the
Corporate
Internet
template
and you're
already half-
way to
getting your
company
online.

NetObjects Fusion lets you publish data that's either stored within your NetObjects Fusion site or housed in some other database format. Either way you go, NetObjects Fusion creates a DataList on a parent page to display a list of the various records that make up your data. Then the program creates a stacked page for each record. To view one of those stacked pages in your Web browser, click the appropriate entry in the DataList.

Job listings, press releases, and product catalogs are just a few examples of the many ways you can put NetObjects Fusion's data publishing capabilities to work. For detailed procedures, see Chapter 14.

An online compartment for your department

More and more companies today are creating what are called *intranets*. An intranet is simply a Web site (or series of Web sites) set up on a company's internal computer network. Unlike sites that you publish on the World Wide Web, an intranet site is available only to the employees on the company network.

Although many of the design considerations are the same, the type of information you want to share with fellow employees may be vastly different from the information you want to share with the rest of the world. Because the whole purpose of an intranet is to provide easy access to useful employee information, you want to publish information that other employees are likely to need to perform their duties more efficiently. If you're wondering what to include on your intranet site, the Department Intranet template is an excellent place to begin.

If you really want to dive head first into this whole intranet thing, you may want to pick up a copy of *Intranet Publishing For Dummies* by Glenn Weadock (IDG Books Worldwide, Inc.).

Feature-wise, the Department Intranet template doesn't offer much different from the Corporate Internet template. Figure 3-5 shows an example of this template in Site view.

If you do happen to be creating a site for your corporate intranet, you should keep two things in mind. First of all, chances are that the IS powers that be have prescribed a particular Web browser to be used by everyone in the company. If that's the case, you can design your intranet site with that particular browser in mind. In particular, if your company has standardized on a 4.*x* browser, you can incorporate 4.*x*-only features, such as Actions, into your site without worrying about who has which browser.

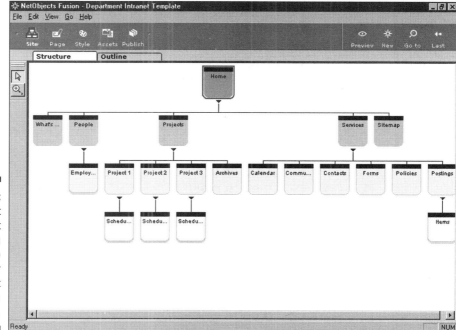

Figure 3-5:
Here's just about everything you need to get your department seen in cyberspace.

Second, you don't need to worry quite as much about bandwidth on an intranet. When you publish on the Internet, you have to give some consideration to people who might access your site via a modem connection. On the other hand, everyone on your intranet is tied together with high-speed data lines. I'm not suggesting that you should load your intranet site with scads of multimegabyte multimedia files; such stuff is typically not appropriate for a business setting anyway. However, if you really *need* some high-bandwidth content to make your intranet site complete, slow modem connections aren't one of the issues you need to address.

Do It with Style

If your graphic arts skills are anything like mine, you welcome any help you can get. Lucky for people like you and me that NetObjects Fusion comes with an assortment of what are called *Styles*. A Style is a collection of related graphics, each of which is designed to serve a specific purpose on your Web page. To be precise, each style consists of the following graphic elements:

- **Background.** A Style background can be either a solid color or a picture of some sort.

- **Banner.** The Banner is the large graphic that appears across the top of your Web page. It usually contains the name of the page.

- **Primary Button.** This is the image you use for each of the buttons in your NavBars. (I cover NavBars in Chapter 8.) The Primary Button is actually a set of two buttons, one for regular and one for highlighted. The highlighted button indicates the current Web page.

- **Secondary Button.** This is an alternate button set that you can use at will instead of the Primary Button.

- **Line Picture.** Instead of using boring HTML-generated horizontal rules, you can choose to replace your rules with this picture. I cover rules in Chapter 7.

- **DataList Icon.** Use this graphic as a bullet character when you publish a DataList. I cover DataLists in Chapter 14.

- **Normal Text Color.** This option controls the color of normal text on your Web page.

- **Regular Link Color.** This option controls the color of linked text before a user has visited the linked-to page.

- **Visited Link Color.** This option controls the color of linked text after someone has visited the linked-to page.

You can change from one Style to another with just a couple of clicks in NetObjects Fusion's Style view. In Chapter 16, I explain everything you need to know about changing the variables for a particular style, as well as how to create new ones of your own. (I've also included on the CD at the back of the book several sets of graphic elements that you can use to create your own Styles.) However, I think it's a good idea to familiarize yourself with the basics of Styles and the Style view early on the Web development process you've now undertaken.

If you don't have NetObjects Fusion running, start the program. If you're a little leery of experimenting on your current site, you may want to create a new one just to fiddle with. The truth is, it doesn't much matter, because switching back to your original Style only takes a couple of mouse-clicks.

With a site loaded, click the Style button in the button bar at the top of the screen. When you do, NetObjects Fusion takes you to the Style view and displays a list of all available Styles, much like Figure 3-6.

Figure 3-6:
NetObjects Fusion provides an impressive array of Styles.

On the left side of your screen, NetObjects Fusion displays the actual list of Styles. On the right side of the screen, you see the various elements that make up whatever Style you click in the list. Let me take a moment to explain the various elements of a Style.

- ✔ The Banner area shows you the banner graphic, the banner text font, and the color of the banner text.

- ✔ The Primary Navigation Bar area shows you what a NavBar that has this Style looks like. The button that looks different from all the others represents the current page.

- ✔ Every Style offers an alternate NavBar that you can use at will. The Secondary Navigation Bar area shows you what a NavBar that has the alternate Style looks like. The button that looks different from all the others represents the current page.

- ✔ The DataList Icon shows the graphic that appears as a bullet character in DataLists (see Chapter 14).

- ✔ The Text area shows the specified colors for normal text, regular links, and visited links.

- ✔ The SiteStyle Line area shows the graphic that you can use in place of HTML horizontal rules.

NetObjects Fusion comes with more than 50 Styles. Some of them are more interesting than others. To see what any Style looks like, simply click its name in the list on the left.

To change the Style for your site, follow these easy steps:

1. **In the Style view, click the name of the Style you want to use.**

   NetObjects Fusion displays that Style on the right side of the screen.

2. **Click the Set Style button on the right side of the button bar at the top of the Screen.**

   NetObjects Fusion displays a message advising you that you have changed the Style, as you see in Figure 3-7.

Figure 3-7:
NetObjects
Fusion lets
you know
when
you've
changed
your Style.

If you want, you can select the Don't Show This Message Again check box. If you do, NetObjects Fusion makes future Style changes without displaying this message, speeding things up a little for you.

3. **Switch to Page view to see what your site looks like with its new Style.**

If you're looking at some Style other than the one your site is currently using and then switch to another view, NetObjects Fusion displays a message box, asking you if you want to use the Style you're looking at. If you choose Yes, a bug in the original shipping version of NetObjects Fusion 3.0 (which may be fixed by the time you read this) causes the program to crash. To avoid this problem entirely, click the Don't Show This Message Again check box and then click No. In the future, you'll only be able to change Styles using the procedures I describe earlier in this section.

Chapter 4

Moving Up to NetObjects Fusion without Confusion

*I*f you've already created a Web site in some other program, you may not want to start all over again with NetObjects Fusion. Well, I've got good news and bad news; which do you want first? The good news? Okay. You can bring your existing Web site into NetObjects Fusion. Now for the bad news: The task is a little more complicated than it may be in other programs.

Every other Web authoring program I've looked at — and I've probably fiddled with at least a dozen or so — saves its files in plain HTML format. That means, for example, that if you wanted to switch from Claris HomePage to Adobe PageMill, you could just fire up PageMill and open the files you originally created in HomePage. For better or worse, it's not quite that easy when you're migrating to NetObjects Fusion, which saves all its files in a proprietary format and doesn't create any HTML code until you actually publish your site.

You can't just open an HTML file in Fusion and start working on it. Instead, you have to go through a process called *importing*. When you import an existing site into NetObjects Fusion, the program examines your old files and then makes a fusionized copy of your site. Your new, fusionized copy is what you actually work on in NetObjects Fusion.

This chapter tells you how to import an existing site into NetObjects Fusion. If, on the other hand, you just want to use a single page from an existing site or even just part of an existing page you should warp yourself to Chapter 10.

Fusionizing Your Current Site

If you have an existing Web site and you shelled out a couple of hundred dollars for NetObjects Fusion, I have to assume that you want to use NetObjects Fusion in modifying that site. In other words, you didn't buy NetObjects Fusion just to sit on your hard drive waiting for the next time you want to modify your site; you want to modify your site right now. NetObjects Fusion lets you import your entire site in one big operation, or one page at a time; it's up to you.

 Before you import your existing site into NetObjects Fusion, think about exactly how extensively you plan to change your site. If you're planning a major site overhaul, you're probably better off starting a new NetObjects Fusion site from scratch. You can still use individual elements from your old site if you want to. However, if you're happy with the overall look-and-feel of your site and just want to add a few fusionistic enhancements, importing is probably the way to go.

Importing the whole enchilada . . . er, site

The quickest way to make the move from some lesser Web authoring program to NetObjects Fusion is to import your entire existing site into NetObjects Fusion. To import an existing Web site into NetObjects Fusion, just follow these steps:

1. **Start NetObjects Fusion.**

   You can choose Start⇨Programs⇨NetObjects Fusion⇨NetObjects Fusion 3.0 or double-click the NetObjects Fusion icon on the desktop.

2. **Choose File⇨New Site⇨Imported Site.**

   The Import Local Web Site dialog box appears, as shown in Figure 4-1.

Figure 4-1: This dialog box enables you to import from your hard drive.

Import Local Web Site	? X
Home page:	Browse...
Options	
Assign MasterBorder:	Import
☐ Limit number of pages to	200
☐ Down to structural level	20
Domain name:	www.domain.com
(This is needed for managing links)	
	OK Cancel

Converting to NetObjects Fusionism

My first Web page was no masterpiece by anyone's standards. I had a basic understanding of how HTML worked, but I only knew a couple of the tags. So I went online, found some Web pages that I liked, and saved them to my hard drive. Then I opened them using a plain old text editor and began experimenting with copy and paste to see exactly what each tag did. It was an interesting educational exercise, but I quickly realized that using a text editor was no way to create presentable Web pages. It was more like deciding one night to make yourself a pizza by first making your own cheese from the jug of milk in your refrigerator.

So I did what any cost-conscious Web wannabe would do and found a reasonable shareware HTML editor. This was in the days before WYSIWYG (what-you-see-is-what-you-get) HTML programs, so I was still working directly in the HTML code.

But my shareware program made it easy. If I wanted a portion of text to appear in bold, I'd just highlight that text with my mouse and click *bold* from a floating palette. In a heartbeat, the program would add the tags for bold type. That was a very good learning experience, too, because I could see all the HTML tags as they were created by the program.

But let's face it: Editing with WYSIWYG shareware programs involves too much trial and error. You do a little HTML work, and then click the Preview button in the shareware program to launch Netscape Navigator and see what the page really looks like. When you find out how bad it really looks, you go back to the drawing board.

Next came Adobe PageMill, which to the best of my knowledge was the first commercial WYSIWYG HTML editor. This program made laying out a Web page almost as easy as laying out a printed page in PageMaker. (Some of you may argue that laying out a page in PageMaker isn't all that easy, but I was already quite proficient in PageMaker at the time.) I liked PageMill so well that I ended up coauthoring *PageMill 2 For Dummies* with Deke McClelland. However, the key word in PageMill is *page*. It's a great little program for creating Web *pages*, but doesn't offer all that much for those interested in creating large, sophisticated Web *sites*.

Finally, along came NetObjects Fusion, which is, in my opinion, the best way yet to edit Web pages *and* manage Web sites. My hard drive contains the pages for several Web sites that were created in programs other than NetObjects Fusion. As time goes by, however, I'll convert these to NetObjects Fusion sites.

Before you continue, take a look at the options available in the Import Local Web Site dialog box:

- The Assign MasterBorder field provides a drop-down list of all the MasterBorders you've defined for the site you're importing into. When you complete these steps, a separate page is created for each page you reference, with the referenced page occupying the Layout area of its respective page. The MasterBorder you select here is applied to each of those pages.

- The Limit Number of Pages To box enables you to control the total number of pages that NetObjects Fusion imports from a site. Leaving this option unchecked imports the entire site.

- The Down to Structural Level box enables you to control how many levels down in the site's hierarchy NetObjects Fusion imports. Again, leaving this option unchecked imports the entire Web site.

- It's not absolutely essential that you type the site's domain name into the Domain Name field, but it helps NetObjects Fusion figure out whether links in the site are relative links or absolute links. A relative link is a link to another page on the same site. In HTML coding, a relative link doesn't need the `http://www.domain.com/` part, which is assumed. Only the name of the Web page (such as `Index.html`) is necessary. An absolute link is a link to a page on some other site.

3. **Click the Browse button.**

   NetObjects Fusion displays a standard Open dialog box.

4. **Use this dialog box to navigate your hard drive and locate the folder that houses your existing site.**

5. **Select the file that represents the site's home page, and then click the Open button.**

   In most cases, the home page for a given site is named *Index*. However, if you used some other name for your home page, select that one.

   After you click the Open button, NetObjects Fusion takes you back to the Import Local Web Site dialog box.

6. **Make sure all the options in this dialog box are set the way you want them.**

7. **Click the OK button.**

   NetObjects Fusion displays a Save Site As dialog box.

8. **Type a name for your new site in the File Name field.**

   You also have the option to save your site in a different location on your hard drive by navigating to that location. However, I recommend keeping all your sites stored together in the User Sites folder.

9. **Click the Save button.**

NetObjects Fusion begins the process of importing your site. Depending on the size of your site and the speed of your computer, this process could take a few minutes. After NetObjects Fusion has finished importing your site, it displays it in Site view.

If you've already started a site and decide that you want to import that old site you created in some other program into your work in progress, just choose File➪Import Web Site➪Local Web Site. Both the procedures and the results are essentially the same as those described earlier in this chapter.

Importing a page here and there

NetObjects Fusion doesn't force you to import an entire site when all you really want is a single page from the old site. If you decide to build a new site without importing the old one, you can still import a single page from your old site whenever you need to.

You import individual pages when you're in Page view. So when you start the process, you need to be on the page in your NetObjects Fusion site where you want the imported page to appear. When you finish the process, the imported page appears in the Layout area of your NetObjects Fusion page.

Importing from the Web

Not only can you import a Web site from your own hard drive, NetObjects Fusion also gives you the capability to import a Web site from directly off of the Web. You do so by simply entering a Web address in the Home Page field of the New Imported Site dialog box. Doing so makes NetObjects Fusion log on to whatever Web site you specify and import the entire site. This can be any site on the World Wide Web.

I can think of two reasons for doing this: Either you want to borrow some Web design ideas for use on your own site or you want to import your own site onto your hard drive.

The first reason can be a little legally sticky. If you've come across an interesting site and want to borrow some design ideas, it's okay — as long as you borrow only ideas and not any copyrighted text, graphics, or Java applets. If you're unsure which category the stuff you want to borrow falls into, contact the owner of the site you want to borrow from and get his or her permission. An ounce of prevention is worth a pound or ton of legal bills later.

I have one other word of caution with regard to your ability to import a site — you import the

entire site, not just the home page. Suppose, for example, you like the way the Yahoo! home page is laid out, so you type in www.yahoo.com to import that home page. Wait a minute! Doing this imports an entire site, and Yahoo! is an enormous site. If you type in www.yahoo.com just to import a copy of the home page, you're going to get much, much more than you bargained for, and the download will probably take hours. If you just want a single page, make sure you limit the number of pages to 1.

You may also want to import your *own* Web site on the Web into NetObjects Fusion. A situation where this can really come in handy is if you lose the contents of your Web site from your hard drive, perhaps due to a hard drive failure. Assuming you have published your site on the World Wide Web, you can import it from the Web server where it lives back onto your hard drive (hopefully a better hard drive). Importing your own site is safe, legally speaking, because as long as you have created the text and graphics, you already own the copyright to it.

The procedures that follow assume that you're already in Page view on the page where you want the imported page to appear. (I know, that's a lot of the word *page*, but I can't help it.) To import an individual HTML page, follow these steps:

1. **Select File⇨Import HTML Page.**

   NetObjects Fusion displays a standard Open dialog box.

2. **Navigate through your system to locate the desired HTML file.**

3. **Click once on the desired HTML file and then click Open.**

That's all there is to it. NetObjects Fusion imports the page you specified. The background of the entire page changes to whatever the background was in the imported page, and the page name changes to whatever page name was used in the imported page.

Imparting Important Importing Portents

Most popular applications today include the ability to import files created with some other competing application. For example, Microsoft Word lets you import files created in WordPerfect, and vice versa. However, if you've had the need to do a lot of this sort of thing, you already know that importing a file from another application doesn't always work perfectly.

NetObjects Fusion is no different. Although the program does a reasonably good job of importing Web sites created in other programs, it's not perfect. In this section, I cover a few areas where I've observed some problems.

Layout lunacy

The simpler the layout of the Web page, the better NetObjects Fusion does in importing it. The more complicated you get, the more the importing process seems to go haywire. For example, I've noticed that NetObjects Fusion doesn't always behave itself when the imported page has a bulleted list.

I've also noticed a problem with imported pages that make heavy use of tables as a layout tool. An invisible table is simply a table in which the borders are hidden so that it's not readily apparent that a table exists. This is a common technique for laying out graphics on a Web page and is, in fact, the very same technique that Fusion uses to provide you with such precise layout control. You can find more information on this topic in Chapter 1.

Because you can't be sure of exactly how NetObjects Fusion will treat each imported page, your best bet is to explore your site as soon as you import it, noting on a sheet of paper any problems you observe. Then you can come back later, using the techniques described in later chapters of this book, and fix what needs to be fixed.

To explore the site you just imported, dance to the following steps:

1. **With your newly imported site displayed in Site view, double-click the Home page.**

   This displays the Home page in Page view.

2. **Use the scroll bars on the right and bottom of the screen to examine the layout of your Home page, noting on a sheet of paper anything that needs to be fixed.**

3. **Click the Site button in the toolbar, or as NetObjects calls it, the control bar, at the top of your screen.**

4. **Repeat Steps 1–3 for each additional page on your imported site.**

If changing views in this manner seems a little like taking the freeway to your next-door neighbor's house, check out Chapter 5 for more direct methods of switching from one page to another.

Mac under attack

Suppose you find yourself, as many people do these days, migrating from Macintosh to Windows, and suppose furthermore that your original site was created on a Macintosh. Because a Mac can read Windows floppies, it's pretty easy to slap the files for your Web site onto a Windows-formatted floppy and copy them over to your current machine.

The hidden danger with moving from Mac to Windows skulks in the long filenames. Even though both Mac and Windows use long filenames, their long filenames aren't compatible with each other. So when you copy a file from a Mac onto a Windows floppy, the filenames get converted to the old DOS 8.3 (eight letters, a period, and then three letter extension) format. If you copy those files to your Windows computer and try to use them with the new truncated names, you'll run into all sorts of problems, because whatever Web authoring program you use with them will look for filenames that no longer exist.

To get around this problem, you just have to take a few minutes to set things right. The steps that follow assume that you've already copied your site's files from the Mac to your Windows system.

To restore filenames lost in a Mac to Windows conversion, follow these steps:

1. **On the Mac, open the folder that contains the files for your site.**

2. **Choose File⇨Print Window.**

   Doing so prints out a list of the files in that folder, giving you a handy printed reference to work from when you restore the filenames on your Windows system.

3. **On your Windows system, launch Windows Explorer and locate the folder that contains the files you copied from the Mac.**

4. **For each file, choose File⇨Rename and type in the long filename from your printed list.**

One alternative to these steps, if you're so inclined, is to revise your site while it's still on the Mac, making sure that every filename conforms to the DOS 8.3 filename format. If you take this route, just remember that the correct file extension for HTML documents is .htm.

Let's get metaphysical

One other problem I noticed when I attempted to import various sites into NetObjects Fusion has to do with the use of a *meta tag* to auto-advance the user from one page to another. A meta tag is a section of HTML code that's not actually displayed on the page, but gives some sort of instruction to the Web browser. What I'm talking about in this particular instance is a tag that looks like this:

```
<META HTTP-EQUIV="REFRESH" CONTENT="5;URL=home.htm">
```

This particular line of code tells a Web browser to refresh the contents of the browser window in five seconds with the page named home.htm. Five seconds later, the browser jumps to home.htm, even though there's no true hypertext link between the first page and the next.

When you import a site, however, NetObjects Fusion follows the *links* it finds on each page in the site until it doesn't find any more. (That's how NetObjects Fusion ensures that it imports all the files it needs and only the files it needs.) But NetObjects Fusion doesn't identify meta tags as links. So if you have a Web page that relies solely on a meta tag to advance to another page, NetObjects Fusion stops when it gets to the page with the meta tag, and any pages that follow the meta tag aren't converted.

The easiest way around this problem is to add a hypertext link that leads from the page containing the meta tag to the page that the meta tag links to *before* you import the site into NetObjects Fusion.

Importing without Really Importing

Suppose you created some Web pages in some other program and want to keep them just the way they are. Maybe you've created some complex form that you'd be just as happy maintaining in the program you used to create it. Or perhaps somebody in your workgroup who does have the benefit of using NetObjects Fusion needs to maintain some pages that you must include on your site.

If you need to include an external HTML page or range of pages in your NetObjects Fusion site without actually importing it, you're in luck. Using what the folks at NetObjects call *reference HTML,* it's a snap.

With NetObjects Fusion, you can include any HTML document or group of documents on your hard drive from within a NetObjects Fusion page by referencing the HTML document. By *referencing,* I mean that you place a pointer to a page in your NetObjects Fusion page that points to the HTML document in a similar way as a Windows 95 shortcut or Macintosh alias points to a program or document. (To make things easier, I call the page you want to include the *reference page,* and I call the NetObjects Fusion page where you want it to appear the *target page.*) When NetObjects Fusion publishes your site, it looks for references of this kind and, when it finds one, NetObjects Fusion includes the contents of the reference page as part of the target page. Any time you make changes to the reference page, the target page is automatically updated the next time you publish your site.

Referencing a single page

You can begin the process of adding a reference page in two ways, but both produce the same result. The first is to use the External HTML button, which, when you're in Page view, is at the very bottom of the toolbar on the left side of the screen. It looks like a tiny grid with a page icon in the middle. The second was is to choose File⇨Reference HTML. In the procedures that follow, I use the External HTML button, but the procedures are nearly identical when you use the menu option. These procedures assume that you're already in Page view on the target page. To add a reference to an external HTML page, just follow these steps:

1. **Click the External HTML button on the toolbar that runs along the left side of the screen.**

   It looks like a tiny page icon on top of a grid.

   The mouse pointer turns into a crosshair.

2. **Click and drag the crosshair within the Layout area to identify the approximate desired location of the reference page; then release the mouse button.**

   A Reference HTML Page dialog appears, as shown in Figure 4-2.

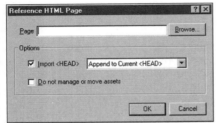

3. **Click the Browse button in this dialog box.**

   A standard Open dialog box appears.

4. **Navigate through your system to identify the desired reference HTML file; then click the Open button.**

   NetObjects Fusion displays the previous dialog box with the filename filled in.

   In the options panel of the Reference HTML Page dialog box, you can control the following:

   - The Import <HEAD> check box controls how NetObjects Fusion handles the information contained within the <HEAD> tag of the reference document. This HTML tag contains basic information about a document, such as its title. I recommend that you leave this box unchecked and stick with the <HEAD> information generated by NetObjects Fusion. If you use this option, use the drop list to the right to control whether NetObjects Fusion appends the information to your target page's <HEAD> information or entirely replaces it.

   - The Do Not Manage or Move Assets check box controls whether NetObjects Fusion treats the page as an Asset. Normally, you should always leave this box *unchecked;* if you check this box, NetObjects Fusion doesn't publish the graphics included on the reference page, which you normally want it to do.

5. **Ensure that the two check boxes are marked according to your desires, and then click the OK button.**

   Rather than showing the contents of the reference page, the box now contains information about the reference page, as shown in Figure 4-3.

Figure 4-3:
NetObjects
Fusion
shows
information
about the
reference
page
instead of
its contents.

Other.htm
Last Modified: 06:55PM, 23 July
1997
File Size: 2.01KB (2061 bytes)

◆ Double-click to edit this html file ◆

When you select the reference box as shown in the previous figure, the Properties palette offers you a few options, as shown in Figure 4-4.

Figure 4-4:
You have a
few options
to control
the display
of the
reference
page.

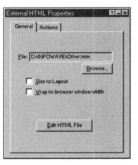

Here's the run-down on each of these options.

- ✔ **The Browse button** allows you to navigate through your system and select a new file to use as the reference page.

- ✔ **The Size to Layout check box** resizes the reference box to fill the entire layout area. If you're referencing a complete HTML page (for example, you're not using this feature to insert just a small amount of code), you should check this box. In all cases, and especially if you decide to leave this box unchecked, you should preview your page using the Preview button to make sure the page really looks the way you want. The reference page may take more space than you allotted for it in your layout.

- ✔ **The Wrap to Browser Window Width check box** adjusts the width of the reference page, if necessary, to fit in the browser window.

- ✔ **The Edit HTML File button** enables you to edit the reference file in a text editor or other Web authoring program. As an alternative to this button, you can simply double-click the reference box.

Referencing a whole site

When you reference an individual HTML page, you start out in Page view. So it only makes sense that when you reference an entire Web site that was created in some other program, you start out in the Site view. The steps that follow assume that you're in Site view and the site that you want to reference is located somewhere on your hard drive or on a network to which you're connected.

To reference an entire site created in another Web authoring program, follow these steps:

1. **Select the page that you want to serve as the parent for the referenced pages.**

   In other words, all of the pages you reference in these steps will appear in your site's hierarchy under the page you select in Step 1.

2. **Choose Edit⇨Reference HTML.**

   A Reference HTML dialog box appears, as shown in Figure 4-5. Note that this dialog box offers more options than those offered when you reference an individual page.

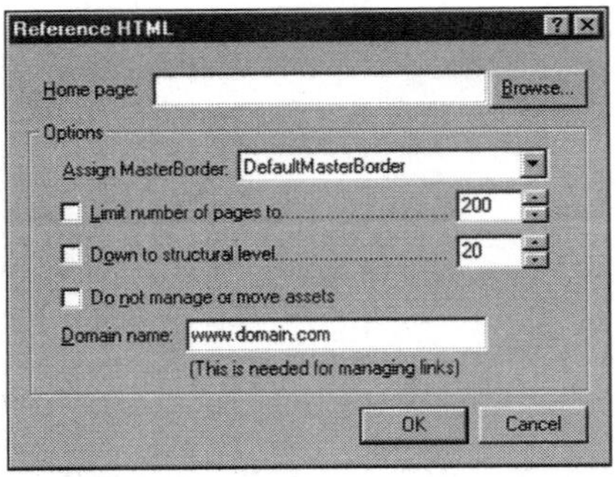

Figure 4-5:
Referencing a site is similar to importing it.

Before I continue, let me explain what each of the options in this dialog box does.

- *Assign MasterBorder field:* This field provides a drop-down list of all the MasterBorders you've defined for the site you're importing into. When you complete these steps, a separate page is created for each page you reference, with the referenced page occupying the Layout area of its respective page. The MasterBorder you select here is applied to each of those pages.

- *Limit Number of Pages To box:* This box enables you to control the total number of pages that NetObjects Fusion imports from a site. Leaving this option unchecked imports the entire site.

- *Down to Structural Level box:* This box enables you to control how many levels down in the site's hierarchy NetObjects Fusion imports. Again, leaving this option unchecked imports the entire Web site.

- *Do Not Manage or Move Assets check box:* This check box controls whether NetObjects Fusion treats the page as an Asset. Normally, you should always leave this box *unchecked;* if you check this box, NetObjects Fusion doesn't publish the graphics included on the reference page, which you normally want it to do.

- *Domain Name field:* It's not absolutely essential that you type the site's domain name in the Domain Name field, but it helps NetObjects Fusion figure out whether links in the site are relative links or absolute links. A *relative link* is a link to another page on the same site. In HTML coding, a relative link doesn't need the `http://www.domain.com/` part, which is assumed; only the name of the Web page (such as `Index.html`) is necessary. An absolute link is a link to a page on some other site.

3. **Set the options in this dialog box as desired.**

4. **Click the Browse button.**

5. **Use the resulting dialog box to navigate your hard drive and locate the folder that houses your existing site.**

6. **Select the file that represents the site's home page and click the Open button.**

   In most cases, the home page for a given site is named *Index*. However, if you used some other name for your home page, select that one.

7. **Back at the Reference HTML dialog box, click OK.**

NetObjects Fusion creates a separate page on your site for each referenced page. The previous section of this chapter explains your options for controlling the individual referenced pages.

Part II
The Site Is
the Castle, but
the Page Is King

The 5th Wave   By Rich Tennant

"Hold your horses. It takes time to build a
home page for someone your size."

In this part . . .

Sure, NetObjects Fusion makes it easy to create and maintain a great Web site. But the people who visit your Web site don't care what program you use or how easy it was to create all those pages. Their biggest concern is what you put on all those pages.

Part II first covers how to perform some basic fine-tuning on your page before you add any content. From there, it moves on to text — in my opinion the single most important thing you can put on a page. Some Web designers promote style over substance but, on the Web, people are looking for information — not just pretty pictures. And as far as Web programs go, NetObjects Fusion is a typographer's dream come true.

This part also offers separate chapters on Web page mainstays, such as graphics, links, and multimedia. Some may find it odd that I offer multimedia under the "basic stuff" category. A couple of years ago, I may have put it with the advanced content, but not any more. Web surfers have come to expect at least a little multimedia pizzazz, and NetObjects Fusion makes adding multimedia content as easy as adding a still graphic.

Chapter 5

Tooling Up for Web Page Creation

● ●

In This Chapter

▶ Exploring some floating palettes
▶ Creating and modifying NetObjects Fusion Layouts
▶ Creating and modifying MasterBorders
▶ Navigating in Page view

● ●

*I*magine that you're opening a fine restaurant. You have a state-of-the-art kitchen and you've hired a master chef. Your kitchen is going to run like a finely tuned machine. But suppose a waiter comes to work sans deodorant, is obnoxious to your customers, and picks his nose while taking orders. No matter how efficient your kitchen is, nobody's going to come to your restaurant because the presentation is poor.

Presentation is just as important at a Web site as it is at a restaurant. Even if you make the absolute most of all NetObjects Fusion's site-management tools, your visitors won't notice that if you create ugly, obnoxious pages. If your presentation is poor, folks won't return to your site.

You don't have to be a professional graphic artist to create a nice-looking Web page. Goodness knows, if I had to make a living as a graphic artist with my current skills, my family would be living in the back seat of a '74 Plymouth. All you need is a little common sense — and a great program like NetObjects Fusion to help you along the way.

Before you can start adding all that good stuff — text, graphics, multimedia, and so forth — you need to know how to get around in the NetObjects Fusion Page view and how to control some of the basic elements of your page layout. That's what this chapter is all about. If you're in Site view right now (or any view other than Page view), just click on the Page button in the control bar. That pops you right into Page view. At first glance — and possibly even at second glance — Page view may seem a little overwhelming. Don't worry, though. It's not as bad as it looks. I promise.

Getting the Hang of Floating Palettes

Floating palettes, eh? That reminds me of my childhood years in Jamestown, New York, watching debris gather under the train bridge that crossed the Chadakoin River near our house. Sure, I've seen plenty of floating palettes in my day. Just not the kind you're likely to come across while using NetObjects Fusion. When you're working on your Web site, the floating palettes you encounter are simply little moveable windows that display information about and present options for whatever you're working on.

NetObjects Fusion offers two floating palettes: the Object Tree and the Properties palette. To display the Object Tree, choose View⇨Palettes⇨ Object Tree. To display the Properties palette (or hide it if it's already visible), choose View⇨Palettes⇨Properties Palette. I describe the use of the Object Tree and the Properties palette in the following sections.

The problem with floating palettes is that they tend to get in the way of your work (the smaller your monitor, the more obtrusive palettes are). The good news is that you can move palettes around on the screen, collapse them to just a title bar, or close them completely. If a floating palette is in your way and you want to see what's behind it, use one of the following methods:

- ✔ **Move the palette.** Move the palette by clicking and holding the left mouse button on the palette's title bar (the area on the top of the palette that shows the palette's name), dragging it to another location, and releasing the mouse button.

- ✔ **Collapse the palette.** Collapse the palette so that you see only its title bar by double-clicking anywhere on the title bar or by clicking once on the Minimize button (the one that looks like a dash) in the upper-right corner of the palette. To expand the palette again, double-click any-where on the title bar or click once on the Minimize button (the one that looks like a dash) in the upper-right corner of the palette.

- ✔ **Close the palette.** Close the palette by clicking the Close button (the one that looks like an X) in the upper-right corner of the palette. To reopen a palette, choose View⇨Palette and select the palette you want to open from the list. (You can also reopen the Properties palette from your keyboard by pressing Ctrl+U.)

The Object Tree

As you add more and more elements to your Web page, identifying what's what on the page becomes harder and harder. The Object Tree provides an easy way to select any element on your page immediately.

You can use the Object Tree both to select any element on your page and to see whether each element is part of the page's MasterBorder or Layout.

The Object Tree shows you every element on your page and exactly what purpose it serves. If you add an element to the Layout portion of your page, that element appears under the Layout name in the Object Tree. Likewise, if you add an element to the MasterBorder, that element instantly appears under the MasterBorder name in the Object Browser.

Figure 5-1 shows the Object Tree. The icon on top indicates the name of the page that you're on, the icon beneath that one shows the name of the MasterBorder you're using, and the bottommost icon shows the name of the Layout you're using. (Check out "Controlling your Layouts" and "Mastering MasterBorders" later in this chapter for a more in-depth look at these important elements.)

Page name MasterBorder

Figure 5-1:
The Object
Tree is
found
nowhere
in nature.

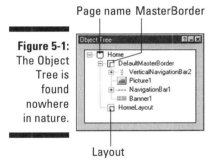

Layout

When you click any element in the Object Tree, it's immediately selected on your page. If you were to click on the Picture 1 icon in the Object Tree shown in Figure 5-1, the Page view would automatically jump down to the bottom of the page and highlight the Built With NetObjects Fusion icon. You may also notice that the title bar on the Properties palette also changes. Check out the section entitled "The Properties palette" for more information.

What the L Is It? "Layout" or "layout"?

In some cases, I say *layout*, and in others, I say *Layout*. What's the difference?

When I say *layout* (with a lowercase *l*), I'm speaking in general terms about the way different elements are laid out on a page. However, *Layout* (with a capital *L*) refers to a specific group of settings that you can create to provide broad control over the layout of one or more pages. I cover exactly how to create and modify these Layouts later in this chapter. And if I say I'm going to lay out, it means I'm headed for one of San Diego's wonderful beaches.

If a component contains other elements, that component appears in the Object Tree with either a plus or minus sign next to it. A minus sign indicates that the subelements (for lack of a better term) are displayed right below the element. A plus sign indicates that the subelements are hidden on the Object Tree list. Clicking the Object Tree's plus sign displays subelements; clicking a minus sign hides subelements.

You can also change the name that the Object Tree uses to identify a particular element, such as a graphic. To do that, just click the element in the Object Tree and then click a second time on the element's name. You're ready to type in a new name. Now any time you use that same element on any other page in your site, it appears in the Object Tree with its new name.

The Properties palette

The Properties palette is like command central for controlling just about every aspect of an individual Web page. You use it to adjust the settings for virtually any aspect of your page, from the overall layout to a specific graphic. Make friends with the Properties palette now, and it will be your closest ally as you develop your Web site.

Whenever you select an element (either by clicking the element on your Web page or by selecting the element in the Object Tree), the title bar on the Properties palette changes to show properties for the selected element, as shown in Figure 5-2. As you select different elements on your page, the Properties palette always changes to show the properties for that element.

Figure 5-2:
The Properties palette changes according to what you've selected on the page.

One Page, Yet Two Parts: Layouts and MasterBorders

Two important elements you can control from the Properties palette are the page Layout and the MasterBorder. If you look at Figure 5-3, you'll notice a little gray box labeled `MasterBorder` in the upper-left corner of the page. Then down a little and to the right, you can see another gray box labeled `Layout`. The thin lines that extend from the gray box marked `Layout` form a box that defines your *Layout area*. The Layout area is where you place any elements — text, graphics, and so on — that are to appear only on this particular page.

Anything outside the Layout area is the *MasterBorder*. The MasterBorder is an area where you place elements that you want to appear on any page that uses the same MasterBorder. The MasterBorder works kind of like the header and footer in a word processing document, except that it can include the sides of a Web page as well as the top and bottom.

MasterBorder marking   Layout marking

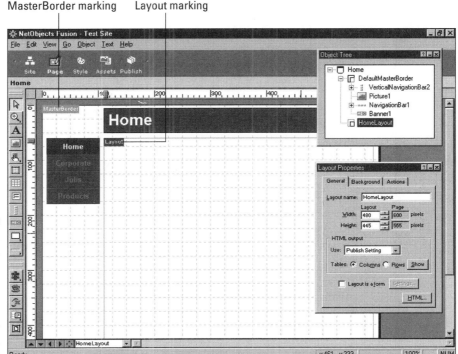

Figure 5-3: Each page is divided into a Layout area and a MasterBorder area.

Controlling your Layouts

In fusionese, a *Layout* is simply a combination of settings and content that controls the look of a particular page. (For example, background color is one such setting.) What makes NetObjects Fusion so powerful in this respect is that you can define several Layouts for the same page. What makes Layouts a little confusing is that any given Layout includes not only certain settings like background color, but also the content you add to your page while using that Layout. In other words, if you add, for example, some text to your page and then create a new Layout on that page, the text you added disappears until you switch back to the original Layout.

When you publish your site, only the Layout currently in use gets published for any given page. This means that using multiple layouts is useful not only for experimenting with various looks for the same page, but also with controlling variable content. For example, suppose you have a page that holds specific content for each day of the week. You could create a Layout for each day of the week, add the appropriate content for each Layout, and then publish the page daily using the appropriate Layout.

You control several aspects of the page Layout through the Properties palette. This section covers the more basic settings; I cover other settings as appropriate elsewhere in this book.

Creating a new Layout

The ability to create multiple Layouts for the same page gives you an incredible amount of flexibility. You can experiment with a new look for that page without fear of losing the old look. Because a Layout includes the content within the Layout area, you can store different content within the same page and change the published content of the page by simply selecting a different Layout.

To create a new Layout, follow these steps:

1. **Click your mouse anywhere in the Layout area.**

   Doing so changes the title of the Properties palette to Layout Properties. On the Properties palette take note of the text field marked Layout Name.

2. **Click the down arrow by the Layout pull-down list located in the lower-left of the screen, as shown in Figure 5-4.**

   A pull-down list appears that includes the names of all available Layouts, plus the word Add.

Figure 5-4:
In the
bottom-left
corner of
Page view,
you can find
the Layout
pull-down
list.

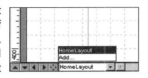

3. Select Add.

The Layout name on the Properties palette changes to the name of the current page followed by the word *Layout*, all with no spaces. For example, if the name of your page is Home, the name of the new Layout is HomeLayout. This in itself can be a little confusing, because you may already have a Layout named, in this example, HomeLayout. For better or worse, NetObjects Fusion allows you to create multiple Layouts with the same name. Hence, the next order of business is changing the name of your new Layout.

4. Use your mouse to highlight HomeLayout **in the Layout Name field on the Properties palette and then type a new name for your Layout.**

You can use only standard alphanumeric characters with no spaces or punctuation.

Notice that as you type in a new name, the Layout name changes in the Layout pull-down list at the bottom of the page, as well as in the Object Tree (assuming that the Object Tree is visible).

Resizing your Layout area

NetObjects Fusion lets you make each Layout a different size. This is handy if you're storing different content versions within your various Layouts and one version needs more room than another.

To adjust the size of the Layout area, do the following:

1. Click your mouse anywhere in the Layout area.

Doing so changes the title of the Properties palette to Layout Properties. Note the fields marked Width and Height under the Layout heading, as shown in Figure 5-5. These fields display the current size of the Layout area in pixels.

What the heck is a pixel, anyway?

When you're working in the real world, you measure in units like feet and inches because they're standard. One inch at my house is the same as one inch at your house. However, in cyberspace, it's not so easy. That's because different computer monitors have different resolutions, and those resolutions are measured in pixels. The image you see on your computer screen is made up of thousands of little dots, and each one of those dots is called a pixel. For that reason, an image that's, say, 100 pixels wide appears smaller on a higher resolution monitor. By measuring in pixels instead of inches, you're using a unit of measurement that's the same from one monitor to the next.

Also note that you're not allowed to change the settings listed under the Page heading. The reason is that the width and height of the page are determined by figuring in the dimensions of the Layout area, plus the dimensions of the MasterBorder, which I cover in the section called "Creating a new MasterBorder" later in this chapter.

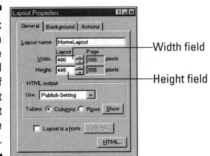

Figure 5-5:
You can change the width and height of the Layout area, but not of the page.

Width field

Height field

2. **Change the width by either highlighting the current width and typing in a new number, or by clicking the small up and down arrows immediately to the right of the Width field.**

3. **Change the height by either highlighting the current height and typing in a new number, or by clicking the small up and down arrows immediately to the right of the Height field.**

How big is big?

You may be wondering exactly how big your page should be. Height isn't as big a concern as width, because people who visit your Web site can always scroll down to see the rest of a page. But if you make your page wider than the typical monitor can accommodate, people will also have to scroll from left to right, which is extremely annoying. The question then becomes, what can the typical monitor accommodate? The lowest of the low-end monitors have a resolution of 640 x 480 pixels — that's 640 pixels wide by 480 pixels high. That means that if you want to make allowances for the greatest number of people, your entire page should be less than 640 pixels wide. Just remember that the total page width is determined by a combination of the Layout width and the width of the MasterBorder.

Coloring your Layout

When it comes to the background color (the color that you see behind everything else on your page), you have three options. You can use the background color that's defined for the Style you're using (I cover Styles in Chapters 3 and 16), you can use some other color of your liking, or you can choose an image that's repeated across the entire length and width of the page.

To change the background color, follow these steps:

1. **Click your mouse anywhere in the Layout area.**

   Doing so changes the title of the Properties palette to Layout Properties.

2. **Click the Background tab on the Properties palette.**

   The palette gives you several options, as shown in Figure 5-6.

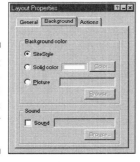

Figure 5-6: You have several options for your background.

3. **To use the background color associated with the style you're using, click the SiteStyle radio button.**

   If you choose this option, you can skip the rest of these steps. If you want to use a background image instead of a solid color, you can skip to Step 7.

4. **To use another color, click the Solid Color radio button.**

5. **Click the Color button to the right of the Solid Color radio button.**

   Doing so displays a Color palette from which you can select any color.

6. **Click the desired color and then click the OK button.**

   The background changes to the color you specified. You can skip the rest of these steps.

7. **To use an image for your background, click the Picture radio button.**

   NetObjects Fusion displays an Image File Open dialog box.

8. **Navigate your computer to find the image you want to use for your background image.**

   The Image File Open dialog box works like any other Open dialog box in any other Windows program. Note that although Web pages use graphics that are in GIF or JPEG format only, NetObjects Fusion also lets you select files in the following formats: PNG, BMP, PCX, or PICT. If you choose a file in one of these alternate formats, NetObjects Fusion automatically creates a copy in GIF or JPEG format for use on your site.

   Also note that the Image File Open dialog box includes a tab called Image Assets. If you click the Image Assets tab, you have the option to select a background image from any of the images that you have already used anywhere in your site.

9. **Click the name of the file you want to use, and then click the Open button.**

   The image you select is tiled across the width and length of the page.

Sounding off in your Layout

NetObjects Fusion gives you the option to include a *background sound* on any Web page (and in fact, lets you include a different background sound for each Layout on a page). A background sound is one that plays immediately when the page is viewed in any late-model Web browser. But before you run off and add your recital of the Gettysburg Address as a background sound, keep in mind that the longer the sound, the bigger the file that contains it. And the bigger the file, the longer your page takes to load. Prior to adding a background sound, stop and consider whether the extra download time is really worth it. Sometimes it is; other times it isn't.

You can add a background sound by following these steps:

1. **Click the mouse anywhere in the Layout area.**

   The title of the Properties palette changes to `Layout Properties`.

2. **Click the Background tab on the Properties palette.**

   Doing so displays several options, including a Sound check box.

3. **Select the Sound check box.**

4. **Click the Browse button.**

   A standard Open dialog box appears.

5. **Navigate the folders of your hard disk to find the sound file you want to use for your background sound.**

   NetObjects Fusion lets you use sound files in AIFF, AU, WAV, or MIDI format. However, not every Web browser can support every sound file format. Because AU files are the most common on the Web, I suggest you use this format for the greatest compatibility with the widest variety of Web browsers.

6. **Click the name of the file you want to use, and then click the Open button.**

   You return to the Background Sound dialog box.

7. **If you want the sound to play continuously (versus just one time through) click the Continuous Loop check box.**

8. **Click the OK button.**

   Now people will not only see your Web page, but they'll hear it, too.

Mastering MasterBorders

A MasterBorder is the area of a NetObjects Fusion page outside the Layout area. You can place elements that you want to appear on more than one page in the MasterBorder. Much like Layouts, you can create or modify a MasterBorder on one page and then use it on any other pages in your Web site. For example, if you create a NavBar (as described in Chapter 8), you'll probably want to put it in the MasterBorder and then use that same MasterBorder on other pages in the same hierarchical level.

You can put just about anything — text, graphics, multimedia (in short, most of the elements described in Chapters 6 through 10) — in a MasterBorder, but you control the general characteristics of the MasterBorder from the Properties palette.

Creating a new MasterBorder

Just as with Layouts, your best bet is to create a new MasterBorder before you start fiddling with any settings. That way, if you find that the results of your MasterBorder experimentation are, shall we say, less than perfect, it's easy to revert to the old one. If you screw up on the new one, just select the old one and you're right back where you started.

Follow these steps to create a new MasterBorder:

1. **Click your mouse anywhere in the MasterBorder area.**

   The title of the Properties palette changes to `MasterBorder Properties`. Note that the Properties palette now has three tabs along the top, as shown in Figure 5-7.

Figure 5-7:
The Properties palette changes to MasterBorder Properties.

   In this chapter, I discuss only the General tab; AutoFrames and Actions are advanced topics that I cover in later chapters. The HTML button in the lower-right corner of the Properties palette also falls into the advanced category.

2. **Click the Add/Edit button to the right of the MasterBorder name.**

   An Edit MasterBorder List dialog box appears, as shown in Figure 5-8.

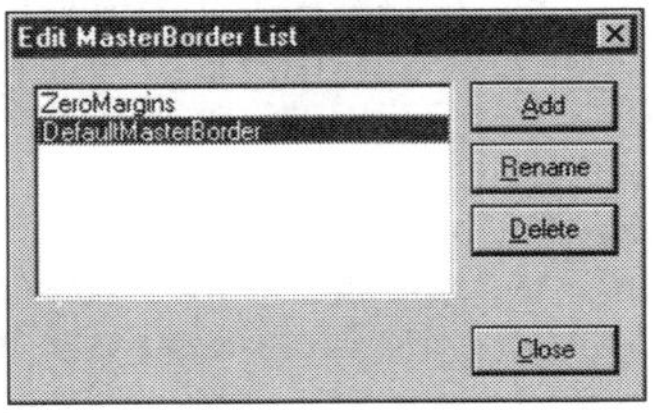

Figure 5-8:
This list shows all the MasterBorders that are currently available.

3. **Click the Add button.**

   A New MasterBorder box appears.

4. **Type in a name for your new MasterBorder.**

   Note that while you can use both upper- and lowercase characters, you can't use any punctuation or spaces.

5. **From the pop-up list in this dialog box, select a MasterBorder as the base for your new one and then click OK.**

No matter what page you're on, you can pop up a list of all available MasterBorders by clicking the little down arrow to the right of the MasterBorder name on the Properties palette. After the list pops up, just click the name of the MasterBorder you want to use.

Getting marginal with MasterBorders

Each portion of a MasterBorder — the top, bottom, right, and left — is called a margin. When you adjust the right or left margin, you affect the width of the entire page. When you change the top or bottom margin, you affect the page height.

You can change MasterBorder margins by following these steps:

1. **Click your mouse anywhere in the MasterBorder area.**

   Again, the title of the Properties palette changes to `MasterBorder Properties`.

2. **To change any one of the margins, either highlight the current size of that margin and type a new number or click the small up and down arrows to the right of the margin size to change the size one pixel at a time.**

Digging through Your Tool Box

I want to cover just a couple more goodies in this chapter. One is the tool palette that appears along the left side of your screen, and the other is a set of navigational buttons on the bottom of the screen. These buttons help you move from page to page when you're in Page view.

You may not realize it, but the tool icons that you see along the left side of your screen are actually in two separate toolbars. One is called Standard Tools and the other is called Advanced Tools. You can hide and redisplay these by selecting the appropriate toolbar name from View➪Toolbars.

Almost all these tools are covered in other, more appropriate sections of this book. The tools that I really want to focus on now are the Selection tool and the Zoom tool. The Selection tool is the one that looks like an arrow. As the name implies, its primary purpose is to select things. You select something by clicking it — this tells the program what item to perform the next operation on.

Table 5-1 lists the tools that I *don't* cover in this chapter, as well as where to look for more information.

Table 5-1		**Standard and Advanced Tools**	
Icon	*Tool*	*Used to...*	*Chapter*
A	Text	enter text on a page	6
	Picture	place a graphic on a page	7
	Hotspot	create hotspots on an image map	8
	Layout Region	create a Layout Region, which is like a page within a page	6
	Table	create a table	10
	Form Area	create a form	11
	Navigation Bar	create a NavBar	8
	Banner	add a new banner	7
	Draw	draw various shapes	7
	Line	add an HTML rule or SiteStyle line	7
	Media	add multimedia elements to a page	9
	Java	add Java applets to a page	9
	ActiveX Control	add an ActiveX control to a page	9
	DataList	add a DataList to a page	14
	External HTML	reference an external HTML file	4

One final comment on both the Standard Tools and Advanced Tools toolbars. I like them where they are by default — along the left side of the screen. However, if you want, you can convert either or both to what amounts to floating palettes. To perform this switcheroo, just click and hold on the double lines at the top of the toolbar and drag to the right. The outline of the toolbar changes to a horizontal orientation, at which time you can put the toolbar anywhere you want on the screen. To put it back, just drag it back to the left side of the screen.

All I wanna do is zooma zoom zoom zoom

The Zoom tool enables you to zoom in and out, making the page appear larger or smaller on your computer screen. To use this tool, just give it a click — it's the one that looks like a magnifying glass. When the pointer turns into a magnifying glass with a plus sign in the middle, click the part of the page that you want to enlarge.

If you find that you've zoomed in too far, you can hold down the Alt key and use the Zoom tool to zoom back out. Notice that when you hold down the Alt key, the plus sign in the middle of the magnifying glass turns into a minus sign. Earlier versions of NetObjects Fusion provided separate Zoom In and Zoom Out tools. For version 3.0, the folks at NetObjects wised up and condensed the whole zoom thing into one tool.

One final note on zooming: Instead of using the Zoom tool to zoom in and out, you can also choose View⇨Zoom.

Movin' around

I also want to discuss the five little buttons near the lower-left corner of your screen. They look like an up arrow, a down arrow, a left arrow, a right arrow, and one button that has arrows pointing in all directions. If you can't find them, take a look at Figure 5-9.

Figure 5-9:
The navigational tools in the lower-left corner.

Table 5-2 explains how each button allows you to navigate in your site's hierarchy.

Table 5-2	Where the Navigation Buttons Take You
Navigation Buttons	*What It Does*
▲	Takes you to the page immediately above the current page in the site's hierarchy. If you don't have a page above the current page (that is, if you're looking at the home page), this button doesn't do anything.
▼	Takes you to the page immediately below the current page, in the site's hierarchy.
◄	Takes you to the page immediately to the left of the current page, as displayed in Site view.
►	Takes you the page immediately to the right of the current page, as displayed in Site view.
✛	Pops up a mini Site view window, like the one shown in Figure 5-10. Use this window to select where you want to go.

Figure 5-10:
You can see a mini version of the Site view while you're still in Page view.

Chapter 6

Getting the Word Out with Text

. . . .

In This Chapter

▶ Adding text to your Web page

▶ Changing the look of your text

▶ Using special characters

▶ Using and creating variables

▶ Running spell-check, word count, and search and replace

. . . .

*P*rose, text, copy. No matter how you say it, the words you present are the most important elements on your Web page. Sure, nice graphics look cool and snappy multimedia makes you say "Wow," but the majority of people surf the Web to find some sort of information. For better or worse, that puts you in the information business.

Just as important as what you say, however, is the way you present your message. If your Web page consists of plain Courier text against a plain gray background, people are going to get plain bored with your Web site, even if your site holds the answers to the Mysteries of Life, a cure for the common cold, *and* a recipe for the perfect martini. Your message needs to be solid and your copy needs to be well edited, but your text also needs to look attractive. Once again, NetObjects Fusion comes to the rescue. With a couple of mouse-clicks here and there, your boring text becomes a virtual work of art!

Adding Text to Your Page

NetObjects Fusion differs from most Web authoring programs in the way it handles text. Most Web authoring programs work like word processing programs: You type from top to bottom, and if you want to type text at the bottom of a page, you have to start at the top and keep typing until you reach the bottom. NetObjects Fusion gives you control over how your text is positioned and, unlike the typical Web authoring programs, NetObjects Fusion lets you position independent blocks of text on a page. In fact, in this respect, NetObjects Fusion works very much like QuarkXPress: First you create a text box, and then you type something in it.

Boxing your text: I coulda been a contenda!

I'm kind of like Dr. Jekyll and Mr. Hyde, or should I say Mr. Hyde and Dr. Jekyll? Take one look at my desk and you'd wonder how I possibly got anything done. But take a look on my hard drive and you'd be amazed at how neat and orderly I am with my computer. I suppose it's my cyber perfectionism that has made me so fond of NetObjects Fusion. Unlike other Web authoring programs, NetObjects Fusion lets me create individual text boxes, fill 'em up with text, and move them around on my Web page, independent of each other or anything else.

The first step, then, in adding text to a page is creating a text box. To create one, make sure you're in Page view on the page where you want to add some text and then follow these steps:

1. **Click the Text tool in the Standard Tools palette on the left side of your screen.**

   This is the Text tool that contains the letter *A*. If the Standard Tools palette isn't displayed, choose <u>V</u>iew➪<u>T</u>oolbars➪Standard <u>T</u>ools to bring it up.

   After you select the Text tool, notice that the mouse pointer turns into a crosshair.

2. **Position the crosshair at any one of the four corners of your intended text box.**

   You can use the grids that appear on the page to help you identify the area for the text box and position the cursor. It's important to realize that these grid lines do *not* appear on your finished Web page. In fact, you can hide the grid lines at any time by pressing Ctrl+D or unchecking Grid in the View menu.

   Also, although you can actually start out at any corner, your best bet is to start in the upper-left corner, because that's where you start typing after you create the text box. For me, it's easier to define the text box in the same direction that I'll eventually be typing — left to right and top to bottom.

3. **Click and hold your left mouse button, and then drag the crosshair to the opposite corner of the imaginary box to define a real text box.**

   As you drag, a dotted line appears around the area you're defining.

4. **Release the mouse button.**

   A new text box appears in the area you defined, with the text cursor blinking in the upper-left corner. Figure 6-1 shows the text box (but unfortunately, on paper I can't show you the blinking cursor).

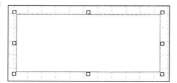

Figure 6-1:
Now you're
ready to
start typing.

Notice the eight little squares positioned around the text box. These are handles that you can use to size the text box. Just click and hold on one of the handles, and then drag in any direction.

5. **Type the desired text into the text box.**

When you finish typing, click the mouse anywhere else on the page and the text box becomes deselected. If you didn't fill up the entire box with text, it automatically resizes itself.

If you ever need to change any of the text, you have two ways to get back into the text box. If you already have the Text tool selected, just click once anywhere in the text box. If you're using the Selection tool, double-click the text box to edit its text.

Wrapping up your box

Of course you can do all sorts of things to affect the appearance of the text in your text box. However, NetObjects Fusion lets you treat each text box as a separate page element. That means that there are certain characteristics that you can apply to the text box as a whole. If you click once on a text box with the Selection tool, the Properties palette shows you some options marked Text Box, as shown in Figure 6-2.

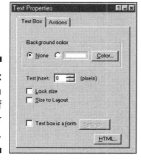

Figure 6-2:
You have a
couple of
options for
a text box.

Here's what these options do:

- ✔ **Background Color.** Clicking the Color button brings up a color palette. Click the color that you want to appear inside your text box.

- ✔ **Text inset.** This option controls the distance between the edge of a text box and its contents. It helps you keep the text box from looking cramped.

- ✔ **Lock Size.** This option lets you lock the size of the text box, preventing it from automatically adjusting its size according to its contents. This is handy if you're going to be changing the text in that box regularly and want to make sure the text box takes up the same space on the page every time you modify it.

- ✔ **Size to Layout.** Clicking this check box automatically resizes the text box to fill the entire layout area.

- ✔ **Text Box Is a Form.** This option makes NetObjects Fusion treat the text as a form. I tell you how to set up a form in Chapter 11.

Touching Up Your Text

While everyone at the Academy Awards ceremonies clearly realizes that regular street clothes aren't appropriate for such an occasion, ideas for what does constitute appropriate clothing vary greatly. Outfits range from the stunning to the ghastly. In this sense, the Web is like the Oscars. Nobody wants plain, boring text on their Web pages. Yet, in their quest for the unique, many would-be Web authors end up with the atrocious.

Trick or treat?

I remember one Halloween in a previous life when I worked for a savings and loan. (I suppose that dates me a little.) My department had a potluck lunch, so I decided to make something especially ghoulish. What I came up with was my usual delicious lasagna — with a couple of modifications. I used food coloring to make the sauce black and the ricotta cheese a disgusting shade of pink. I also used green lasagna noodles.

My lasagna tasted the same as it always tastes — pretty good, in all modesty — but much to my surprise, several people in my department refused to eat it. Despite my assurance that there was nothing extra except food coloring, these people couldn't bring themselves to take even one bite. That day, I learned a lesson that I would one day apply to Web authoring: No matter what the content, you have to make your finished product look good or you'll turn people away.

NetObjects Fusion gives you every bit as much control over your text as you're likely to find in any word processor. Your challenge is to use these text-control features without misusing or abusing them.

Going boldly where no italic has gone before

When I was a kid, I had to type my book reports on a manual typewriter. If I wanted bold type, I had to backspace and retype the word. If I wanted italics . . . well, I was out of luck. Thanks to computers, now all this special formatting stuff is a snap. That's a good thing and a bad thing.

It's a good thing because special formatting, when used sparingly, can really drive a point home. It's a bad thing because it's so easy that it tempts you to go overboard. If you add special formatting to every other word in your text, the words you really should accentuate become de-emphasized by the all those other words that don't deserve any special formatting. That, plus too much special formatting just looks lame. Table 6-1 shows Fusion's formatting options.

Table 6-1	Formatting Options in NetObjects Fusion	
Formatting Attribute	*Button*	*What You Get*
Bold	**B**	**Bold**
Italic	*I*	*Italics*
Underscore	U	<u>Underscore</u>
Strikethrough	S	~~Strikethrough~~
Superscript	a^b	Superscript
Subscript	a_b	Subscript

 Right now, you should be in Page view. The page you're viewing should have a text box on it, and you should see some text in that box. You should also have the Properties palette displayed. Now, on with the procedures. To add special formatting to text, just follow these steps:

1. **Using the Selection tool, double-click the text box that contains the text to be formatted.**

   This makes the text box active and positions the text cursor wherever you happened to double-click. I call this active state *edit mode*. Notice

Figure 6-3:
Click one
of these
buttons to
change the
appearance
of your text.

that when you go into edit mode, the title bar on the Properties palette
changes to `Text Properties`.

2. **Use your mouse to highlight the portion of text to which you want to
   apply special formatting.**

   Note: Double-clicking a word highlights the whole word; triple-clicking a
   word highlights the entire paragraph.

3. **With the text still highlighted, click one of the special formatting
   buttons on the Properties palette, as shown in Figure 6-3.**

   Notice that when you click one of the formatting buttons, the button
   turns a darker shade of gray. This lets you know that this particular
   formatting has been applied to the current text selection.

Keep in mind that you can apply more than one type of special formatting to
a text selection. For example, bold and italic is a common combination. The
only two that you can't combine are superscript and subscript, because
they're the opposite of each other.

Size on the rise and the great shape escape

I don't have hard figures, but I'd guess that 90 percent of all text produced
on this planet uses 12-point type in a Times font or some variation thereof.
That makes for a lot of text that looks just like a lot of other text.

With NetObjects Fusion, you don't need to be just another Times font in the
crowd. You have complete control over what fonts you use on your page and
to a somewhat lesser extent, the size of those fonts. In short, you have the
power to create text the likes of which no man, woman, or child has ever
seen. You can make a stand! You can . . . okay, okay, I'm getting a little
carried away here. My whole point is that NetObjects Fusion doesn't force
you to live with 12-point Times type.

Adjusting type size

NetObjects Fusion gives you the maximum control possible over fonts and type size. To demonstrate this to yourself, start out (again) in Page view, viewing a page with a text box on it and some text in that box. You should also have the Properties palette displayed. To change your type size, step through the following:

1. **Using the Selection tool, double-click the text box that contains the text to be changed.**

   This puts the text box in edit mode and changes the Properties palette to Text Properties.

2. **Use your mouse to highlight the portion of text that you want to change the size of.**

   Note that double-clicking a word highlights the whole word; triple-clicking a word highlights the entire paragraph.

3. **With the text still highlighted, click the down arrow just to the right of the Size field on the Properties palette.**

   This pops up a list of your possible choices for text size.

4. **Click the desired text size from the list.**

Changing the font

NetObjects Fusion lets you choose specific fonts to include on your Web page. Although the use of specific fonts is not an official part of HTML — not yet, anyway — the current versions of both Navigator and Internet Explorer recognize instructions to use specific fonts when displaying a Web page. That means that you can use any font on your system to create your Web page.

Before you make the decision to specify a particular font in your Web page, bear in mind that you're unlikely to find two computers in the whole world that contain exactly the same set of fonts. If your visitors don't happen to have the font you specify, their browsers display your page in its default font. This means that it can end up with quite a different look from what you planned.

In general, I avoid using specific fonts on my Web pages. If you're creating a site for the whole world to see, and you insist on using special fonts, you should consider creating those portions of your page as graphics, which I cover in Chapter 7.

If you want to change a font on your Web page, follow these steps:

1. **Using the Selection tool, double-click the text box that contains the text to be changed.**

   This puts the text box in edit mode and changes the Properties palette to *Text Properties*.

Does size really matter?

One of the drawbacks of HTML is that it's not nearly as flexible at handling text as, say, your word processor. You can change the type size on your Web page, but it's only a relative change.

If you don't specify any particular size for the type on your page, it will display on someone's screen at whatever type size they've specified for the default in their Web browser. For most people, that's 12-point type. If you want to specify a smaller or larger type size, it's expressed in HTML as a relative numerical value. For example, if you want your type one increment larger than normal, *+1* is added to the HTML code — not an exact type size. Again, for most people, *+1* will translate to 14-point type.

The problem here is that some people may change their default type size to something else. If someone, for example, already has their default type size set to 14-point type, changing the type size on your page to *+1* will bump that person up to 18-point type.

This doesn't mean that you should never change your type size. Certain portions of text should be larger than other portions. What you want to avoid, however, is creating a page layout that relies on type fitting precisely into a specific area. For example, don't design a page that relies on a single line of text exactly filling the width of a text box. It may look OK on one person's system but wrong on someone else's.

2. **Use your mouse to highlight the portion of text whose font you want to change.**

   Note that double-clicking a word highlights the whole word; triple-clicking a word highlights the entire paragraph.

3. **With the text still highlighted, click the down arrow just to the right of the Font field on the Properties palette.**

   This pulls down a list of your possible font choices.

4. **Click the desired font from the list.**

   Note that the first two options on this list are `Browser Proportional` and `Browser Fixed`. If you select Browser Proportional, the Web page loads using the default proportional font for whatever Web browser you use to view the page. Likewise, if you select Browser Fixed, the Web page loads using the default fixed-width font for whatever Web browser you use to view the page. The most common default proportional font is Times or some variation of it; the most common default fixed-width font is Courier.

Coloring your world (and words)

How many times have you heard the expression, "It's right there in black and white"? For hundreds of years, virtually all published words really were all right there in black and white. Today on the Web, however, published words are just as likely to be right there in yellow and blue, brown and green, or purple and gold. Even if the thoughts conveyed by your Web words are on the drab side, the words themselves can be as colorful as you want.

Unless you tell it to do otherwise, NetObjects Fusion colors your text according to whatever Style you happen to use. (See Chapter 3 for more information about Styles.) Although NetObjects Fusion makes it easy to change the color of selected portions of text, I have to caution against it. The problem with coloring text is that hypertext links (covered in Chapter 8) also appear in a different color, and people who use the Web on a regular basis tend to assume that any different-color text represents a hypertext link.

Text coloring can come in handy when you alter the color of an entire text block to set it off from other text blocks on the page. For example, if you have a small block of text that provides extra information about the text in the main body of the page (something commonly called a *sidebar*), you may want to change the color of that text.

To change the color of text, again start out in Page view and follow these steps:

1. **Using the Selection tool, double-click the text box that contains the text to be recolored.**

   This puts the text box in edit mode and changes the Properties palette to *Text Properties*. Pay particular attention to two radio buttons next to the word *Color*, as shown in Figure 6-4.

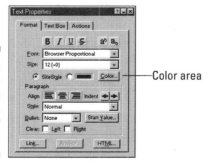

Figure 6-4: These options control the color of your text.

—Color area

One of the radio buttons is the SiteStyle button; the other just has a colored box next to it. When you check the SiteStyle radio button, text color is set according to the Style you use. When you choose an alternate color, NetObjects Fusion selects the unmarked radio button for you.

2. **Use your mouse to highlight the portion of text for which you want to change the color.**

   Note: Double-clicking a word highlights the whole word; triple-clicking a word highlights the entire paragraph.

3. **With the text still highlighted, click the Color button to the right of the two radio buttons.**

   This pops up a standard Color palette that shows the colors you can choose from.

4. **Click the color you want and then click OK.**

Prettying Up Your Paragraphs

If you passed second-grade English, you know that groups of words make sentences and groups of sentences make paragraphs. (I know Sister Mary Athanacius drilled this into my head with the help of her trusty solid-oak yard stick.) And you also know that some formatting — indents, alignment, and so on — applies to entire paragraphs. And that brings us to this section. You read on while I go pop a Prozac and reminisce about my days in parochial school.

Adjusting your alignment

HTML (and by extension, NetObjects Fusion) offers you the standard text alignment options found in your word processor. Specifically, you can choose left alignment, right alignment, or center alignment. The one thing you can't do to the alignment is justify text (that is, align text) so that its edges are flush with both the right and left side of the text box at the same time. Tip-toe through the following steps for changing text alignment:

1. **Using the Selection tool, double-click the text box that contains the text to be realigned.**

   Doing so puts the text box in edit mode and changes the Properties palette to `Text Properties`.

2. **Click your mouse anywhere in the paragraph that you want to realign.**

   If you want to realign more than one consecutive paragraph, highlight just enough text to select some portion of each paragraph. For example, in Figure 6-5, I can change the alignment of the second and third paragraphs.

3. **Click the desired alignment button.**

Figure 6-5:
You don't
have to
highlight
the entire
paragraph
to change
alignment.

Smoothing out those indents

You can indent a paragraph on your Web page much as you would with a
word processor. The difference here is that you can't control the amount of
the indent. An HTML indent is an HTML indent; what you see is what you
get. If you want the paragraph to be indented more, you just indent it a
second time. Don't worry; it will all make sense when you work through the
following steps for indenting:

To indent a paragraph, follow these steps:

1. **Using the Selection tool, double-click the text box that contains the
   text to be indented.**

   Doing so puts the text box in edit mode and changes the Properties
   palette to `Text Properties`. Take note of the two Indent buttons on
   the Properties palette. They're the two little arrow buttons next to the
   word *Indent*.

   Actually, only the second button, the one with the right arrow, is the
   indent button. The first button, the one with the left arrow, is really the
   "unindent" button. You use this button to unindent a previously indented paragraph.

2. **Click your mouse anywhere in the paragraph that you want to
   indent.**

   If you want to indent consecutive paragraphs, highlight just enough
   text to select some portion of each paragraph.

3. **Click the Indent button (the one with the right arrow).**

   To indent that paragraph farther, click the Indent button a second time.
   To unindent a paragraph, click the Unindent button (the one with the
   left arrow).

Getting the lead out with bullets

In other Web authoring programs, you likely can find several paragraph styles for creating lists. As you may have guessed, you use list styles to organize lists (as opposed to tables) of information. Take a look at Figure 6-6 if you're not sure what I'm talking about.

Figure 6-6:
Here's a
simple
HTML list.

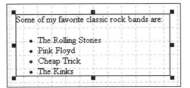

Unlike other programs, NetObjects Fusion presents no paragraph styles with which to define lists. NetObjects Fusion takes a simpler approach. Rather than choosing a specific type of list such as ordered, unordered, and so on, you only have to choose which type of bullet character you want to precede each list item. If you specify a bullet character for a particular paragraph, NetObjects Fusion knows you're creating a list and handles all the underlying coding for you.

Your lists can be preceded by the following bullet characters:

- Solid circle
- Solid square
- Open circle
- Uppercase letters
- Lowercase letters
- Uppercase Roman numerals
- Lowercase Roman numerals
- Standard numbers

When you choose letters or numbers, each list item is lettered or numbered consecutively. To create a list, just follow these steps:

1. **Type your list items into a new or existing text box.**

   Don't worry about any formatting right now. Just be sure to separate each list item by a paragraph return. As you complete Step 1, the Properties palette displays `Text Properties`.

2. **Drag your mouse to select the items in your list.**

3. **Click the down arrow just to the right of the Bullet field on the Properties palette, as shown in Figure 6-7.**

   This pulls down a list of available bullet characters.

Bullet field

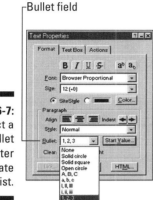

Figure 6-7:
Select a
bullet
character
to create
a list.

4. **Select the bullet character you want to display in your list.**

5. **If you want the numbering or lettering in your list to begin at some point other than the beginning, click the Start Value button to the right of the Bullet field.**

   This displays a Start Value of Numbered List dialog box.

6. **Type in the desired start value as a standard number; then click OK.**

   For example, if you choose lettering and want the list to start with *B*, type in the number **2**. Also, if you do choose lettering and you specify a number greater than 26, the list will go to double-digit lettering. For example, the twenty-eighth item would be listed as *AB*.

The last two items in the Paragraph area are the Clear Left and Clear Right check boxes. You use these check boxes in conjunction with *wrapped graphics* — graphics that have text flowing around them. Selecting the Clear Left or Clear Right check box specifies that you want a particular paragraph to start beneath a wrapped graphic instead of wrapping around it. Select the Clear Left check box if the text that you want to start beneath the graphic wraps on the left side of the graphic; select the Clear Right check box if the text wraps on the right side of the graphic.

Writing in style

You'd think that with all the thousands of words in the English language, you'd be able to create a Web page without using the word *style* to describe two different things. Well, sorry, Charlie. Chapter 3 covers the NetObjects Fusion SiteStyles; however, in HTML-land you also find *paragraph styles* — that's with a small *s*. A paragraph style is simply a combination of formatting characteristics that you can apply to an entire paragraph with a single click.

Table 6-2 lists the different paragraph styles available in NetObjects Fusion and describes what each style does.

Table 6-2	Paragraph Styles in NetObjects Fusion
Style	*Result*
Address	Italic type; browser proportional font; default size
Caption	Italic type; Arial font; -1 size
Code	Normal type; browser fixed font; default size
Credits	Centered paragraph; Times New Roman font; -1 size
Footnotes	Numbered list; Arial font; -1 size
Formatted	Normal type; browser fixed font; default size (same as Code)
Heading 1	Bold type; browser proportional font; +3 size
Heading 2	Bold type; browser proportional font; +2 size
Heading 3	Bold type; browser proportional font; +1 size
Heading 4	Bold type; browser proportional font; default size
Heading 5	Bold type; browser proportional font; -1 size
Heading 6	Bold type; browser proportional font; -2 size
Normal	Normal type; browser proportional font; default size
Quotes	Italic type; indented paragraph, Times New Roman; +1 size
Subheads	Normal type; Arial font; -1 size

Most of the time, you're likely to use Normal. The various levels of headings also come in quite handy. You may wonder why Formatted style and Code style appear the same. In strict HTML coding, you use Code to identify lines of computer code or screen output. The Formatted style isn't used much today. In the days before HTML tables, the Formatted style was used to line up row and columns of information. (Check Chapter 10 for more on tables.)

Way back when HTML was coded by hand in simple text editors, using the correct style (for example, Code for computer code and Formatted for formatted text) made it easy to identify various elements in the mumbo-jumbo of HTML code.

To change a paragraph style, perform the following steps:

1. **Using the Selection tool, double-click the text box that contains the paragraph to be changed.**

   Doing so puts the text box in edit mode and changes the name of the Properties palette to `Text Properties`.

2. **Click anywhere in the paragraph that you want to change.**

   To change consecutive paragraphs, highlight enough text to select some part of each paragraph. (It's not important to select all of it.)

3. **Click the down arrow just to the left of the Style field on the Properties palette.**

   Doing so pulls down a list of available styles.

4. **Click the style you want to apply.**

Making Paragraph Styles Your Way

Paragraph styles are pretty handy, but face it. Everyone who creates Web pages uses these same exact styles. The good news is that NetObjects Fusion never forces you to follow the crowd. The program lets you change various characteristics of each paragraph style and even lets you create your own custom paragraph styles to make the road to the perfect Web site more pleasant.

Changing paragraph styles to match your style

When you apply any given paragraph style, the most you can expect to see is a change in type size and the application of bold and/or italic formatting. Sometimes that just isn't enough. Suppose you want all your first-level headings to be centered or all your captions to be red. No problem. Just go in and change the paragraph style just the way you want, using these oh-so-easy steps:

1. **Choose Text⇨Edit Text Styles.**

   Doing so displays a Text Styles dialog box, as shown in Figure 6-8. This dialog box lists all the paragraph styles available for your site.

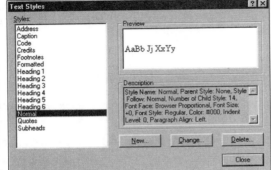

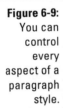

Figure 6-8:
Start
here to
modify any
paragraph
style.

2. Click the desired paragraph style in the list and then click Change.

The Change Style dialog box pops up, as shown in Figure 6-9.

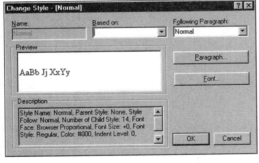

Figure 6-9:
You can
control
every
aspect of a
paragraph
style.

The following is a description of the various options available from the Change Style dialog box:

- *Name field:* This field is always grayed out (unavailable) when you are changing a style. If you want to change the name of your style only, you have to add a new style with the name you want that has all of the same options as in the old style. Then delete the old style. The following section, "Creating a style all your own," gives you the steps for creating a new style.

- *Based on field:* If you want to begin by borrowing the characteristics of another paragraph style, you can select that paragraph style from the drop-down list associated with the Based On field.

- *Following Paragraph field:* It's not uncommon to have one paragraph style that's always followed by some other paragraph style. For example, maybe your first-level headings are always followed by normal text. If you select another paragraph style from the drop-down list associated with the Following Paragraph field, NetObjects Fusion will handle this switcheroo for you.

- *Paragraph button:* Clicking the Paragraph button presents you with another dialog box that allows you to define the paragraph style as a list.

- *Font button:* Clicking the Font button presents you with another dialog box that allows you to adjust various aspects of the type, such as size, font, color, and so on.

- *Preview area:* This area shows you an example of the paragraph style as it's currently defined.

- *Description area:* This area provides a summary of the various characteristics of the paragraph style.

3. Adjust the desired options and click OK.

Doing so takes you back to the Text Styles dialog box.

4. Click Close.

Making styles disappear (forever)

It may be that after using your Web page for a long time, you decide to do some house cleaning. If you want to get rid of a style (maybe it's offended you in some way), you can do so easily (perhaps too easily).

When you delete a style, it's gone. The Undo command doesn't retrieve it. NetObjects Fusion converts text in your site that is formatted with the deleted style to Normal style. The bottom line? Be darned sure that you want to delete a style before you actually delete it.

To delete a style, make sure you're in page view, and follow these steps:

1. Choose Text⇨Edit Text Styles.

This brings up the Text Styles dialog box.

2. Click the paragraph style you want to do away with and then click the Delete button.

You can't delete Normal style under any circumstances and you can't delete a style that has another style based on it. You can, however, delete any other style.

3. Click Yes when NetObjects Fusion asks if you're sure you want to delete the style.

Think long and hard. Clicking Yes permanently deletes the style. Clicking No leaves the style in tact.

4. Click the Close button to close the Text Styles dialog box.

Creating a style all your own

Where most web authoring programs limit you to the standard HTML paragraph styles, NetObjects Fusion allows you to create as many custom paragraph styles as you want. Imagine the possibilities. You can create a set of red and green paragraph styles that you use just during the holiday season. You can create a variation of the Normal style that right-aligns text. If you'd rather define a list by applying a paragraph style, you can do that, too. The possibilities are endless. Just follow these steps:

1. **Choose Text⇨Edit Text Styles.**

   Doing so displays a Text Styles dialog box. This dialog box lists all the paragraph styles available for your site.

2. **Click the desired paragraph style in the list, and then click New.**

   Doing so displays the New Style dialog box. The options in this dialog box are almost identical to the options for the Change Style dialog box that I describe in the previous section, "Changing paragraph styles to match your style." The big difference is that the Name field is available, and you must supply a name for your new style. The name can contain spaces and punctuation.

3. **Adjust the desired options and click OK.**

   Doing so takes you back to the Text Styles dialog box.

4. **Click Close.**

Specializing in Special Characters

Perhaps you're wondering about special characters like the copyright symbol (©) or the registered trademark symbol (®). Or perhaps you're not. In any event, chances are you'll need to use some of them somewhere along the way to Web nirvana.

Representing symbols

HTML code uses a combination of regular characters to represent these special characters. For example, HTML uses the code ® for the registered trademark symbol. Of course, you have better things to do with your brain cells than to waste them on remembering stuff like that. You want to be able to tell NetObjects Fusion which special character you need and then have the program type all that HTML voodoo for you. You're in luck.

Figure 6-10 shows some of the special characters that NetObjects Fusion can type in the code for.

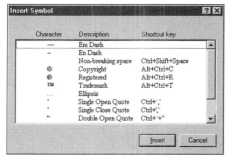

Figure 6-10:
You don't
have to
remember
any HTML
code to
use these
characters.

Notice in Figure 6-10 that some of the special characters have keyboard shortcuts. Once you remember some of these shortcuts, you probably won't go to the menu for them very often. To add a special character to your document by selecting it from a menu, follow these steps:

1. **Position the text cursor in the text box where you want the special character to be added.**

2. **Select Insert Symbol from the Text menu.**

   This displays an Insert Symbol dialog box like the one shown in Figure 6-10.

3. **Click the desired character and then click Insert.**

   The character you want appears right where you want it.

Varying variables

One of my favorite aspects of the NetObjects Fusion design philosophy is that once you type something in one place, you shouldn't have to type it again. To further that idea, NetObjects Fusion enables you to insert pre-defined *variables* (which NetObjects Fusion calls *fields*) into your text with just a couple of mouse-clicks. If you use a word processor, you've probably already encountered variables. *Variables* are placeholders for some information you want the program to enter for you, such as page numbers, the date, and so on. NetObjects Fusion breaks down the variables you can use into three categories: Date and Time, Site and General, and User Defined.

In the Date and Time Category, your options are

- ✔ Now
- ✔ Site Created
- ✔ Site Modified
- ✔ Site Generated

For Site and General, your options are

- ✔ Site Name
- ✔ Author Name (see Chapter 2)
- ✔ Number of Pages (in the entire site)
- ✔ OS Platform (Windows 95/NT)
- ✔ Generated by (NetObjects Fusion 3.0)

While these are all handy, I think the user-defined variables are the most useful. If you have any text that you want to use in various places around your site, you can just add it as a user-defined variable. The next time you need the text, don't worry about retyping. A couple of mouse-clicks and it pops right in where it belongs.

Using a variable

To add a variable to your text, just follow these steps:

1. **Click in the text box where you want to add the variable.**

2. **Choose Text➪Insert Field.**

   Doing so displays the Insert Field dialog box.

3. **Click the down arrow to the right of the Type field.**

   This displays your three options for variable type: Date and Time, Site and General, and User Defined.

4. **Select the type of variable you want to use from the list.**

   NetObjects Fusion displays a list of variables for the variable type that you choose. See the preceding section "Varying variables" for the list of variables of each type.

5. **Select the variable you want to use; then click OK.**

   Notice that when you click a particular variable, NetObjects Fusion displays its current value at the bottom of the dialog box. Also notice that when you select Date and Time, you have the option to set the format using the Date Format button. Figure 6-11 shows the dialog box that greets you when you click the Date Format button.

   The variable appears on your page with a gray background. The gray background simply identifies for you which parts of your text are variables and which aren't; the gray background doesn't appear on your finished Web page. However, because a variable controls that particular part of the text, you cannot edit any text that appears with this shading.

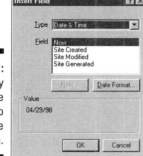

Creating your own variable

When you create a variable, you start out like you're going to insert one. Then the fun begins. These are the steps for creating a variable:

1. **Position the text cursor in the text box where you want the new variable to appear.**

2. **Choose Text⇨Insert Field.**

   This displays an Insert Field dialog box.

3. **Click the down arrow to the right of the Type field.**

   This displays your three options for variable type.

4. **Select User Defined from the list.**

   This displays a list of variables, which most likely only has one entry right now — some goofy address variable. Unfortunately, you can't modify an existing variable from here. That's done in the Assets view, which I cover in Chapter 17.

5. **Click New.**

   This displays a New Variable dialog box like the one shown in Figure 6-12.

6. **In the Variable Name field, type the name for your new variable as you want it to appear in the list in the Insert Variable dialog box.**

7. **Press the Tab key to move the text cursor to the Value field.**

8. **Type in whatever text you want; then click OK.**

   NetObjects Fusion highlights the new variable in the Insert Field dialog box.

9. **Click the OK button one more time to insert your new variable.**

Searching and Checking Your Text

Borrowing again from your word processor, NetObjects Fusion offers the following features to help make light of your text-handling chores:

- Find
- Replace
- Spell check
- Word count

These features all work pretty much the way you'd expect them to work — with one possible exception. Unfortunately, all of these options only examine the current page. That means, for example, that to spell-check your entire site, you have to check each page individually. In a perfect world, you'd be able to cover your whole site with one spell-check. I have that down on my wish list for NetObjects Fusion 4.0.

Chapter 7

Picture the Perfect Web Page

• •

In This Chapter

▶ Converting unacceptable file formats

▶ Inserting and enhancing graphics

▶ Using lines and rules

▶ Drawing with NetObjects Fusion

▶ Working with regions

• •

*A*nybody remember gopher? No, I'm not talking about the critter that ate up the golf course in *Caddyshack*. And I'm not talking about the dork on *Love Boat* either. I'm talking about the Internet application named gopher. Before the Web came along, many people predicted that gopher would revolutionize cyberspace. Some people even began experimenting with gopher-based online commerce. But gopher is entirely text-based — no graphics. When the World Wide Web came along with all its pretty pictures, gopher all but vanished from the cyberscape almost overnight.

The truth is, people like to look at pictures. Even pictures that serve no utilitarian purpose. *Especially* pictures that serve no utilitarian purpose. If you create a Web site with no graphics whatsoever, the only people you'll attract to your site are residents at the Sunnybrook Home for the Terminally Uninteresting. (On the flip side, load your pages with too many graphics and you're likely to tick people off because the pages take too long to download.) With NetObjects Fusion, you can easily makes it easy to add as many graphics as you want.

NetObjects Fusion inserts quite a few graphics in your page for you. NavBars (which you can read about in Chapter 8) and other SiteStyle elements (more on those in Chapters 3 and 16) are graphic images. By using only these graphics, you could probably come up with a reasonably attractive Web page. Chances are, however, that you already have company logos, product pictures, employee photos, and so on waiting to find homes somewhere in your Web site. Plus, NetObjects Fusion offers some of its own basic tools that you can use to create additional graphic elements on your Web pages.

Too much of a good thing

Many years ago when my wife and I had only achieved boyfriend/girlfriend status, we were out cruising the Pacific Coast Highway and decided to stop for pizza. Unfortunately, the pizza parlor we stopped at was just about to close. The workers agreed to make us a pizza, but only if we took it to go. We were hungry, so we agreed.

Well, the joke was on us. A few minutes later we found a picnic table and opened the pizza box, only to discover that our the clever pizza workers had dumped what was probably a 5-gallon drum of black olives on our pizza. What could have been a tasty dinner turned out to be plain disgusting. We scraped off as many olives as we could, each ate a piece of pizza, and threw the rest in the trash.

Black olives are good on pizza — as long as you don't overdo it. The same goes with graphics on a Web page. If you can find the right balance of text and graphics, you can create an award-winning Web site.

Determining the perfect balance between text and graphics is not an exact science. The correct balance varies from site to site. If you're setting up an online art gallery or a site to showcase the offerings of a real estate brokerage, you clearly need plenty of graphics. If you're building a Web site for some sort of service business — a dry cleaning company or an insurance agency, on the other hand — you don't need nearly as many graphics. (Whatever type of business you're in, please don't feel compelled to put a big picture of company headquarters on your home page. Nobody cares.)

Formatting Frenzy

Computer graphics have more file formats than you can shake a mouse at. Photoshop (the industry-leading image-manipulation program from Adobe) offers 16 different file format options in addition to its own proprietary format. Furthermore, many formats offer subformats, for lack of a better term. For example, when saving a file as a TIFF (Tagged Image File Format), you have the option to save the image as a regular TIFF or as a compressed TIFF. Indeed, fumbling around for just the right file format can be fairly frustrating.

Creating Web-friendly formats

The World Wide Web simplifies graphic file formats somewhat by limiting your choices. Traditionally, the Web has only supported two graphic formats: GIF (Graphic Interchange Format) and JPEG (Joint Photographic Experts Group). Typically, you use JPEG for photographic images because JPEGs are capable of 24-bit, photorealistic color, and you use GIFs for everything else. GIFs are capable of only 8-bit color, so they aren't well suited for photographic images.

GIF and JPEG formats have served the Web well for two reasons. First, both formats are widely used across all computing platforms. Other formats, like PCX (for Windows) and PICT (for Mac), don't usually find their way outside their respective platforms. Second, both formats are compressed formats, meaning that they scrunch the image information to produce smaller file sizes.

Smaller file sizes translate into faster download times for your Web pages. For example, I just converted a 10K JPEG image to an uncompressed TIFF, the result of which was a 50K file. Going from 10K to 50K may not seem like a big deal, but it's a factor of five. If the JPEG had started out at 50K, the resulting TIFF would have been 250K. That's a big difference.

Most everyone believed GIF to be a freely usable format for years, given as a gift to the world by the online service CompuServe. Then, a couple of years ago, Unisys Corp. decided that because it had developed the compression technology used in the GIF format, Unisys should be entitled to royalties from any program that supports the GIF format.

Based on the sudden costliness of the GIF format and other reasons, a consortium of Internet and graphics folks developed a format to replace GIF, called PNG (Portable Network Graphic). In addition to providing some boring, technical advantages over GIF, the PNG format is free for anyone to use.

Although PNG is a legitimate format for Web graphics, only the latest Web browsers support it. For example, only 4.*x* and later versions of Navigator/ Communicator and Internet Explorer recognize this format. Because millions of people still use earlier-version Web browsers, you may want to hold off for a while before you begin using graphics in the PNG format.

Converting the infidels . . . I mean graphics

JPEGs, GIFs, and PNGs may be all well and good for the Web, but chances are that the existing graphics you want to put on your Web page are in some other format. Now what? The answer depends on exactly what format they're in.

If your existing graphics are in BMP, PCX, or PICT format, you're in luck. NetObjects Fusion can convert images in these formats into either JPEGs or GIFs for you as you put them on your Web page. (In case you're wondering, you can pronounce PICT just like it's spelled; I've never even attempted to pronounce PCX or BMP.)

How do you pronounce that, anyway?

The computer world is full of acronyms and abbreviations, and for better or worse, people attempt to pronounce most of them as words. JPEG, which you sometimes see written simply as JPG because of its *.jpg* name extension, is an easy one to pronounce. Just say *jay-peg*. PNG is an easy one, too. It's *ping*, as in Ping-Pong or "ping the server."

GIF is the problem child of this Web graphic family. Many people, including myself, prefer to say *giff* (with a hard *g*), while many others say *jiff*, as in, "Choosy mothers choose Jif."

The strange thing is that some people on both sides of this discussion are quite fanatical about their preferences (choosy mothers, if you will), sometimes engaging in heated debate over the matter.

So which is correct? I've talked to many reliable industry resources and haven't found a definitive answer. I base my choice on the fact that the *g* stands for *graphic*. However, you can say GIF any way you want; at least half the world will agree with you.

If you have graphics that are in any other format, you have to convert them to GIF or JPEG on your own. I do my converting in Adobe Photoshop. However, I've seen utility programs in software catalogs that are designed to handle such conversions.

If you're on a budget, you may want to consider the shareware alternative. For example, at the time of this writing, the ever-popular Paint Shop Pro is on Version 4.14. This latest version supports just about every format you can imagine, including PNG. You can find it on Shareware.com (located conveniently at www.shareware.com).

Dipping into Your Personal Gallery

Say that you have a graphic on your hard drive that you want to use on your Web page. The graphic is already saved as a JPEG, GIF, or PNG (which NetObjects Fusion can use with no conversion) or a BMP, PCX, or PICT (which NetObjects Fusion can convert to GIF or JPEG for you). What next? (A little confused? Check the previous "Formatting Frenzy" section.)

Getting your graphics onto your Web page is easy, but that is only the beginning. You can do a whole bunch of other cool stuff with the graphic after you get it on your page. In this section, I explain how to put graphics on your page and what you can do with them after they're there.

Graphic insertion without too much exertion

Whether you're placing a native Web graphic or one that NetObjects Fusion has to convert for you, you use the same basic steps. The steps that follow assume that you're already in Page view, the Standard Tools palette is showing, and you have some idea where on the page you want to put your graphic. To put a graphic on your Web page, just follow these steps:

1. **Click once on the Picture tool (just below the Text tool) in the Standard Tools palette.**

   The mouse pointer turns into a crosshair.

2. **Click and hold your left mouse button; then drag the crosshair to form a box into which NetObjects Fusion will insert your graphic.**

   As you drag, a dotted line appears around the area you're defining. You don't have to worry about precision when it comes to the size and shape of the box. After you choose a graphic, NetObjects Fusion automatically adjusts the size of the box to the exact size of the graphic.

3. **Release the mouse button.**

   An Image File Open dialog box appears on your screen, as shown in Figure 7-1. If no dialog box appears, you probably tried to place a graphic where one doesn't belong. For example, you can't place a graphic partially in the Layout area (the content area unique to any given page) and partially in the MasterBorder (the content area shared by many pages).

Figure 7-1: Time to locate your graphic.

Notice that the Image File Open dialog box has two tabs: Folders (which you're on now) and Image Assets. After you place a graphic on any Web page in your site, it becomes an asset. (I discuss assets in Chapter 17.) The next time you want to use a graphic that's defined as an asset, you can click on the Image Assets tab and select the graphic from the list. Doing so saves you the trouble of navigating through your system to find the graphic.

4. **If the image you want to insert is not a GIF, JPEG, or PNG, click the Files of Type field and select the correct file format.**

5. **Navigate through your system to locate the graphic file that you want.**

6. **When the filename appears in the dialog box, click the filename once and then click Open.**

   If your file type is GIF or JPEG, you're done. If you inserted a PNG, BMP, PCX, or PICT file, you have one more step to go. NetObjects Fusion warns you that the original file format isn't recognized by most Web browsers and asks you whether you want to convert the file and store it as a GIF or JPEG, just like in Figure 7-2. About the only time you'd choose not to convert the image is if you're intentionally using a PNG file and want to keep it in that format.

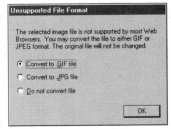

Figure 7-2: You get to choose between GIF or JPEG.

As I mention previously in this chapter, if the image is a photograph, you should select JPEG. Otherwise, go with GIF.

7. **Click on the file format you want and then click OK.**

After, the image appears in your document, you can

- Move the image around by simply clicking and dragging.
- Delete the image by selecting it with the Selection tool and then pressing the Delete key.
- Replace the image with a different graphic by clicking the Browse button in the Picture Properties palette (see Figure 7-3) and selecting a different file.

Figure 7-3:
You can
control
many
aspects of
a graphic's
appearance
with the
Properties
palette.

You should do one more thing for the graphically impaired Web surfer. Direct your attention to the Alt Tag field in the Picture Properties palette. In the interest of saving time, some people turn the graphics viewing option off on their Web browsers. Although this step speeds up Web surfing, people have no idea what graphics they're missing — unless you type an Alt Tag. An *Alt Tag* is a line of text that appears in place of a graphic when graphic viewing is turned off. This field is not required, so whether you use it or not is entirely up to you; it's not required.

Stretching the limits — and then some

When you select a graphic that you've placed on your Web page, eight small handles appear around it, as shown in Figure 7-4. You can use these handles to do one of three things: crop your image, change its size, or tile it across a portion of the page.

If you're ever unsatisfied with the results of your cropping, resizing, or tiling, you can choose Object⇨Restore Original Size to get back where you started.

If you want to resize the bounding box proportionally, hold down the Ctrl key while dragging one of the corner handles.

The Display panel in the Properties palette is shown in Figure 7-3. The panel contains the following options, which determine what happens when you drag one of the handles.

✔ **The Normal option** lets you crop the image by dragging one of the handles. The weird part is that NetObjects Fusion only lets you crop from the bottom or the right (or both). If you want to crop from the top or left, you're SQL . . . oops, I mean SOL. This option is the only one available for an unconverted PNG file. (See the "Creating Web-friendly formats" section earlier in this section to get up to speed on PNGs.)

Figure 7-4:
These handles resize the bounding box, not the graphic.

- ✔ **The Stretch option** allows you to resize the graphic by dragging any one of its handles.

- ✔ **The Tile option** lets you tile copies of the image across an area of your page. You determine the size of the area by dragging one of the image handles.

Adding special image effects

When you select a graphic on your Web page, the Effects tab on the Properties palette offers three options that you can use to further fine-tune the appearance of your graphic: Transparency, Text in Element, and Rotate. (However, note that none of these effects are available for unconverted PNG files.)

Making colors transparent

Choosing the Transparency option on the Properties palette's Effects tab lets you make one — and only one — color in a GIF (not a JPEG or PNG) image transparent when viewed with a Web browser. This feature comes in handy if you want to place an odd-shaped image over the background on your page. For example, Figure 7-5 shows two copies of the same image, one with no transparency and the other with. You can see that the background color in the first image would obscure the Web page's background. The problem is solved with the second image.

You have to be careful with transparency. When you make a particular color transparent, every occurrence of that color within that graphic becomes transparent. For example, suppose you have a picture of a man in a white shirt, with white also as the background color. If you make white transparent, the background becomes transparent, but so does the white area of the man's shirt. Oops.

To use the Transparency option, follow these steps:

1. **Select a GIF image that you've added to your Web page.**

Figure 7-5:
The first
image
uses no
trans-
parency;
the second
does.

2. **Click the Effects tab on the Properties palette; then click the Eyedropper button in the Transparency panel.**

   Note that the mouse pointer turns into an eyedropper.

3. **Within the graphic, click the eyedropper on whatever color you want to make transparent.**

   The color bar on the Properties palette changes to the color you clicked on.

4. **Click the Use Color check box next to the eyedropper button.**

   When you look back at your GIF image, the color you specified is invisible.

Adding text to graphics

In Chapter 6, I warn against using unusual fonts on your Web pages because everyone viewing your page may not have the font you specify. If you insist on using some fancy typeface, you can work around this font problem by adding your text to a graphic, which is an option on the Effects tab. You can freely edit this text in NetObjects Fusion, but when you publish your site, NetObjects Fusion makes the text part of the graphic. That way, whether or not your visitors have the right font doesn't matter; what appears to be text is really just a picture of text. (This option is not available for unconverted PNG files.)

Making text into a graphic is also handy if you design a graphic that you want to use as some sort of link button. I describe how to add linking buttons in Chapter 8, but you can use this option to add the text to your button.

To add text to a graphic, follow these steps:

1. **Select the graphic to which you want to add text.**

2. **Click the Effects tab on the Properties palette.**

3. **In the Text in Element area, click the Enable check box.**

   The words Your text here appear over your graphic.

4. Click the Settings button to the right of the Enable check box.

The Text in Element Settings dialog box appears, as shown in Figure 7-6.

Figure 7-6:
You can
control
exactly
how the text
appears
with the
graphic.

You can type your text in a field at the top of the Text in Element Settings dialog box. The other settings in this dialog box work as follows:

- The *Relative Alignment buttons* control how various lines of text are aligned in relation to each other — not in relation to the graphic.

- The Set button next to the *Font field* lets you select any font that's installed on your computer.

- The Set button next to the *Color field* lets you select a different color for your text.

- The *Horizontal Position* and *Vertical Position radio buttons* control the alignment of the text in relation to the bounding box.

- The *Orientation settings* enable you to rotate the text. When you select the Right Angles option, you can only rotate the text in 90-degree increments. With this option unselected, you can rotate the text in 1-degree increments.

5. Type the text you want, make any adjustments to the settings, and then click the Close button.

Rotating and bordering

The last two options on the Effects tab are Rotate and Border. (Neither of these options is available for unconverted PNG files.) By using the arrows next to the Rotate field, you can rotate your graphic in 90-degree increments.

This rotation does not affect any text that you added to the graphic (see the "Adding text to graphics" section). With the arrows next to the Border field, you can add a black border to the bounding box — not necessarily the graphic — that ranges in width from 1 pixel to 100 pixels.

Lines and Rules Are Not for Fools

The Line tool is the last tool on the Standard Tools palette. The button for this tool has a simple, diagonal line running through it. When you click and hold on this button, as shown in Figure 7-7, you see that NetObjects Fusion enables you to add three different types of lines: a horizontal rule, a regular line (for lack of a better term), and a Style line.

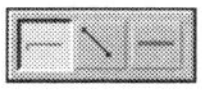

Figure 7-7:
The Line tool gives you three options.

The rules of horizontal rules

A horizontal rule is a standard HTML element. In other words, when you create a horizontal rule, no graphic file is involved. Instead, you define the horizontal rule with HTML code. Although you can't do any fancy tricks with a horizontal rule like you can with the other line types that NetObjects Fusion makes available to you (a regular line and a Style line), horizontal rules download much more quickly. This quick download time is the main reason to choose a horizontal rule over one of the other two line types. To add a horizontal rule to your Web page, follow these steps:

1. **Click and hold the Line tool.**

2. **When the three options appear, select the Horizontal Rule option, which is the first of the three.**

3. **Click and drag on your cursor to identify the starting and ending points of the horizontal rule.**

   When you release the mouse button, the rule appears where you specified. If the rule does not appear, you probably tried to place it partially in the Layout area and partially in the MasterBorder, which is a Bozo-no-no. Try again.

   Assuming that you place the rule correctly, observe that the title bar on the Properties palette changes to *Rule Properties*.

4. **Adjust the settings on the Properties palette the way you want.**

   You can't do much to a horizontal rule. The Thickness setting controls the thickness of the rule in pixels. With the Shading option selected, the horizontal rule appears with a beveled look; with it unselected, the horizontal rule appears as a simple black line.

You may have noticed that when you select a horizontal rule, it only appears with two handles. That's because the only thing that you control with these handles is the length of the rule.

A line in the sand... er, on your page

NetObjects Fusion refers to the second option on the Line tool as Draw. You can use this option to draw a line. These lines are much more flexible than horizontal rules. You can point them in any direction, change their colors, and add arrow heads to the beginnings and ends.

To draw a line, just follow these steps:

1. **Click and hold the Line tool.**

2. **When the three options appear, select the Draw Shape option, which is the second of the three.**

2. **Drag your cursor to identify the line's starting and ending points.**

   When you release the mouse button, the line appears where you specified.

   Creating a line that spans both the Layout and the MasterBorder doesn't work. That's because items in the Layout area appear only on one page, while items in the MasterBorder area can appear on several pages.

4. **Adjust the settings on the Line Properties palette the way you want.**

   The Line Properties palette allows you to control the appearance of your lines, as shown in Figure 7-8.

The Line Properties palette gives you the following options:

 - The **Alt Tag field** lets you specify an Alt Tag, which allows you to show text describing a graphic to folks who choose not to download them.

 - **The Line width setting** adjusts the width of the line in pixels.

 - **The Line, Head, and Tail color settings** control the colors of the various parts of your line. If you check the All Parts Use One Color check box, all three colors change according to the color you specify for the line.

✔ **The Style area** allows you to choose the shapes for both the head and tail of the line, including line, point, arrow, diamond, circle, and square. If you check the Head/Tail Same Style check box, both the head and tail change according to the style you select for the head. If you check the Outline check box, the head and tail shapes are outlined in the color of you specify for the line.

Figure 7-8:
You can do more with these lines than with horizontal rules.

Lines with style

As I explain in Chapter 3, one of the elements of a NetObjects Fusion Style is a barlike graphic that you can use in place of a horizontal rule. You use the Line tool to put these Style lines onto your Web page. To draw a Style line, follow these steps:

1. **Click and hold the Line tool.**

2. **When the three options appear, select the SiteStyle option, which is the third of the three.**

3. **Click your mouse on the point where you want the left end of the Style line.**

   You don't have to specify an ending point for this type of line because, as a graphic, it pops in at its regular size.

   If the Style line doesn't appear, it may be partially in the MasterBorder and partially in the Layout area. You can't place it in the MasterBorder.

   Notice that on the Properties palette, your only option for one of these lines is rotation. The Rotate buttons let you rotate the line in 90-degree increments.

4. **Adjust the rotation however you want it.**

The Shapes of Things to Come

The Shape tool, which is on the Standard Tools palette just above the Line tool, enables you to create the following geometric shapes on your Web pages: rectangle, rounded rectangle, oval, and polygon. NetObjects Fusion is the only Web authoring program I've seen that offers its own built-in drawing tools. To draw a shape, follow these steps.

1. **Click and hold the Shape tool; when the four options appear, select the shape you want.**

2. **If you selected one of the first three shapes, click and drag to identify an area for the shape. If you selected a polygon, click once on each intended corner of the polygon; when you reach the final corner, double-click on it.**

   Your shape appears where you specified, unless you tried to stick it on that Layout/MasterBorder border.

Take a look at the Properties palette. The following shapes have many of the same options as other graphics that you can place on your page:

- ✔ **The Alt Tag field** lets you type a text description of the graphic for people who have graphics viewing turned off in their Web browsers.

- ✔ **The Line Width** setting controls the width of the line in pixels.

- ✔ **The two Color buttons** control the colors of the line and the fill, respectively.

- ✔ **The Text in Element option** works just like the one I describe in the "Adding text to graphics" section of this chapter.

A Regional Slant

If you've ever worked with an illustration program like Freehand or Illustrator, you know that one of the handiest features is the ability to group individual objects together so that you can move and manipulate them as a single object. This feat is just plain impossible in any ordinary Web authoring program. However, as you already know, NetObjects Fusion is no ordinary program.

Through the use of *regions*, you can group objects together and manipulate them as a single element. A region is simply a container into which you can place text boxes, graphics, or anything else that you can put on a Web page. When you create a region, you essentially create a mini Layout area within the Layout area — or within the MasterBorder, for that matter. (See Chapter 5 for more on Layouts and MasterBorders.)

Why would you want to group your images together in regions? Suppose that you have a graphic and some text you want to go with it; and you know exactly how you want the text laid out in relation to the graphic, but you're not quite sure where you want to put the whole thing. By creating a region, you can lay out the text and graphic just the way you want; then experiment by putting the region in different places on the page. If you don't like the way it looks, just move the whole region to a different location.

To create a region, follow these steps:

1. **Select the Region tool and click and drag to mark the outline of the region on your page.**

2. **After the region appears on your screen, just start dropping in text, graphics, multimedia — anything you can think of. If you want to add an element that already appears on the current page, just drag it over to the region.**

Creating a region results in a corresponding change to the Properties palette. As you can see from Figure 7-9, a region has many of the same options as a Layout (see Chapter 2). You can control the appearance and spacing of the grid and output options. You also have almost the same background options as you do for a Layout. Background sound is the only thing missing.

Figure 7-9:
Regions have many settings in common with Layouts.

To resize a region, just click on and drag one of its handles. You can press the Ctrl key while dragging a corner handle to resize the region proportionally. Just be careful when you delete a region, because everything in that region gets deleted right along with it.

Chapter 8

Hot Rod Linkin'

* *

In This Chapter

▶ Creating hypertext links

▶ Using graphics as links

▶ Creating image maps

▶ Using anchors

▶ Getting around with the NavBars

* *

*L*et's face it. Putting words and pictures on a page is no big deal. Sure, the fact that the page exists on your computer screen is cool, but all gee-whiz considerations aside, people have been putting words and pictures on pages for thousands of years.

What sets the World Wide Web apart from any medium that came before it is *hypertext* — the ability to create mouse-clickable links from one page to any other page on the entire Web. That's why the coding used to create Web pages is called hypertext markup language, or HTML. For the first time in history, you can present information to the masses in a nonlinear format.

The Web functions much like the way people think: When you're just sitting there pondering the meaning of life, your mind can wander off in a million different directions. On the Web, you operate the same way. Start clicking one link after another, and you can soon find yourself many cybermiles away from the original Web page.

This chapter revs the engine and spins the wheels, giving you everything you need to know about linking in NetObjects Fusion.

Cruisin' Your Own Hypertext Highway

Creating hypertext links in your documents is a decidedly cool thing to do. Used correctly, hypertext links help your readers find the information they're looking for.

Just because you can create links, don't feel that you have to provide hypertext links to every site on the Web that has some possible relevance to your site. Your main purpose is to provide information and, ultimately, to keep people at your site for as long as possible.

When you select a portion of text to serve as a hypertext link, NetObjects Fusion offers you four different choices for the type of link you want to create:

- ✔ An Internal Link is simply a link to another page on your site, and optionally an *anchor* on that page. (I cover anchors under "Anchors Aweigh," later in this chapter.)

- ✔ A Smart Link is a relative link. For example, one of the options for a Smart Link is *Up*. If you select this option, NetObjects Fusion figures out for you which page is one level up in the hierarchy and creates the appropriate link.

- ✔ An External Link is a link to any page outside your site. Once you type in a Web address for an External Link, it becomes an Asset, as I explain in Chapter 17. You never have to type it again. The next time you need it, you can select it from a list.

- ✔ A File Link is a link to a file that you created in some other program besides NetObjects Fusion. For example, you can use this option to create a link to a ZIP or EXE file that users can download from your site. The good news is that no matter where the file currently resides on your hard drive, NetObjects Fusion will include the file when it publishes your site, and adjust the link according to where it places the file.

Linkin' text, not Nebraska

Although the steps for the different types of links start out the same, they get very different later on. Rather than provide one set of steps to cover all three options, I've written four separate sets of steps.

Adding internal text links

An internal link is simply a link to some other page on your site. While NavBars create internal links to pages related to each other in your site's hierarchy (see "NavBars: The Fast Lane for Your Linkin'" later in this chapter), you can create your own internal link to any other page on your site, no matter where it lies in the hierarchy. To create an internal link, just cruise through these steps:

1. **Use your mouse to select the word or words you want to serve as the link.**

   The Properties palette switches to *Text Properties*.

REMEMBER

Keepin' 'em at home

Just as with any other element you put on your Web page, you have to be careful not to go overboard with links. Consider the following sentence, which could appear on a Web page for Callahan Auto Parts:

With a customer list that includes <u>Zalinsky Discount Auto Parts</u>, <u>Callahan Auto Parts</u> is recognized by the <u>American Brake Pad Institute</u> as the <u>leading supplier of brake pads</u> nationwide.

That's not so bad as far as sentences go, but suppose each one of those underlined portions is a hypertext link. The first link leads to the Web site for Zalinsky Discount Auto Parts, the second link leads back to the home page of the current site, the third link leads to the home page of the American Brake Pad Institute, and the final link leads to the specific page on the ABPI Web site that shows the survey results on which this statement is based.

If you have four links in every sentence, your visitors probably won't stay at your site through the first paragraph. They'll click one link, follow another link from the resulting page, and in a few minutes they'll forget they were ever at your site.

2. **Click the Link button in the lower-left corner of the Properties palette.**

   A Link dialog box appears on your screen, as shown in Figure 8-1. This dialog box has four tabs: Internal Link, Smart Link, External Link, and File Link. NetObjects Fusion always starts you out on the Internal Link tab.

Figure 8-1:
The Link dialog box offers a separate tab for each type of link.

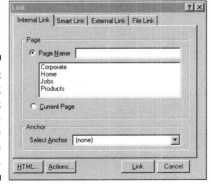

The center of this dialog box contains a list of all the pages that are currently part of your site. Perhaps you're wondering why there's also a radio button marked *Current Page*, and more specifically why you'd want to create a link to the page you're already on. You use this option in conjunction with anchors. Although I cover anchors later in this chapter (see "Anchors Aweigh"), here's the quick definition: By creating an anchor, you can link not only to a specific page on your site, but also to a specific location on that page. Typically, for example, if you have a very long page, you may want to provide a link from the top of the page to some point further down on the same page.

3. **Click once on the page to which you want to link, then click the Link button at the bottom of the dialog box.**

   When NetObjects Fusion has created the link, the text you selected in Step 1 changes color according to the SiteStyle (see Chapter 3) and becomes underlined. This means that when someone views the page through a Web browser, clicking anywhere on that text takes the user to the page you specified.

Adding smart links

NetObjects Fusion provides a quick and easy way to add a link to a page that has some direct relation to the current page (even if you don't know the name of the page you want to link to). Using the Smart Link feature, all you have to do is decide whether you want to link to the next page in the hierarchy, the first child page under the current page, or your home page. NetObjects Fusion handles the rest.

1. **Use your mouse to select the word or words you want to serve as the link.**

   The Properties palette switches to *Text Properties*.

2. **Click the Link button in the lower left corner of the Properties palette.**

   A Link dialog box appears on your screen.

3. **Click the Smart Link tab.**

   See Figure 8-2 for an example of the Smart Link tab.

   The dialog box now lists the four different Smart Links: Home, which represents the site's Home page; Next Page, which refers to the next page at the same level in your site's hierarchy; First Child Page, which refers to the next page down in the hierarchy; and Blank, which you use when the purpose of the link is to activate an Action, as described in Chapter 15.

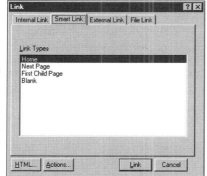

Figure 8-2:
You have four Smart Links to choose from.

4. **Click once on the desired Smart Link, then click the Link button at the bottom of the dialog box.**

   When NetObjects Fusion has created the link, the text you selected in Step 1 changes color according to the SiteStyle (see Chapter 3) and becomes underlined. This means that when someone views the page through a Web browser, clicking anywhere on that text takes the user to the page you specified.

Adding external links

An external link is a link to anything other than a page on your site. Table 8-1 lists each type of external link and what you use it for. In the procedures that follow, you specify which type of link you want, and then type in an address for the link.

Table 8-1	External Link Types
Type	*Purpose*
http://	Use this type for all external Web pages, except for secure pages (see later in table).
ftp://	Use this type if you want the link to automatically initiate a file download from an FTP (File Transfer Protocol) site. For the address, enter the Internet address of the file, including the complete server name and path.
mailto:	Use this type to initiate a preaddressed outgoing e-mail message to the e-mail address you specify.
news://	Use this option to launch the user's newsreader program and connect to a specific Usenet newsgroup.

(continued)

Table 8-1 *(continued)*

Type	Purpose
shttp://	This is one of two formats that you use to indicate secure Web pages. Check with your system administrator to see which of these two is correct for your system.
https://	This is the other format for secure Web pages.

Here are the steps for creating an external link:

1. **Use your mouse to select the word or words you want to serve as the link.**

   The Properties palette switches to *Text Properties*.

2. **Click the Link button in the lower-left corner of the Properties palette.**

   A Link dialog box appears on your screen.

3. **Click the External Link tab.**

   See Figure 8-3 for an example of the External Link tab.

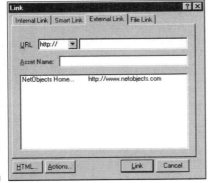

Figure 8-3:
You have
several
options for
External
Links.

Take a moment to examine the External Link tab. The first field has the label *URL* and contains *http://*. Note also the little down arrow at the end of this field. You click that arrow to display a list of external link types for which you can create links (see the table at the beginning of this section).

Secured Web Pages?

When you create a form (see Chapter 11), you might ask the user for some sort of sensitive information, such as a credit card number. Although it's highly unlikely that the form information will be intercepted by a cyber thief as it travels from the user's computer to your computer, you can safeguard against interception by putting the form on a secured page. This means that before the information is transmitted from the user's computer, it's encrypted (scrambled into hacker-proof code), rendering it useless to the cyber thief. The information is not decrypted (unscrambled) until it reaches your computer.

4. **Select the correct URL type and then type in the remainder of the Internet address for this link.**

   Just below all this, notice the Asset Name field. After you enter an address for an External Link once, you never have to retype the address. In the Asset Name field, you can type a descriptive name for this link. The next time you create an External Link, this link will be shown by Asset Name in the list at the center of the dialog box.

   As you add more and more external links to your site, the list of links on the External Links tab may become quite long. If this happens, instead of scrolling through the list, you can start typing the name you gave to the link into the Asset Name field. Assuming you spell the name right, NetObjects Fusion scans the list and locates the link for you.

5. **Type the name you want to assign to this link into the Asset Name field and click the Link button at the bottom of this dialog box.**

   When NetObjects Fusion has created the link, the text you selected in Step 1 changes color according to the SiteStyle (see Chapter 3) and becomes underlined. This means that when someone views the page through a Web browser, clicking anywhere on that text takes the user to the page you specified.

Adding a file link

A file link is a link to a non-HTML file. For example, suppose you've created a program you want users to download from your site. You can create a file link to the program; clicking on the link then initiates the download of that file. Follow these steps to create a file link:

1. **Use your mouse to select the word or words you want to serve as the link.**

   The Properties palette switches to *Text Properties*.

2. Click the Link button in the lower left corner of the Properties palette.

A Link dialog box appears on your screen.

3. Click the File Link tab.

See Figure 8-4 for an example of the File Link tab.

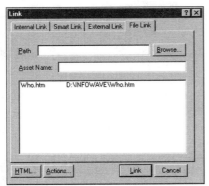

Figure 8-4:
NetObjects
Fusion
gives you
several
ways to
choose
a file.

You have the option to type in the exact pathname to your file or use the Browse button to locate the file on your hard drive. After you've linked to a file once, it appears in this dialog box as an Asset. You can select an Asset from the list by clicking it, or if you know the Asset's name, you can type it in the specified field.

4. Select the desired file, then click the Link button at the bottom of the dialog box.

When NetObjects Fusion has created the link, the text you selected in Step 1 changes color according to the SiteStyle (see Chapter 3) and becomes underlined. This means that when someone views the page through a Web browser, clicking anywhere on that text takes the user to the page you specified.

Undoing the deed

Changing and unlinking links is very easy stuff. To do it, just select the linked text and click the Link button on the Properties palette again. Nearly the same Link dialog pops up as when you created the link in the first place, with a couple of subtle differences. First of all, instead of three tabs, NetObjects Fusion only presents you with the options that go along with the type of link you are changing. For example, if you're changing an External

Link, you only see the External Link options. If you're changing to another External Link, you can do so at this point. However, if you want the selected text to link to an Internal Link, a Smart Link, or a File Link, you have to click the Unlink button, which completely cancels the existing link, and start over again.

Cute as a Button — Literally

Text isn't the only page element that can serve as a hypertext link. You can also make a link out of any graphic on your page. Just follow the same steps I describe earlier in this chapter for linking text, but instead of selecting text, select a graphic. In effect, this creates a clickable button for that particular link. It's that easy. You can tell quickly whether a graphic is linked because when it is, a little arrow appears in its upper left corner, a shown in Figure 8-5. This arrow is there only for your reference; it won't appear on your published site.

Figure 8-5:
The arrow tells you this graphic is linked.

Check out the following list for some reasons why you may want a graphic to serve as a link:

- ✔ **Corporate logo.** It's a good idea to put your company logo on every page in your site. That way, users always know whose site they're visiting. You make the logo even more useful by having it serve as a link to your home page.

- ✔ **NavBars.** NetObjects Fusion creates NavBars — groupings of navigational buttons — on command. NavBars take care of moving your visitors up and down or side to side in your site's hierarchy, one step at a time. I give you the skinny on NavBars in the section entitled "NavBars: The Fast Lane for Your Linkin'" in this chapter.

- ✔ **Navigation buttons.** Navigation buttons link you to an entirely different part of a site. Some buttons speak for themselves without any text. For example, you can be pretty sure a button that looks like a mailbox has something do with e-mail. On the other hand, many buttons need to include text so people know what they do. Furthermore, you may want to use the same basic design — just with different text — for all such buttons on your site, for a consistent look and feel. Before NetObjects Fusion, if you wanted several buttons to have the same basic design you had to start with a blank button image, open it in a program like Photoshop, add the desired text, then save the file with a new name — and repeat this process for each button. That's a lot of tedious work for one stinking button — but those days are over.

If you've already read Chapter 7, you know that NetObjects Fusion lets you add text right on top of any graphic, via the Text in Element option on the Properties palette. What a great feature for creating buttons! You just insert the blank button graphic on your Web page, add the appropriate text using the Text in Element feature, and create a link for the button. BAM! Instant button. Once you get a little time under your belt, you can probably zip through the whole process in under a minute.

One Big Picture, Many Little Links

If you've spent any time at all on the Web, you've probably encountered your share of image maps. An *image map* is a single graphic that is divided into several links. Click one *hotspot* (an individual link on an image map) and one thing happens; click a different hotspot and something else happens. These hotspots can be rectangular, round, or polygonal.

Figure 8-6 shows a graphic that functions as an image map.

Figure 8-6:
Clicking different hotspots yields different results.

This is a clever trick, but not quite as amazing as it may seem. Hidden in the HTML code for such a page is a simple list of the hotspots that the image map contains. The code defines each hotspot by the coordinates (how many pixels in, how many pixels down) that form its boundary. When you click a hotspot, your Web browser compares the coordinates of your click to the coordinates for the various hotspots to figure out which hotspot you clicked. Then it requests whatever link is associated with that hotspot. Pretty spiffy, eh?

For a while, image maps were *the* big thing in Web pages. However, I think their popularity is waning. Why waste all that time fiddling with an image map when you have power tools like NetObjects Fusion's NavBars? A fancy image map may look a little snazzier than a NavBar, but it also takes a lot more time to download. Today's Web surfers want function more than anything else.

Nevertheless, sometimes an image map may be appropriate. For example, suppose you're developing a site for a nationwide retail chain and you want to include a page that helps people find store locations. You could create an image map from a map of the United States: Click California and see a list of all the stores in California, click New York and see the same for New York. This is a nice, visual way to get at the information.

Before I continue with the steps for creating an image map, let me offer one more bit of advice on the topic. If you're going to use an image map, make sure the image you use to create it has clearly identifiable hotspots. And for added measure, include a line of text advising people that they're looking at an image map.

For example, five or six versions ago, I used the graphic in Figure 8-7 as an image map on my personal Web site. I think it's pretty clear where to click to see different samples of my work, but just to make sure, I included some instructions just below the image.

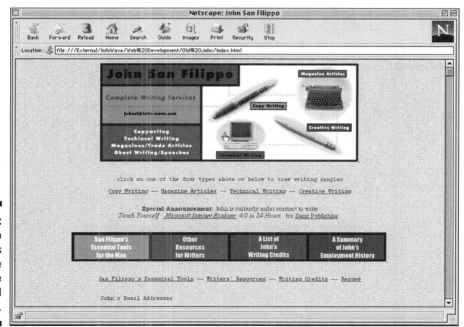

Figure 8-7: Leave no question as to where people are supposed to click.

In the steps that follow, I assume that you've already created a graphic that you want to use as an image map, and that you've inserted that graphic somewhere on your Web page. Here are the steps for creating an image map:

1. **Click and hold on the Hotspot tool on the Standard Tools palette.**

   This is the one that looks like a little finger pointing at a red button. When you click and hold, a subpalette pops up that shows you the three choices for hotspot shapes: rectangular, round, or polygonal.

2. **Select the desired shape and release the mouse button.**

   The mouse pointer turns into a crosshair.

3. **Move the crosshair over the graphic.**

   If you selected the rectangle or circle hotspot, as you move the crosshair over the graphic, a gray box appears around the graphic, as shown in Figure 8-8. (Somebody at NetObjects apparently forgot to add this for the polygon hotspot.) This lets you know that you're more or less in the right place.

Figure 8-8:
The gray box lets you know that you're ready to create a hotspot.

The Hotspot tool works just like the Shape tool I discuss in Chapter 7. If you selected a rectangle or circle, you click and drag to identify an area for the shape. If you selected a polygon, you click once at each intended corner of the polygon; when you reach the final corner of the polygon, double-click it.

4. **Define the shape of the hotspot.**

   The instant you finish creating the hotspot, a Link dialog box appears just like the one I describe earlier in this chapter. If you need a refresher course, skip back a few pages.

5. **Identify the page to which the hotspot should link and click the Link button.**

   Presto! You've created the first hotspot for your image map.

As you create additional hotspots for your image map, be careful not to overlap them. If you overlap them and click one of the overlapping sections using your Web browser, it won't know what the heck to make of the image map.

6. Repeat these steps for any other required hotspots.

To move a hotspot, just click and drag it anywhere on the graphic. You can also resize and reshape it using any of the handles that appear around its edge.

Anchors Aweigh

I don't know who came up with the term *anchor* as it's used in HTML, but whoever it was should be tied to a boat anchor and tossed into the sea. As you know, out there in the nautical world, an anchor is a big chunk of metal that keeps a ship from moving. In contrast, an HTML anchor is a special type of link designed to keep you *moving* to specific locations on a page.

If I had been the guy in charge, I would have called anchors *bookmarks*. Of course, then I would have had to come up with a different term for what we now call bookmarks. But an HTML anchor by any other name is still an anchor, and here's how anchors work:

The anchor itself is an invisible marker that you place anywhere on a Web page. Later on, when you're creating a link from somewhere else — either on the same Web page or a different one — you link not only to the page with the anchor, but directly to the anchor. Then when someone clicks that link using a Web browser, the anchored part of the page appears.

Here's one example in which an anchor is handy. One of the best uses of anchors that I've seen is in the creation of a FAQ (pronounced *fack*, stands for frequently asked questions). A FAQ is an online document that provides users with basic information in question-and-answer format. For example, if I were to write a FAQ for myself, one question might read: Why does John always seem to have pizza on his mind? Then I'd write an answer to that question.

Depending on the topic, FAQs can be quite long. The format I like to see for longer FAQs is to have all the questions listed at the beginning of the document, with links to the answers further on down the page. This is all done with anchors. You see a question you'd like to know the answer for, you click it, and in a jiffy you're looking at the answer, without any tedious scrolling.

If you decide to create your own FAQ using this technique, you should also add an anchor at the very top of the page and provide a link to it at the end of every answer. That way, it's easy for users to get back to the top of the page no matter where they are in a FAQ. A little button with an up arrow on it is common for this sort of thing.

One last note: An anchor needs to be attached to *something* — you can't just stick one out in the middle of a blank layout. That something can be either a graphic, or a specific point within text. It doesn't much matter which of these you choose.

Just follow these steps to create an anchor.

1. **Click the point on the page where you want to create an anchor.**

   If you want to drop anchor inside a text block, simply position the text cursor where you want the anchor. If you're going to use a graphic as the anchor, select the graphic.

2. **Click the Anchor button at the bottom center of the Properties palette.**

   This button is in the same position no matter whether you're viewing Picture Properties or Text Properties. Clicking this button displays an Add Anchor dialog box, as shown in Figure 8-9. If other anchors already exist on the current page, they're displayed in the list in this dialog box so that you can make sure you don't create two anchors with the same name on the same page.

Figure 8-9:
You drop
anchor
from this
dialog box.

3. **Type a descriptive name for the anchor in the field provided, then click OK.**

   The key word here is *descriptive*. Remember that when you link to this anchor, you're going to be selecting it from a list of all the anchors on that page, so you want the name to be as distinguishable as possible. The only limitation is that the name cannot include any spaces. I usually use periods instead of spaces to make the name easier to read.

If you used a graphic for the anchor, a little red circle with what I assume is an anchor but looks more like an upside-down T appears in the upper-left corner of the graphic. This is for reference only and won't appear on your published page. If you placed the anchor in text, the red circle appears in gray until the text box is no longer in edit mode.

Removing an anchor or changing its name is easy. If the anchor is a graphic, select the graphic and click the Anchor button again. The result is a Change Anchor dialog box that looks just like the Add Anchor dialog box. You then have the option to change the name or click the Remove button.

If the anchor is in a text box, make sure that the text box is in edit mode. Then move the mouse pointer over the anchor. When the mouse pointer is over the anchor, it changes from an I-bar back into a pointer. One mouse-click at that point displays the Change Anchor dialog box.

Follow these steps to link to an anchor:

1. **Use your mouse to select the word or words you want to serve as the link.**

   The Properties palette switches to *Text Properties*.

2. **Click the Link button in the lower-left corner of the Properties palette.**

   A Link dialog box appears on your screen. The center of this dialog box contains a list of all the pages that are currently part of your site, as well as a button marked *Current Page*.

3. **Click once on the page that contains the anchor, or optionally on the Current Page radio button.**

   Near the bottom of this dialog box is a field marked *Select Anchor*. When you create a new link, this field defaults to *none*. Clicking the down arrow at the end of this field displays a list of all the anchors on the page you selected.

4. **Select the desired anchor from the list, then click OK.**

If you should later remove the anchor to which you just linked, NetObjects Fusion automatically changes the link to an anchor value of *none*. Also note that you can use the same basic procedures for linking a graphic to an anchor.

NavBars: The Fast Lane for Your Linkin'

In the past, the biggest problem with managing a large Web site has been keeping track of all the Internal Links. For example, if you happened to rename a page, you had to dig through your site and manually change all the links to the page. Believe me, that's no fun. NavBars go a long way toward eliminating problems like this.

A NavBar is simply a group of buttons linked to various other pages that relate to the current page in the site hierarchy. You can have NetObjects Fusion create a NavBar on any page that provides links to the following:

- **First Level.** The first level includes all pages at the hierarchical level just below the home page.

- **Parent Level.** The parent level includes all pages at the level immediately above the page on which you place the NavBar.

- **Current Level.** The current level includes all pages at the same level as the one on which you place the NavBar.

- **Child Level.** The child level includes all pages immediately below the page on which you place the NavBar.

Furthermore, you also have the option to include a link to the home page on any NavBar.

The most amazing thing about NavBars is that once you create one, you never have to fiddle with it again. When you add a page to your site, NetObjects Fusion automatically adds a button to every NavBar on your site that the addition affects. The same applies when you delete a page; NetObjects Fusion deletes any NavBar buttons that link to that page.

Before you continue, I'd like to offer some other suggested reading. First of all, the appearance of the buttons in a NavBar is based on which SiteStyle you use. Because I cover Styles in Chapter 3, you may want to take a look there for additional information.

Also, there's a good chance that you'll want to use the same NavBar for all the pages across a particular level in your site hierarchy. That means creating a new MasterBorder for that particular level. If you want to discover exactly how to do that, flip back to Chapter 5.

To create a NavBar, follow these steps.

1. **Click the Navigation Bar tool on the Standard Tools palette.**

   This is the one that looks like four blocks piled on each other. When you click the Navigation Bar tool, the mouse pointer turns into a crosshair.

You have the option to create either a horizontal NavBar (with the buttons next to each other) or a vertical NavBar (with the buttons one above the other). If you define an area that's wider than it is tall, NetObjects Fusion creates a horizontal NavBar. Likewise, if you define an area that's taller than it is wide, NetObjects Fusion creates a vertical NavBar. If you screw up, just delete the NavBar and start over; you can't change the orientation of a NavBar once you've created it.

2. **Click and drag to define an area for the NavBar.**

   You don't need to be precise about the size as long as you get the shape right.

When you create a new NavBar, NetObjects Fusion defaults to a First Level NavBar. This is easy enough to change — just follow these steps.

1. **If the NavBar you want to change isn't already selected, select it using the Selection tool.**

   The title bar on the Properties palette changes to either *Navigation Bar Properties* or *Vertical Navigation Bar Properties*, depending on which type of NavBar you're changing. Aside from the title bar, the Properties palette is the same in either case.

2. **Click the Options button to the right of the Display field.**

   A NavBar Display dialog box like the one shown in Figure 8-10 appears on your screen. This dialog box provides a good visual representation of what each option does. In each illustration in this dialog box, the current page appears in red, and the pages for the NavBar to include appear in yellow.

Figure 8-10:
The NavBar
Display
dialog box
offers a
visual
description
of each
option.

3. Click the radio button for the desired display; if you want to include a link to your home page, make sure to check the Include Home Page check box. Then click OK.

The NavBar instantly changes to reflect the display you just selected. Assuming you placed the NavBar in the MasterBorder, all pages that share the same MasterBorder now include this NavBar. (See Chapter 5 for more on MasterBorders.)

The Properties palette also includes several options for controlling the appearance of your NavBar. Here's a description of each option:

✔ The Border field lets you create a beveled border around the entire NavBar. I suggest you experiment with this to see if you like it; I don't much care for it.

✔ The Spacing field controls the spacing between individual buttons on the NavBar. This spacing is measured in pixels.

✔ The Button Type radio buttons control the actual appearance of the buttons. The Primary and Secondary buttons let you choose between the primary or secondary button that's defined for the current Style (check Chapter 3). You can use the Text button to convert the NavBar to a text-only format that doesn't use any graphics. Unfortunately, you don't have any control over the font or other type characteristics in such a NavBar.

✔ The Button Style radio buttons let you choose between the buttons that are defined for the current Style or the buttons defined for any other Style on your system. I suggest you stick with the current Style.

✔ The Use Highlighting check box controls whether the NavBar displays a different button to indicate the current page. With this option checked, the NavBar not only provides links to other pages, but can also tell you what page you are on. See Chapter 3 for more details.

✔ The Background tab gives you the option to add a background color to the NavBar. This color fills in the area you define in the Spacing field.

I cover the Actions tab in Chapter 15.

Chapter 9
Multimedia: The Real Sizzle

*T*he Web is no longer just about text and static images. Though these are still Web mainstays, the most excitement today revolves around multimedia. NetObjects Fusion lets you easily add all sorts of multimedia — Macromedia Shockwave, Apple QuickTime, video and audio files, Java applets, and ActiveX controls — to your Web pages:

Furthermore, the folks at NetObjects didn't want to limit you to just these types of multimedia elements. That's why they also built in the ability to add any type of plug-in–driven elements that may be available now or in the future. Of course, to preview an element, you need the appropriate browser plug-in.

Electrifying Visitors with Shockwave

Shockwave is a file format developed by Macromedia that allows multimedia content created in Macromedia's Director program to be presented on the Web. It can make for some shockingly interactive and exciting Web pages.

Before you start jazzing up your site, think about this

As tantalizing as Web multimedia is, you should address several concerns before adding loads of multimedia to your Web pages. Every multimedia element you add to your site presents a trade-off from the user standpoint.

First, multimedia files are often large. If you suspect that most of your visitors will access your site via standard modem connections, you may want to think twice about adding multimedia. Many users won't appreciate having to wait several minutes for an otherwise simple page to load.

Make your multimedia optional by putting it on a clearly identifiable page. This way, those people who have high-speed Internet connections or are willing to wait for your multimedia files to load can see the goodies, and others aren't forced into it. I may be in the minority on this, but I advise you to never put large multimedia elements on your home page.

Another shortcoming of Web-based multimedia is that much of it requires extra plug-ins or other special software. For example, if you add Shockwave media to a Web page, your visitors must have the Shockwave plug-in installed for their Web browser. Likewise, if you add ActiveX controls, your page can only be viewed properly by users of Microsoft Internet Explorer; Netscape Navigator doesn't support ActiveX. That leaves out a large segment of the online population.

If you're developing a site for a corporate intranet, you have it a little easier. You already know that everyone has a high-speed connection to your site. You can also determine what software the employees in your company use.

On the other hand, if you're developing a site for the general public, you can't predict what software any given visitor may use. My rule is that if the multimedia adds real functionality to your site, go ahead and use it. Conversely, think twice about adding multimedia just for the sake of having it.

I may sound like I'm trying to discourage you from using multimedia, and to a certain extent, I am. The purpose of any Web site is to attract visitors — and, even more important, to attract *repeat* visitors. The more elements you add to your site that exclude one visitor or another, the more trouble you'll have achieving this goal. That said, I devote the rest of this chapter to adding various multimedia elements to your Web pages.

Exactly where you get your Shockwave media files from — whether you develop them yourself, buy them from a designer, or use freeware media from the Web — is a matter left to you. Just be aware that NetObjects Fusion supports the following types of Shockwave files:

- Shockwave for Director 4.0 and 5.0 (.dcr extension)
- Director (.dir extension)
- Protected Director (.dxr extension)
- Flash (.swf extension)
- Splash (.spl extension)

To add a Shockwave file to a page, make sure that you're in Page view on the page where you want to add Shockwave media and that you know the location on your hard drive of the Shockwave file in question.

1. **Click and hold the Media *flyout* (or pop-up menu) on the Advanced Tools toolbar.**

   A pop-up menu appears.

2. **Select the Shockwave tool and release the mouse button.**

3. **Click the page where you want to add the Shockwave element.**

   NetObjects Fusion displays a standard Open dialog box — except that it only displays valid Shockwave files.

4. **Navigate through your system to locate the Shockwave file you want and then click the Open button.**

   A gray placeholder appears in the spot you clicked in Step 3. The Properties palette switches to Shockwave Director Properties, Shockwave Flash Properties, or Shockwave Splash Properties, depending on which type of Shockwave file you choose. In any event, the Properties palette looks like the one shown in Figure 9-1.

   The title bar on the Properties palette changes to reflect the type of file that you choose. Instructions specific to the particular file types appear in the sections "Directing Director files" and "Flashing and splashing" later in this chapter.

Figure 9-1:
Your initial options are the same regardless of the type of Shockwave file you use.

5. **Type some text in the Alt Tag field, such as** The Shockwave plug-in is required to properly view this page.

   The Alt Tag field indicates the text that displays to users who don't have the Shockwave plug-in installed. This text appears on the page where the Shockwave media is supposed to be.

You can't preview Shockwave files unless you have published your site and you have the Shockwave plug-in installed on your browser. The plug-in is available from Macromedia's Web site at `www.macromedia.com`. If you use Shockwave on your site, I suggest that you provide a link to the Macromedia site for people who don't have the plug-in.

Directing Director files

If you want to insert a Shockwave Director file into your Web page, you may have to fill in several blanks in the Properties palette under the Controls tab (see Figure 9-2). Because the information that you input requires an intimate knowledge of Macromedia Director and Shockwave, a thorough description is beyond the scope of this book.

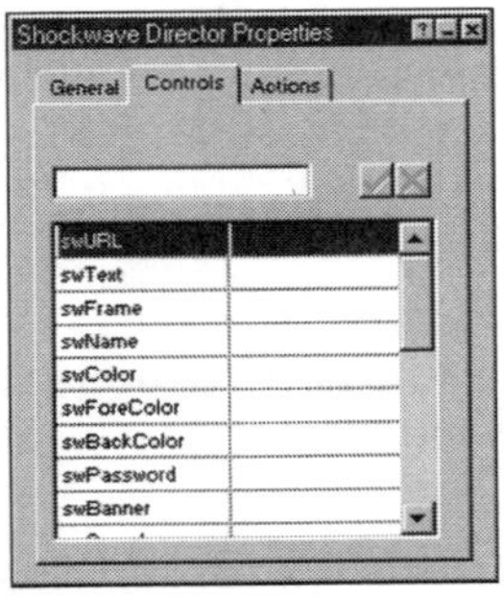

Figure 9-2:
The settings for Director files can get a little hairy.

If you want to put a file of this type in your NetObjects Fusion page, consider the following possibilities for getting the file to work properly:

- ✔ Try it to see if it works. Many Shockwave Director files don't require any special settings at all.

- ✔ Ask the creator of the file (if you can), for the settings you are unsure of.

- ✔ Pick up *Shockwave For Dummies,* 2nd Edition, by Greg Harvey (IDG Books Worldwide, Inc.) to get the scoop on Shockwave Director files in a style that the rest of us can understand.

Flashing and splashing

No, this isn't a discussion of skinny-dipping. Where full-blown Shockwave files can provide true interactive multimedia, the Flash and Splash formats were designed to provide simple animation.

This section explains how to use the Controls tab that appears on the Properties palette when you select a Shockwave Flash or Splash file. At this point, you should be in Page view and should have selected the Shockwave placeholder.

1. **Click the Controls tab of the Properties palette.**

   The Properties palette displays several options, as shown in Figure 9-3.

Figure 9-3:
The settings
for Flash
and Splash
files are
more
manageable
than the
ones for
Director
files.

2. **To change the anti-aliasing quality setting, click the arrow to the right of the Quality field and select the desired option.**

   These options control how *anti-aliasing* is handled. Anti-aliasing is the blurring of the edges of two adjoining images to reduce the choppy effect known as jaggies. Here's what each option does:

   - *AutoLow* sets the default anti-aliasing to low; the host computer uses high if it can.

   - *AutoHigh* sets the default anti-aliasing to high; the host computer uses low if it can't handle high.

   - *High* sets anti-aliasing to high on any computer.

   - *Low* sets anti-aliasing to low on any computer. Animations play faster with this option.

3. **To change the scale, click the arrow to the right of the Scale button and select the desired setting.**

   The *scale* setting controls how the animation fits in the space allotted for it. Here's what each does:

   - *Show All* displays the animation proportionally within the specified area. Empty space may appear on the side or bottom of the area.

- *No Border* maintains the proportions of the animation, but also fills the area. Some of the animation may get cropped on the side or bottom.

- *Exact Fit* stretches or scrunches the animation to fit exactly within the designated area.

4. **If you selected Show All or No Border in the previous step, click the arrow to the right of the Alignment field and select the alignment you desire.**

   This setting controls the alignment of the animation in relation to the designated area for the animation. Since Exact Fit fills the entire area, Alignment isn't an option.

5. **If you want the animation to begin as soon as the page loads, click the Auto Start check box.**

   With this option unchecked, users must click the animation to start it.

6. **If you want the animation to run in a continuous loop, click the Loop check box.**

   With this option unchecked, the animation plays once.

A Quick Look at QuickTime

QuickTime is an audio and video playback technology developed by Apple Computer for both the Mac and Windows platforms. On the Web, QuickTime is another type of media that requires a special browser plug-in. The plug-ins for both Mac and Windows are available from the Apple Web site at www.apple.com. On the Web, a QuickTime file uses the .mov file extension and is commonly called a movie, even if it's just an audio track.

To insert a QuickTime movie on your Web page, make sure you're in Page view on the page where you want to display the movie and follow these steps:

1. **Click and hold the Media flyout on the Advanced Tools toolbar.**

   A pop-up menu appears.

2. **Select the QuickTime tool and release the mouse button.**

3. **Click the page and draw a box where you want to add the QuickTime movie.**

   NetObjects Fusion displays a standard Open dialog box that contains valid QuickTime files.

Flattening Mac movies for use on Windows

Because QuickTime was developed by Apple, it's a very common format on Macintosh computers. As such, the QuickTime movies you use may have been developed on a Macintosh. If that's the case, you cannot simply copy the QuickTime file from a Mac system to a Windows system. To understand why, you need to understand a little about the Mac file structure.

Unlike the files on most other platforms, a Mac file consists of two parts, or forks. The *data fork* contains the actual contents of the file, and the *resource fork* contains extra information, such as the file type and creator ID. Since

this two-fork format is incompatible with other platforms, any Mac-originated QuickTime movies must be put through a process called flattening. When you *flatten* a QuickTime movie, you essentially combine the two forks to make the file compatible with other systems.

Many commercial video editing programs can do the flattening for you. Shareware programs such as flattenMooV, a Mac-based program, also do the trick. In any event, you must flatten any Mac-originated QuickTime movie before you can use it on your Web site.

4. **Navigate through your system to locate the desired QuickTime file and then click the Open button.**

A gray placeholder appears in the box you drew, and the Properties palette switches to QuickTime Properties, as shown in Figure 9-4.

Figure 9-4:
Control your
QuickTime
movies
here.

Here's a description of each option on the General tab of the Properties palette.

✔ **The Browse button** lets you select a different QuickTime movie if you happen to change your mind.

✔ **The Alt Tag field** allows you to specify text for users who don't have the proper plug-in installed.

✔ **The Display radio buttons** control whether the movie is displayed on the current page or in a separate browser window. If you elect to have the movie displayed in a separate window, you can use the Browse button next to the Launch from Picture field to select the image that serves as the link to the movie.

On the Controls tab, you can set the relative audio volume from 1 to 256. Keep in mind that the actual volume also depends on the settings on the user's computer. The Controls tab also provides the following Display Options:

✔ **The Hide All option** is useful if the movie is an audio file that you want to use as a background sound because this option makes the movie invisible. You normally use this option in conjunction with the Auto Start option.

✔ **The Control option** determines whether a small toolbar is displayed with the movie, thereby giving the user certain control over the movie. You cannot use this option if you use the Hide All option.

✔ **The Auto Start option** causes the movie to begin playing as soon as the page is loaded.

✔ **The Loop option** causes the movie to repeat continuously.

✔ **The Back and Forth option,** which is available if you select the Loop option, causes the movie to play in a loop, first playing forward, then in reverse, then forward again, and so on.

Finally, the Keep Movie in User's Cache check box controls whether the movie is stored in the browser cache or vaporized when the user moves on to another page. I suggest that you use this option. If someone comes back to the same page later, they certainly don't want to be forced into download-ing your QuickTime movie a second time.

Hey, Mom, I'm Makin' Movies!

NetObjects Fusion allows you to add movies in any of the following formats to your Web pages:

✔ **MPEG (Motion Picture Experts Group) movies** use .mpg, .mpeg, .mpe, or .mpv file extensions, and both Mac and Windows plug-ins are available.

✔ **AVI (Audio/Video Interleaved) movies** use the .avi file extension and are common on the Windows platform.

✓ **VIV (Vivo Active Producer) movies** use the .viv extension, and both Mac and Windows plug-ins are available.

✓ **RPM (Rapid Prototyping Model) movies** use the .rpm extension.

To add an MPEG, AVI, VIV, or RPM movie, just follow these steps:

1. **Click and hold the Media flyout on the Advanced Tools toolbar.**

   A pop-up menu appears.

2. **Select the Video tool and release the mouse button.**

3. **Drag the mouse to draw a box where you want to add the movie.**

   NetObjects Fusion displays an Open dialog box that contains valid movie files.

4. **Navigate through your system to locate the desired movie file; then click the Open button.**

   A gray placeholder appears in the box you drew in Step 3, and the Properties palette switches to Video Properties, as shown in Figure 9-5.

Figure 9-5:
Control your movies here.

Here's a description of each option on the General tab of the Properties palette.

✓ **The Browse button** next to the File field allows you to select a new file if you change your mind.

✓ **The Alt Tag field** is the place to specify the text that is displayed for users who don't have the proper plug-in installed.

✓ **The Display radio buttons** control how your movie is displayed. If you select Inline, your movie is displayed as part of the current page. If you select Icon or Picture, your movie is displayed in a separate browser window. The Icon option allows you to select one of three icons as the link to your movie. The Browse button associated with the Picture options allows you to select any image file to serve as the link to your movie.

> ✔ **The HTML button** allows you to edit the HTML code for the multimedia file or to add extra HTML code. I cover HTML scripting briefly in Chapter 13.

The Sound and the Flurry

Anybody can create a Web page that looks nice. How about a Web page that sounds nice? You can add music, a message from the company president, burping sounds. (Okay, maybe that last one wouldn't sound so nice.) The point is, your Web page doesn't have to be only a visual experience. NetObjects Fusion allows you to add sounds in any of the following formats to your Web pages:

- ✔ **Wave files,** which use the .wav extension.

- ✔ **Audio Interchange File Format files,** which use the .aiff extension.

- ✔ **MIDI (Musical Instrument Digital Interface) files,** which use either the .mid or .midi extension.

- ✔ **AU files,** which use the .au extension. This sound file format is the most common one on the Web.

- ✔ **RealAudio files,** which use either the .ra or .ram extension. However, note that to use these files, server software from RealAudio must be installed on your Web server. For more information, visit the RealAudio Web site at www.realaudio.com.

- ✔ **Rich Music Format files,** which use the .rmf extension.

The procedures that follow assume that you're in Page view on the page where you want to add a sound and that you know the location on your hard drive of the sound file in question.

1. **Click and hold the Media flyout on the Advanced Tools toolbar.**

2. **Select the Sound tool and release the mouse button.**

3. **Click the page where you want to add the sound.**

   NetObjects Fusion displays an Open dialog box that contains valid sound files.

4. **Navigate through your system to locate the desired sound file and then click the Open button.**

   A gray placeholder appears in the spot you clicked in Step 3, and the Properties palette switches to Sound Properties, as shown in Figure 9-6.

Figure 9-6:
Control your
sounds
here.

Here's a description of each option on the General tab of the Properties palette.

- ✔ **The Browse button** next to the File field allows you to select a new file if you change your mind.

- ✔ **The Alt Tag field** lets you specify the text users see when they don't have the proper plug-in installed.

- ✔ **The Display radio buttons** control how your sound is represented. If you select Inline, a small control panel like the one shown in Figure 9-7 is displayed on your Web page. This control panel allows users to stop and start the sound as well as control the volume. If you select Icon or Picture, users hear your sound by clicking on a link. The Icon option allows you to select one of three icons as the link to your sound. The Browse button associated with the Picture options allows you to select any image file to serve as the link to your sound.

- ✔ **The HTML button** allows you to edit the HTML code for the multimedia file or to add extra HTML code. I cover HTML scripting briefly in Chapter 13.

Figure 9-7:
This control
panel lets
users
control how
they hear
your sound.

Do-It-Yourself Multimedia

Although NetObjects Fusion supports a wide variety of multimedia formats, creating a program that supports every plug-in in use on the Web would be impossible. Besides that, new formats and plug-ins are added almost daily. With this limitation in mind, the programmers at NetObjects included the ability to add files in formats that aren't directly supported by NetObjects Fusion. This way, you are ready to add the latest files no matter what new formats and plug-ins come along.

If you want to add a multimedia element that uses a special plug-in, make sure you're in Page view on the page where you want to add the plug-in–based file and that you know the location on your hard drive of the file in question. Remember, to preview the results, you need the appropriate plug-in installed with your Web browser.

1. **Click the Media flyout on the Advanced Tools toolbar.**

   A pop-up menu appears.

2. **Select the Plug-In tool and release the mouse button.**

3. **Click the page and draw a box where you want to add the movie.**

   The size of the box is particularly important here, because NetObjects Fusion has no idea what type of file you're putting on your page. Make sure you provide enough space for whatever type of file you're using.

   NetObjects Fusion displays a standard Open dialog box.

4. **Navigate through your system to locate the desired file; then click the Open button.**

   A gray placeholder appears in the box you drew in Step 3, and the Properties palette switches to Plug-In Properties, as shown in Figure 9-8.

Figure 9-8:
NetObjects
Fusion lets
you control
how your
plug-in–
based file is
displayed.

Here's a description of each option on the General tab of the Properties palette.

- ✔ **The Browse button** allows you to select a different file if you happen to change your mind.

- ✔ **The Alt Tag field** is where you specify what text is displayed for users who don't have the proper plug-in installed.

- ✔ **The Display radio buttons** control whether the file is displayed on the current page or in a separate browser window. If you elect to have the file displayed in a separate window, you can use the Browse button next to the Launch from Picture field to select the image that serves as the link to the movie.

When you click the Advanced tab, as shown in Figure 9-9, NetObjects Fusion gives you the option to define any necessary parameters for your plug-in file. These parameters, if any, vary from plug-in to plug-in. You can contact each plug-in's creator for specific details.

Figure 9-9:
NetObjects
Fusion
lets you
define any
necessary
parameters
for your
plug-in file.

To add a parameter, just click the plus sign (+) and type a name and parameter in the resulting dialog box. You can add as many parameters as you need.

Spilling the Beans on Java

I don't know if Java will ever become the premier programming language that Sun Microsystems (its creator) is hoping for, but it's sure great for adding little multimedia thingies to your Web site. What makes it so powerful is that most popular Web browsers support it on most platforms without the need for any special plug-ins. What's more, NetObjects Fusion makes implementing Java applets and servlets easy, as well as letting you control their parameters from right within NetObjects Fusion. (FYI, an *applet* is a Java program that runs on the user's system; a *servlet* is a Java program that runs on the Web server.)

The procedures that follow assume that you're in Page view on the page where you want to add a Java applet or servlet, and that you know the location on your hard drive of the file in question.

1. **Click the Java tool on the Advanced Tools toolbar.**

2. **Drag the mouse (while holding down the button) to draw a box where you want to add the Java program.**

   NetObjects Fusion displays a standard Open dialog box that contains valid Java files that use the .class file extension.

3. **Navigate through your system to locate the desired Java file; then click the Open button.**

   A gray placeholder appears where you drew the box in Step 3, and the Properties palette switches to Java Properties, as shown in Figure 9-10.

Figure 9-10:
NetObjects
Fusion lets
you adjust
applet/
servlet
parameters
without
using
another
program.

Here's a description of each option on the General tab of the Properties palette.

✔ **The arrow to the right of the Class field** lets you display a list of all Java .class files currently in use on your site and select another one if you desire.

✔ **The List button** displays a list of all Java .class files currently in use on your site and gives you the opportunity to add new ones for later use.

✔ **The Alt Tag field** lets you specify what text is displayed for users who have older, Java-incapable browsers.

✔ **The Parameters list** displays the various parameters established for your particular Java program. These parameters vary from program to program. Contact the supplier of the program for details on possible values for each parameter.

To change the value for a parameter, double-click on it and type a new value in the resulting dialog box. You can also add and delete parameters by clicking the plus (+) and minus (-) signs below the list.

✔ **The radio buttons** at the bottom of the Properties palette let you indicate whether your Java program is an applet or a servlet.

Leading an ActiveX Lifestyle

NetObjects Fusion makes adding functionality to your Web pages using ActiveX controls easy. However, keep in mind that Netscape Navigator/ Communicator does not support ActiveX — it's a Microsoft-only product, which means that using ActiveX controls on your Web pages prevents Netscape users from taking full advantage of your site. If you're developing a site for your company's intranet and you know that your company has standardized on Internet Explorer, though, this is a nonissue.

The procedures that follow assume that you're in Page view on the page where you want to add an ActiveX control and that you know the location on your hard drive of the file in question. These procedures also assume that you have a reasonably solid understanding of how ActiveX controls work; an ActiveX tutorial is beyond the scope of this book.

1. **Click the ActiveX tool on the Advanced Tools toolbar.**

2. **Click the page and draw a box where you want to add the ActiveX control.**

   NetObjects Fusion displays an Insert ActiveX Control dialog box, as shown in Figure 9-11. This dialog box lists ActiveX controls that are available on your system.

3. **Click on the ActiveX control you want to add (and optionally click the Set Codebase check box); then click OK.**

   The appropriate ActiveX control appears in the box you drew in Step 3, and the Properties palette switches to ActiveX Properties, as shown in Figure 9-12.

Figure 9-11:
NetObjects
Fusion tells
you which
ActiveX
controls are
available
on your
system.

Figure 9-12:
NetObjects
Fusion lets
you adjust
ActiveX
control
parameters.

The list of parameters varies from control to control, so I can't tell you exactly what to specify for any given parameter. You need to get that information from whoever provided the ActiveX control. To change any given parameter, click it and then type the new value in the field at the top of the Properties palette. You can also specify the native properties of the ActiveX control by clicking the Properties button at the bottom of the Properties palette.

Part III
Advanced Goodies to Put on Your Page

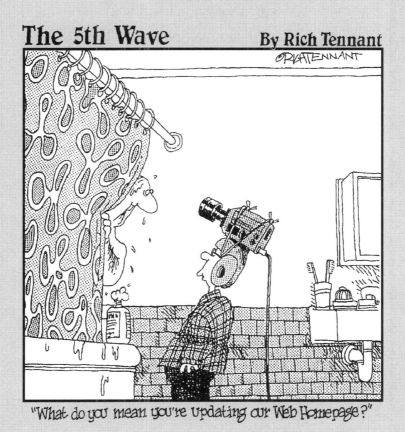

The 5th Wave   By Rich Tennant

"What do you mean you're updating our Web Homepage?"

In this part . . .

The plot thickens in Part III, which addresses some of the more complex elements you can add to your Web pages. Forms and tables are fairly common Web page elements, but they aren't for everybody. You may go years without using them. Especially with forms, getting them to perform the way you want can be a little tricky.

The meat of this part, however, consists of chapters that deal with some of the unique and powerful capabilities of NetObjects Fusion. Perhaps my favorite are NetObjects Components — mini-applications that you can add to your pages with just a few mouse clicks. The results are quite impressive.

Also in this part, I explain how you can convert your page borders to HTML in a matter of seconds. Try doing that with any other Web authoring tool!

Do you have information stored in a database program that you need to publish on your Web site? In the hands of lesser program, publishing a database on the Web can be a real nightmare. Not so here, my friend. NetObjects Fusion has built-in data publishing capabilities that reduce the task to the simplest of steps.

Finally, NetObjects Fusion puts the power of dynamic HTML at your fingertips. For the latest crop of Web browsers, you can create animated pages that were just a gleam in the programmer's eye a few years ago.

Chapter 10

Turning the Tables

● ●

In This Chapter

▶ Creating an HTML table

▶ Adjusting the spacing within a table

▶ Changing a table's background color

▶ Adding text and graphics to a table

▶ Resizing a table

● ●

1 want you to close your eyes and think back to those ancient days when most computer users — not to mention the rest of the world — had never heard of the World Wide Web. Back then, the people who did use the Web weren't worried about multimedia and animation and how to generate a gazillion hits a day. No; back then, the concerns were much more basic.

Among the biggest beefs that users had with HTML in the old days was that it offered no simple and effective way to format *tabular data*. By tabular data, I mean information that you would normally set up in table format so it looks kind of like a spreadsheet: You know, columns and rows. If you absolutely, positively had to present a table, your only option was to format that portion of your Web page with a monospaced font and type periods to separate the fields, all the time praying that people in your audience hadn't adjusted their browser preferences to display monospaced type as proportional.

Luckily, the Web forces that be weren't willing to tolerate such a fundamental flaw, so they invented a set of HTML tags that can be used to organize information into table format within Web pages. My biggest reason for upgrading to Navigator 2.0 was to attain the ability to view HTML tables.

Building a Basic Table

NetObjects Fusion makes creating basic tables a snap. However, I have to be perfectly honest: The program does not offer the most robust set of tools for customizing your tables. For example, combining two or more table cells into one bigger cell by using the *collspan* and *rowspan* HTML tags isn't an uncommon maneuver. Yet, the table tools in NetObjects Fusion don't offer this capability. Other table features that are conspicuously missing are captions (the ability to automatically position a caption either directly above or below the actual table) and table headers (the ability to tag individual cells as column headings, thereby making them look different from the regular cells).

The lack of table captions and column heads is only a minor irritation. You can manually add a text box as a table caption wherever you want it. Likewise, you can manually change header cells to bold type, which is the most common formatting for these cells.

Unfortunately, NetObjects Fusion offers no manual process that can substitute for collspan and rowspan. If you need to create such a table, your best bet is to create it in another program, save it as a separate HTML file, and then incorporate it into your Web page as reference HTML, as described in Chapter 4.

If you're willing to live with the table limitations imposed by NetObjects Fusion, here's how you create a table. These procedures assume that you're already in Page view:

1. **Click the Table button in the Standard Tools palette.**

   This is the button that looks like a 9 x 9 green grid. Clicking it turns the mouse pointer into a crosshair.

2. **Click and drag the crosshair to identify the approximate area for the table; then release the mouse button.**

   You don't have to be exact here, because the initial size of the table is determined in part by how many rows and columns you create in the next step.

   When you release the mouse button, a Create Table dialog box appears, as shown in Figure 10-1.

Figure 10-1:
Just how
big do you
want your
table?

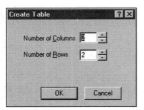

3. Specify the number of columns and rows you want your table to contain, then click OK.

You can type a number in the field provided, or you can click the little arrows to change the numbers in single-unit increments. Also, don't worry if you don't get the numbers right, because you can add and delete rows and columns later.

A row is a horizontal set of cells and a column is a vertical set of cells.

After you click the OK button, your new table appears right about where you specified.

Setting (Up) Your Table

Granted, NetObjects Fusion leaves a lot to be desired when it comes to tables. Nevertheless you can make a few adjustments from the Properties palette.

Giving those cells some elbow room

When you create a new table, or any time you select an existing table, the Properties palette offers you a few Table Properties, as shown in Figure 10-2. I cover forms in Chapter 11; I cover Actions (the third tab) in Chapter 15.

Figure 10-2: The Properties palette lets you control various aspects of table spacing.

Here's what each one of the options shown in the Properties palette does (Note that all measurements are in pixels.):

✔ The Border field controls the width of the border that runs around the outside of the table. When you increase the border size — either by typing in a number or clicking the little arrows — notice that HTML table borders have a somewhat beveled look, which I think is pretty cool.

   ✔ The Padding field controls the distance between the edge of a cell and
     its contents. For example, if you have the padding set to zero, any text
     you type in a cell bumps right up against the edge of the cell, possibly
     making it more difficult to read. By increasing the padding, you can give
     each cell a roomier look and feel.

   ✔ The Spacing field controls the space between one cell and the next. You
     can use this as well to give your table a less cramped feel.

Using backgrounds like a virtual tablecloth

NetObjects Fusion allows you to set the background color of a table inde-
pendently from any background you use on the rest of your page. Here's all
you do.

1. **If you haven't already, select the table by clicking it with the Selection tool.**

   Doing this displays the Table Properties on the Properties palette.

2. **Click the Background tab on the Properties palette.**

3. **Click the Color button on the Properties palette.**

   NetObjects Fusion displays a Color Picker dialog box.

4. **Click the desired color, then click OK.**

   NetObjects Fusion displays the table background in the color you
   specified.

Adding text and graphics to your table

Adding text to a table cell is as simple as can be. Using the Selection tool,
just double-click the cell where you want to add the text. A text cursor then
appears in the cell, at which point you can start typing away.

Note that NetObjects Fusion treats a table cell just like any other text box.
That means that all the formatting options that are available for a text box
through the Properties palette (which I discuss in Chapter 6) are available
for each individual cell.

To add a graphic to a table cell, follow the procedures covered in Chapter 7
for adding a graphic. Using the Picture tool, just make sure you position the
graphic in the desired cell.

Getting the Size Right

As you're working on your table, you may discover that it's not quite the right size. Perhaps you don't have the right number of rows or columns, or maybe you just don't like the overall dimensions of the table. Fixing either of these problems takes only a couple of mouse-clicks.

More rows and columns: Adding a leaf or two to your table

Whether you want to add or delete rows or columns, the same basic procedures apply. After you select the table using the Selection tool, click the Object menu and select Table. This displays a submenu, as shown in Figure 10-3.

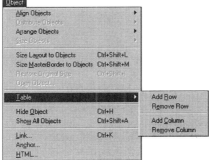

Figure 10-3:
It's easy to
add and
delete
rows and
columns.

Table 10-1 shows you how to make various additions and deletions to and from your table. All submenu references refer to the submenu shown in Figure 10-3.

Table 10-1	Adding and Deleting Rows and Columns
Where You Want It	**What to Do**
To add a row to the bottom submenu	Choose Table⇨Add Row
To add a row below some other row	Double-click any cell in the row below which you want to add a row, and then choose Table⇨Add Row

(continued)

Table 10-1 *(continued)*

Where You Want It	What to Do
To add a column to the right side of the table	Select the table and choose Table⇨Add Column
To add a column to the right of any other column	Double-click any cell in the column to the right of which you want to add a column, then choose Table⇨Add Column
To delete the bottom row	Select the table and choose Table⇨Remove Row
To delete any other row	Double-click any cell in the row you want to delete and choose Table⇨Remove Row
To delete the far-right column	Select the table and choose Table⇨Remove Column
To delete any column other than the far-right column	Double-click any cell in the column you want to delete and choose Table⇨Remove Column

Resizing your table

NetObjects Fusion leaves something to be desired when it comes to resizing your table. You'd expect it to work just like resizing a graphic (see Chapter 7); drag one of the eight handles and the size changes. Unfortunately, that's not so. Here are the results you can expect from various handle drags:

- ✔ If you drag one of the side handles left or right, the width of the table changes accordingly. However, inside the table, only the width of the rightmost column changes.
- ✔ If you drag one of the top handles up or down, all you do is move the table.
- ✔ If you drag one of the bottom handles up or down, nothing happens.

As I said, the program leaves something to be desired in this area.

Changing the width of an individual cell is a little more tedious. You need to keep a couple of things in mind, too. When you change the width of one cell, you change the width of every cell in the same column, and you also change the width of the next column over. That's because the overall size of the table doesn't change. Hence, the size of the next column changes to accommodate the resizing of the column you intend to change. In short, any time you change the width of one column, you really change the width of two. NetObjects Fusion doesn't let you change row height.

Here are the steps to follow to change the width of a table cell:

1. **Select the table using the Selection tool.**

2. **Move the mouse pointer over one of the inner vertical borders of the cell that you want to resize.**

   The mouse pointer turns into a double arrow, as shown in Figure 10-4.

3. **Click and drag the inner border to resize the cell.**

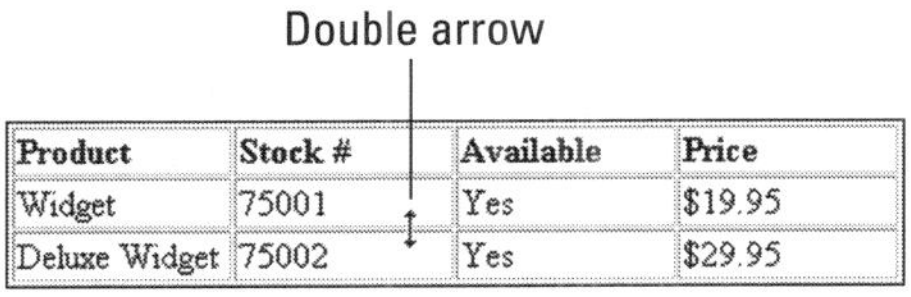

Figure 10-4:
Position
the mouse
pointer, as
shown, to
adjust
a cell's
height.

Double arrow

Product	Stock #	Available	Price
Widget	75001	Yes	$19.95
Deluxe Widget	75002	Yes	$29.95

Chapter 11

Interactive Forms in an Instant

. . . .

. . . .

*W*hile most of the pages on your Web site are devoted to delivering information to visitors, from time to time you may want your visitors to deliver information to you (or your computer). For example, you may want to create an online survey to collect demographic information or solicit opinions. If you're attempting to sell something online, you want to provide a mechanism for people to place orders. The easiest and most efficient way to gather information from your users is to provide an online *form*. A form is simply a Web page (or portion of a Web page, because it's possible to put more than one form on a page) where users can type information and push buttons to select various options and then have their input passed on to you. The data is handled by a CGI (Common Gateway Interface) script — a small program that runs in the background and is designed specifically for the purpose of handling the form data.

Where Will You Put Your Form?

The first decision you face in creating a form in NetObjects Fusion is to determine exactly where you want to put the form. The program allows you to create a form inside any of the following page elements:

✔ **A layout region.** Of the four possible options, the layout region is the most flexible. You have total control over the formatting of the form, plus you can add multiple layout regions to a page to create multiple forms on that page. (For more information about layout regions, see Chapter 7.)

Anatomy of a form

You can make use of a variety of form elements that allow users to provide their input. Specifically, you can create fields into which they type information, radio buttons and check boxes they can use to specify various options, and lists of items from which they can make selections.

Perhaps the most important element in a form is the Submit button, which users click to send all the information they've entered to you or your computer. The reason I say *you or your computer* is that exactly what happens to the information is controlled by a program running in the background on your Web server called a *CGI script*, which stands for Common Gateway Interface script. A CGI script is a little program written in one of several popular programming languages that receives the form input and then does something with it.

Exactly what the CGI script does with information that users enter in a form depends on the script itself. For example, a programmer may write a script that formats the information into an e-mail message and then forwards that message to your e-mail address. A more complicated CGI script may add the information to a database that resides on your Web server. In an online commerce environment, a series of sophisticated CGI scripts can handle

processing an order, verifying the credit card information, checking the inventory database, and fulfilling the order.

Note that if your Web server is Windows-based, certain executable (.exe) files may also handle forms. However, because CGI scripts are more common, I discuss only CGI scripts in the remainder of this chapter. The same basic rules apply to any .exe files you use for forms handling.

NetObjects Fusion provides you with both the tools to create your various form elements and a simple CGI script that can either send the form data to you via e-mail or write it to a text file on your Web server. This CGI script is available via the Forms Handler Component. For details on using the Forms Handler, refer to Chapter 12.

If the Forms Handler doesn't meet your needs and you don't have the programming expertise to write your own CGI scripts, you need to find someone who does. A good place to start is with your Web server's system administrator or webmaster. If you're putting your site on an Internet service provider's server, your ISP may already have form-handling CGI scripts in place that you can use.

- ✔ **A table.** With a table, you're limited in your layout options. With tables and text boxes, you're limited in your layout options. (For more information about tables, see Chapter 10.)
- ✔ **A simple text box.** With a text box, you're limited in your layout options. (For more information about text boxes, see Chapter 6.)
- ✔ **The entire Layout area.** Using the whole Layout area limits you to one form on the page. (For more information about the Layout area, see Chapter 5.)

For the sake of this discussion, I refer to these elements collectively as *form containers*.

The advantage to the first three form containers is that they let you put more than one form on a page. In other words, you can add any combination of layout regions, tables, and text boxes to your page, each containing its own form. If you make the Layout area the form container, that limits you to a single form on that page.

In the procedures that follow in this chapter, I explain how to create a form in a layout region. Just remember that the same information applies to creating forms in the other containers, subject to certain limitations.

Forming Your Form

The form creation process has three basic parts. First, you create a container for your form. Then you add various user-input elements — text fields, radio buttons, lists, and so on. Finally, you add a Submit button (which submits the data to the CGI script) and a Reset button (which clears the form and allows the user to start over).

Creating a new form

Regardless of which container you plan to use, you can start any form in the same manner. In the procedures that follow, I explain how to create a form in a layout region, but the same basic procedures apply regardless of which form container you use. These procedures also assume that you're already in Page view on the page on which you plan to create the form.

1. **Click the Form Area button on the Standard Tools toolbar.**

   This is the button just below the Table button. It looks something like two text fields.

   The mouse pointer turns into a crosshair.

2. **Click and drag to mark off the layout region for your form. Then release the mouse button.**

   A Create Form box appears, as shown in Figure 11-1. It has four options to choose from: Layout Region, Text box, Table, and Layout area.

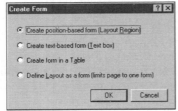

This box defaults to the Layout Region option. Because I'm providing the steps for creating a form in a layout region, you can accept the default.

3. Click the OK button.

A layout region appears where you specified. Note that the Properties palette changes to Layout Region Properties and the Layout Region Is a Form check box is checked. The Form Tools toolbar also appears, as shown in Figure 11-2. You can toggle the display of this toolbar on and off by choosing View⇨Toolbars⇨Form Tools.

Figure 11-2:
The Form
Tools
toolbar.

That's the easy part. Now you need to add form elements to the layout region.

Adding a little text here

The first element you're likely to add to a form is a simple text field. This is a single-line field that can be used for things like name, e-mail address, credit card number, and so on. To add a text field to a form, follow these steps.

1. Click the Forms Edit Field button on the Form Tools toolbar.

The mouse pointer turns into a crosshair.

2. Click and drag with the layout region to mark the area for the text field, then release the mouse button.

Regardless of the area you specify, this field will only be one text line in height because that's the nature of this type of form element. You can, however, control its width.

When you release the mouse button, the text field appears where you specified. Note that the Properties palette has now changed to Forms Edit Field Properties, as shown in Figure 11-3.

Figure 11-3:
You have several options for a text field.

3. **Adjust the options for this field according to the following:**

   - *The Name field* on the Properties palette specifies the field name that your CGI script will use to identify information in that particular field. You can use any name that will be useful to you, but it can't include punctuation or spaces.

   - *The Text field* is where you type in text that you would like to have displayed in this field automatically. The user then has the ability to use the text you have provided, or change it to something else.

   - *The Password Field check box* modifies the text field so that when a user types in that field, the typed input appears as bullet characters. However, keep in mind that the field truly serves as a password field only if your CGI script is designed to handle it as such.

   - *The Visible Length field* controls the width of the field, measured in characters. You can also control the width of the field by dragging its handles.

   - *The Max Length field* controls how many characters a user can actually type in. This number can be higher than the Visible Length field, but it shouldn't be lower. If you make it lower, users will wonder why they can type to the end of the field.

   - *The HTML button* is addressed in Chapter 13.

 4. **Use the Text tool to add some sort of caption to the field so users know what they're supposed to type there.**

The finished field should look something like Figure 11-4.

Figure 11-4:
Don't forget
to put a
caption on
your field
so people
know what
to type.

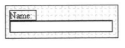

Adding a lotta text there

Suppose the information you want your users to provide isn't likely to fit on one line. For these occasions, you can create a multi-line text field in much the same way you create a single-line text field.

1. **Click the Forms Multi-Line button on the Form Tools toolbar.**

   The mouse pointer turns into a crosshair.

2. **Click and drag within the layout region to mark the area for the multiline text field, and then release the mouse button.**

   When you release the mouse button, the multi-line text field appears where you specified. Note that the Properties palette has now changed to Forms Multi-Line Properties, as shown in Figure 11-5.

Figure 11-5:
You have
several
options for
a text field.

3. **Adjust the options for this field according to the following:**

   • *The Name field* on the Properties palette allows you to specify the field name that your CGI script uses to identify information in that particular field. You can use any name that will be helpful for you, but it can't include punctuation or spaces.

- *The Text field* is where you type in text that you would like to have displayed in this field automatically. The user then can use the text you have provided or change it to something else.

- *The Visible Length field* controls the width of the field, measured in characters. You can also control the width of the field by dragging its handles.

- *The Visible Height field* lets you choose the height of the field, measured in lines.

- *The HTML button* is addressed in Chapter 13.

 4. Use the Text tool to add some sort of caption to the field so users know what they're supposed to type there.

Giving options to your users

When you display a list of options on your form, you need to decide whether you want users to be able to select just one of those options or as many as they want. For example, if you're providing a list of shirt sizes on an order form, you want a user to be able to specify only one size. On the other hand, if you want users to select several different topics that interest them from a list, you want to let them pick more than one. Which of these two options you need determines what type of button you use.

Radio buttons: This or that

If you want users to be able to select only one option from a list, the radio button is your tool of choice. Here's how to add a group of radio buttons.

1. Click the Forms Radio Button button on the Form Tools toolbar.

 The mouse pointer turns into a crosshair.

2. Click the mouse where you want the radio button to appear.

The radio button appears where you specified.

3. Repeat Steps 1 and 2 for as many radio buttons as you need for your list.

Note that each time you create a radio button, the Properties palette changes to *Forms Radio Button Properties,* as shown in Figure 11-6.

4. In the Forms Radio Button Properties dialog box, adjust the options for each radio button in the list according to the following:

- *The Group Name field* identifies which radio buttons on your form are part of the same list. You need to type in the same group name for each button in the list. If you don't use the same group name

on all the radio buttons in the list, users will be able to select more than one option from the list. You can use any name that will be useful to you, but it can't include punctuation or spaces. For example, if you're presenting a list of shirt sizes, you could make the group name *size*.

• *The Value Sent field* specifies what information is sent to your CGI script if a particular button is selected. That means that this information must be different for each radio button in the group. For example, if you're presenting a list of shirt sizes, the value sent for one field might be *xxl*, the next *xl*, and so on.

• *The Selected and Not Selected buttons* control which radio button in the group is selected as the default option when the form is first displayed. You can have only one Selected radio button per group.

• *The HTML button* is addressed in Chapter 13.

5. Use the Text tool to add some sort of caption to each radio button.

The text tool is in the Standard Tools toolbar and has an *A* on it.

The finished field should look something like Figure 11-7.

□ Sm
□ Med
□ Lg
□ XL

Check boxes: This and that

For those times when you want users to be able to choose more than one option from a list, the check box is the tool of choice. Unlike radio buttons, which work together as a group, each check box functions as an independent form element. When you present a list of check boxes, users are free to choose as many options as they like.

1. **Click the Forms Checkbox button on the Form Tools toolbar.**

   The mouse pointer turns into a crosshair.

2. **Click the mouse where you want the check box to appear.**

   The check box appears where you specified.

3. **Repeat Steps 1 and 2 for as many check boxes you need for your list.**

   Note that each time you create a check box, the Properties palette changes to Forms Checkbox Properties, as shown in Figure 11-8.

Figure 11-8: Each check box is an independent form element.

4. **Using the Forms Checkbox Properties dialog box, adjust the options for each checkbox in the list according to the following:**

   • *The Name field* specifies the name by which your CGI scripts identifies the information that particular check box submits. You can use any name that will be useful to you, but it can't include punctuation or spaces.

   • *The Value field* specifies what information that particular check box submits to the CGI script when a user selects it.

   • *The Checked and Unchecked buttons* control the default setting of the check box.

   • *The HTML button* is addressed in Chapter 13.

5. Use the Text tool to add some sort of caption to each check box.

The finished field should look something like Figure 11-9.

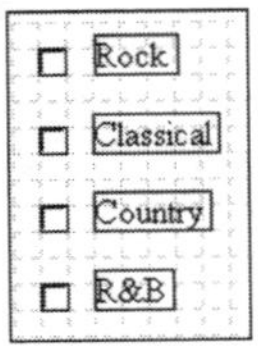

Figure 11-9:
Users can
select any
or all of
these
options.

Combo boxes: The other things

Radio buttons and check boxes enable you to display lists of information with each list item as an individual element on your Web page. However, you can also display a list of information as a true list using what NetObjects Fusion calls a *combo box*. You add list items using the Properties palette, and NetObjects Fusion creates the list for you. To add a combo box to a form, just follow these steps:

1. Click the Forms Combo Box button on the Form Tools toolbar.

The mouse pointer turns into a crosshair.

2. Click the mouse where you want the combo box to appear.

The combo box appears where you specified.

Note that when you create a combo box, the Properties palette changes to Forms Combo Box Properties, as shown in Figure 11-10.

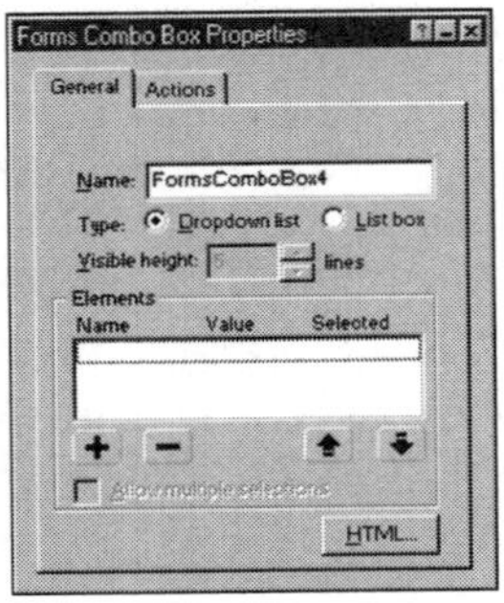

Figure 11-10:
You add
list items
through the
Properties
palette.

3. **In the Forms Combo Box Properties dialog box, adjust the options for the combo box according to the following:**

   - *The Name field* specifies the name by which your CGI script identifies the information submitted by the combo box. You can use any name that will be useful to you, but it can't include punctuation or spaces.

   - *Dropdown List and List Box,* the two Type options, control how the list appears. A drop-down list displays only one option from the list and provides a little clickable arrow to display the rest of the list. A list box displays a portion of the list and provides a scrollbar for viewing the rest of the list, as shown in Figure 11-11.

   - *The Visible Height field* controls how many list items are displayed if you elect to display the list as a list box. In other words, this field controls the physical size of the list box.

   - *The Allow Multiple Selections check box,* if checked, lets users select more than one item from the list. With this box unchecked, users can select only a single list item.

   - *The HTML button* is addressed in Chapter 13.

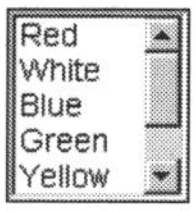

Figure 11-11:
Here's a list
displayed as
a list box.

4. **To add an item to the list, click the plus sign (+) under the Elements field on the Properties palette.**

   The Enter Value dialog box appears, as shown in Figure 11-12.

5. **In the Name field, type the name of the list item as you want it to appear in the list.**

6. **In the Value field, type the value that you want sent to your CGI script when this particular list item is selected.**

7. **If you want this list item to show as selected when the list first appears, click the Selected by Default check box.**

8. **Click the OK button.**

9. **Repeat Steps 4 through 8 for each item you want to add to the list.**

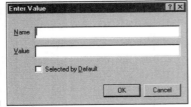

Figure 11-12:
You need to
enter a
name and
a value.

You can delete any item from this list by clicking it in the Properties palette and then clicking the minus sign (–). You can also scroll through the list items using the up and down arrows on the Properties palette. Finally, you can edit any list item by double-clicking it.

Popping in the Reset and Submit buttons

Once you've added all the different parts for your form, you still need to provide some way for the user to submit the information to you. It's also helpful if you provide some means for a user to clear the entire form and start over, if necessary. The two standard buttons for these purposes are, respectively, the Submit button and the Reset button.

You can use the Forms Handler Component to process the form data. I provide complete procedures for this in Chapter 12. Among other things, the Forms Handler creates its own Submit button for your form. Therefore, if you're using the Forms Handler, skip the steps below for creating a Submit button.

To create one of these buttons just follow these steps:

1. **Click the Forms Button button on the Form Tools toolbar.**

   The mouse pointer turns into a crosshair.

2. **Click the mouse where you want the button to appear.**

   Normally, you put the Submit and Reset buttons at the end of the form.

   Note that when you create a button, the Properties palette changes to *Forms Button Properties*, as shown in Figure 11-13.

3. **In the Forms Button Properties, adjust the options for the button according to the following:**

   • *The Name field* is where you can type a new name if you want to rename the button (for example, to make it easier to identify in the Objects Tree).

Figure 11-13:
Here's
where you
manage
your
buttons.

- *The Text field* determines what text appears on the actual button. The most common approach here is to simply type **Submit** for a Submit button and **Reset** for a Reset button, but you can use any text you want.

- *The Image option* is what you select if you want to specify a graphic file to use as a button instead of a simple button. However, a standard button is more efficient (because there's no graphic to download), and I prefer them for this reason.

- *The Type pop-up* provides three options: Submit, Reset, and Button. You can use the Button option if clicking the button will initiate some sort of Action, as described in Chapter 15. Normally, though, you'll choose from one of the first two options.

Applying the Finishing Touches

Once you finish adding various elements to your form, it may look like you're done. However, unless you used the Forms Handler (see Chapter 12), you still have a few more steps. Specifically, you need to provide NetObjects Fusion with some information to make sure that the form communicates properly with your CGI script.

The exact information you provide depends entirely on the CGI script you use. The following is a description of each of bit of information you need to provide:

✔ **Name** refers to the name of your form. Some CGI scripts require a form name, so check with the person who provided the script.

✔ **Action** specifies the complete path to the CGI script you want to handle the form data, and probably some more information you need to get from the person who designed the CGI script. If the CGI script resides on your computer, you can use the Browse button to locate it. You usually need to specify some additional parameters along to the CGI script. You can find out what parameters to type in from the person who provided you with the CGI script.

✔ **Method** distinguishes how your form passes information to and from the CGI script. The two methods available are *get* and *post*. Each CGI script uses one or the other. You can find out which to use from the person who provided you with the CGI script.

✔ **Encoding Type** refers to any data encoding type, such as MIME or BinHex, that your CGI script may require. Obtain this information for the person who provided the CGI script.

✔ **Hidden Fields** are fields that do not appear on your form. They're used to pass necessary information along to the CGI script and their values vary from script to script. Some scripts don't require them at all. Obtain this information for the person who provided the CGI script.

I've got my CGI on you

You can access all these attributes via the Settings button on the Properties palette. To adjust the settings for your form, just follow these steps:

1. **Click the layout region that contains the form to select it.**

2. **Make sure that the Layout Region Is a Form check box in the Properties palette is selected.**

3. **Click the Settings button on the Properties palette.**

   A Form Settings dialog box appears, as shown in Figure 11-14.

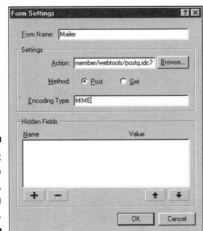

4. **Type a name for your form in the Form Name field as necessary.**

5. **Specify the settings that appear in the Settings panel of the Form Settings dialog box (refer to Figure 11-14).**

   Specify the Action field, Method radio button, and Encoding Type text box according to the information you receive from whoever has the scoop on the CGI script you're using.

   Chances are this is all you need to do. However, depending again on the CGI script you use and what it does, you may need to automatically pass predefined data on to the CGI script. You do this by creating hidden fields.

6. **Click the OK button (unless you need to define hidden fields).**

   I describe hidden fields in the following section.

Hidden fields

A *hidden field* contains extra information that your CGI script needs to do its thing. When you create a hidden field, its value is passed on to the CGI script like any other form information. The only difference is that the user has no control of the information and, in fact, doesn't even know it's being passed along.

1. **If you haven't done so already, open the Form Settings dialog box, enter a form name, and define the Action, Method, and Encoding Type fields.**

   Detailed instructions for this appear in the previous section, "I got my CGI on you."

2. **Click the plus sign (+) in the Hidden Fields area.**

   This displays an Enter Value dialog box, as shown in Figure 11-15.

Figure 11-15: Your form can pass hidden information along to the CGI script.

3. **Type a name for the hidden field in the Name field, as specified by your script provider.**

4. **Type a value for the hidden field in the Value field, as specified by your script provider.**

5. **Click the OK button in the Enter Value dialog box.**

6. **Repeat steps 2 through 5 as necessary.**

   This brings you back to the Form Settings dialog box.

7. **Click the OK button in the Form Settings dialog box.**

Chapter 12

NetObjects Components: Your Secret Bag of Tricks

. . . .

In This Chapter

▶ Creating dynamic buttons

▶ Adding a ticker-tape message to your page

▶ Creating a site map on the fly

▶ Providing visitors with a message board

▶ Creating forms without CGI scripting

▶ Adding cool effects to pictures

▶ Adding and using new components

. . . .

*N*etObjects Fusion gives you a secret weapon in your quest for making a really cool Web site: *NetObjects components.* Components are mini-applications that you can add quickly and easily to enhance the functionality of your Web pages. These components let you enhance the usability and "cool factor" of your Web pages without having to do a lot of programming.

If you've ever messed with Microsoft FrontPage, you've seen similar stuff, but unlike the goodies that Microsoft throws in with FrontPage, NetObjects components don't require you to have a Web server that runs special software for them to work. NetObjects components are based on Web standards like Java and CGI.

Looking at Your Bag of Components

Components are little programs that you can put into your NetObjects Web pages to do cool stuff on the Web. You can access NetObjects components via the Component toolbar. To display the Component toolbar, choose View⇨Toolbars⇨Component Tools. The Component toolbar is shown in Figure 12-1.

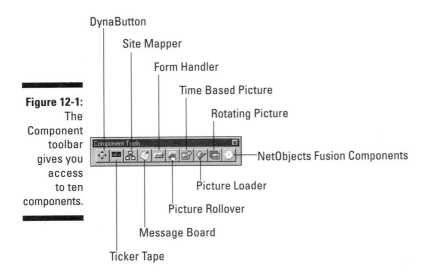

Figure 12-1: The Component toolbar gives you access to ten components.

DynaButton

Site Mapper

Form Handler

Time Based Picture

Rotating Picture

NetObjects Fusion Components

Picture Loader

Picture Rollover

Message Board

Ticker Tape

The following list describes the use of each button on the Component toolbar:

- **DynaButton:** Have you ever been to a Web site where a button changes its looks as you pass the mouse pointer over it? Pretty cool, eh? The DynaButton adds this capability to your Web pages.

- **Form Handler:** If you have a form whose output you simply want to save to a text file or have e-mailed to you, this component provides all the necessary CGI scripting so you don't need to worry about tracking down some other CGI program to do the job. (See Chapter 11 for more information about forms.)

- **Message Board:** This component lets you add a fully functioning, Web-based discussion group to your site. Users can post messages and read others' messages.

✔ **NetObjects Fusion Components:** NetObjects intentionally designed its component architecture to be open, meaning that other companies can (and do) develop their own NetObjects Components. (Check the NetObjects Web site at `www.netobjects.com` for information about available third-party Components.) This component lets you install and use those third-party Components.

✔ **Picture Loader:** This component gives you an easy way to include images that are stored on another site. For example, if you want to put banner advertising for another company on your site, you can tell Picture Loader the location of the banner graphic on the other company's site, and it will appear on your page right where you want it.

✔ **Picture Rollover:** DynaButtons use the button images associated with whatever SiteStyle you're using. If you want to create the same effect with some other graphics, you can do so with the Picture Rollover component.

✔ **Rotating Picture:** This name is a little confusing; your images don't physically rotate. This component lets your page automatically switch among several images at various predefined intervals. For example, you can have an image that switches back and forth every ten seconds.

✔ **Site Mapper:** This component adds a Site Map button to your page. When users click this button, a separate window pops up that shows a map of your entire site. Users can then click any page and go right to that page.

✔ **Ticker Tape:** This Java applet adds a scrolling banner that displays the text you specify.

✔ **Time Based Picture:** This component lets you specify different pictures to occupy the same space at different times of the day. For example, you could have a "good morning" picture display in the morning, a "good afternoon" picture display in the afternoon, and so on.

Components don't work when you simply preview your site. To see them in action, you have to publish the site. Fortunately, most of them work fine when you publish them on your own hard drive. Check out Chapter 18 for instructions on how to publish your site on your hard drive.

Using Those Dynamite DynaButton Bars

DynaButtons make your pages come alive. When you use a *DynaButton bar* instead of a regular NavBar, buttons become highlighted when visitors pass their mouse pointers over them. To pull off this magic, DynaButtons use the buttons assigned to whatever SiteStyle you're using. While making the buttons change as you move your mouse over them doesn't necessarily add a whole lot of functionality, it sure looks cool.

In addition to looking cool, DynaButtons can be used for any type of link, including e-mail links, and can link to pages on other sites (regular NavBars can only link to other pages on your site).

Another powerful feature of DynaButtons is the ability to add sub-buttons. In effect, this lets you add graphical drop-down menus to your page. When the user clicks a button in the button bar, the sub-buttons appear below it. Each DynaButton can have up to 20 sub-buttons.

Creating a basic DynaButton bar

The procedures that follow assume that you're in Page view on the page where you want to add the DynaButtons. They also assume you have displayed the Component toolbar by choosing View➪Toolbars➪Component Tools.

To add a DynaButton bar to a page, follow these steps.

1. **Click the DynaButton button on the Component toolbar.**

2. **Click the mouse where you want the DynaButton bar to appear.**

   A gray box marked DynaButtons appears where you clicked and the title bar Properties palette changes to DynaButtons Properties, as shown in Figure 12-2. The gray box serves as a placeholder for the DynaButtons.

Figure 12-2:
You define
your
DynaButtons
using the
Properties
palette.

3. **To change the orientation of the DynaButton bar, double-click the word Orientation in the list on the Properties palette.**

4. **To change the number of buttons, double-click Number of Buttons in the list, type the new number in the DynaButtons field, and then press the Enter key.**

For example, if you type the number **3**, NetObjects Fusion places three DynaButtons on the toolbar. The placeholder for the DynaButton bar changes size to accommodate the number of buttons you specify. NetObjects Fusion also adds the new buttons to the list on the Properties palette.

5. **To specify the link for a particular button, double-click that button in the list on the Properties palette.**

   For example, to set the link for the first button, double-click Button 1 in the list.

   NetObjects Fusion displays a Link dialog box, as shown in Figure 12-3.

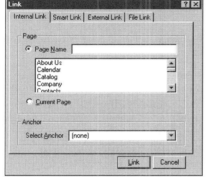

Figure 12-3:
You define
DynaButton
links just
like any
other link.

This is the same dialog box that appears anytime you create a link. Chapter 8 provides the scoop on how to define a link in the Link dialog box.

6. **Specify the link; then click the Link button.**

7. **Repeat Step 5 for each button.**

To see your DynaButtons at work, you need to publish your site. Chapter 18 explains how to publish your site on your own hard drive. This is the easiest way to test your DynaButtons.

Adding sub-buttons to a DynaButton bar

You can use DynaButtons to create graphical drop-down menus on your Web pages. Each item in the drop-down list is called a sub-button. The sub-buttons remain hidden until the user clicks on the main button.

If you plan to use sub-buttons, don't create links for the main button. If you create a link for the main button, then clicking the main button doesn't display the sub-buttons beneath it; instead, it takes the user to some other page.

Before you can create sub-buttons, you must first create a basic DynaButton bar, as I outline in the preceding section "Creating a basic DynaButton bar." Then make sure you're in Page view, and follow these steps:

1. **Select the DynaButton bar by clicking its gray placeholder.**

   The Properties palette changes to DynaButtons Properties. You can refer to Figure 12-2 to see this palette.

2. **On the Properties palette, find the button under which you want to put some sub-buttons and double-click Use Sub-buttons below that button.**

   For example, if you want to add sub-buttons under Button 1, double-click Use Sub-buttons 1. This adds a Number of Sub-buttons option, which defaults to 1, and an entry for that new sub-button to the list on the Properties palette.

3. **Double-click Number Sub-Buttons in the list, type the number you want, and press the Enter key.**

   The dimensions of the placeholder change to reflect the number of sub-buttons you specify. NetObjects Fusion also adds each button to the list on the Properties palette. Note that the dimensions of the placeholder change, even though the sub-buttons aren't visible when someone first views the page. This helps you ensure that you don't place something else on the page that the DynaButton Bar may cover when someone clicks the bar.

4. **To specify the link for a particular sub-button, double-click that sub-button in the list on the Properties palette.**

   For example, to set the link for the first sub-button, double-click Sub-Button 1,1 in the list.

   NetObjects Fusion displays a Link dialog box. This is the same dialog box that appears any time you create a link. Check out Chapter 8 for an explanation of how to create links.

5. **Specify the link; then click the Link button.**

6. **Repeat Step 4 for each button.**

To see your DynaButtons at work, you need to publish your site. Chapter 18 explains how to publish your site on your own hard drive. This is the easiest way to test your DynaButtons.

Parading Messages with the Ticker Tape Component

The NetObjects Fusion Ticker Tape component lets you parade any text you want horizontally across your screen. This is a fun way to call attention to late-breaking news or anything else of importance. You can add up to 50 different messages to your Ticker Tape. Plus, you can specify a unique link for each one of those messages. In other words, you can make it so that clicking the Ticker Tape banner produces different results depending on which message the user sees.

Adding a Ticker Tape banner

To add a Ticker Tape banner to a page, first make sure that the Component toolbar is visible (View⇨Toolbars⇨Component Tools), that you're in Page mode, and that you are on the page where you want to add the Ticker Tape banner (probably the site's home page). Then follow these steps:

1. **Click the Ticker Tape button on the Component toolbar.**

2. **Click and hold to draw a box where you want the Ticker Tape banner to appear.**

   A black and green placeholder marked Ticker Tape appears where you specified, and the Properties palette changes to Ticker Tape Properties, as Figure 12-4 shows.

Figure 12-4:
You direct the parade from the Properties palette.

Ticker Tape Properties	
Component	Actions

Ticker Tape:

Number of Messages	1
Text for Message 1	
URL for Message 1	
Speed	25
Frame Color	lightGray
Background Color	black
LED Color	green

3. **If you want more than one message to appear in the ticker, double-click Number of Messages and type the number of messages you want in the Ticker Tape field; then press the Enter key.**

   NetObjects Fusion adds the additional messages to the Ticker Tape Properties palette.

4. **Double-click Text for Message 1, type the text you want in the Ticker Tape field, and press the Enter key.**

   You can also click the check mark button instead of typing the Enter key. If you make a typing error, you can click the X button to cancel and type your entry again.

5. **If you want to add a link for the Ticker Tape banner, double-click URL for Message 1.**

   NetObjects Fusion displays a Link dialog box. Refer to Figure 12-3 to have a look at this dialog box. Chapter 8 tells you how to handle links in NetObjects Fusion, so check there if you're unsure how to deal with the Link dialog box.

6. **Specify the link that you want your message to connect to; then click the Link button.**

7. **Repeat Steps 4 and 5 for each message in the list.**

8. **If you want to change the scrolling speed of the message, double-click Speed and type a number from 1 to 50 in the Ticker Tape field.**

   Keep in mind that these are relative speeds; 1 is the slowest and 50 is the fastest. However, the exact speed of the message will vary from user to user, based on operating system, browser, and so on.

To see your parading text, you need to publish your site. Chapter 18 explains how to publish your site on your own hard drive. This is the easiest way to test your Ticker Tape banner.

Changing the color of a Ticker Tape banner

After you follow the steps described in the section "Adding a Ticker Tape banner" earlier in this chapter, you can change the color of the frame and background of the Ticker Tape component by

✔ Double-clicking either Frame color or Background color in the Ticker Tape Properties palette. Doing so changes the color to the next option in the list.

✔ Clicking either Frame color or Background color in the Ticker Tape Properties palette and then clicking the arrow on the right of the Ticker Tape field to display a drop-down list of all the colors. You select a color by simply clicking it.

You can choose from the following colors:

✔ black

✔ blue

✔ cyan

✔ dark gray

✔ gray

✔ green

✔ light gray

✔ magenta

✔ orange

✔ pink

✔ red

✔ white

✔ yellow

Giving Your Visitors a Map of Your Site

One of the most useful features you can add to a Web site is a site map. This is a page that shows the hierarchy, or page-by-page structure, of your entire site and allows users to click any page to go to that page. If you put a link to the site map on every page, users can get from any page to any other page with just two mouse-clicks. That's handy.

Although site maps are valuable to visitors, many webmasters don't provide them because of the hassle of manually maintaining a site map. Every time your site changes, you need to make the appropriate changes to your site map page. With the Site Mapper component, however, NetObjects Fusion creates the site map for you and updates it every time you publish your site.

On your Web pages, the site map is represented by a little button. When you add the button, NetObjects Fusion knows to create all the necessary stuff for the site map when it publishes your site.

When a user clicks a site map button, the site map appears in a separate browser window. When the user selects a page, the site map window disappears and the user is taken to the appropriate page.

To add a site map button, make sure you're in Page view on the page where you want to add the site map button and that the Component toolbar is visible.

To add a site map button to a page, follow these steps:

1. **Click the Site Mapper button on the Component toolbar.**

2. **Click the page where you want the button to appear.**

    This is such a useful tool that I suggest you add the site map button to the MasterBorder.

    A button marked Site Map appears where you clicked and the Properties palette changes to Site Mapper Properties, as shown in Figure 12-5.

Figure 12-5:
The Site Mapper component offers only one option.

The only aspect of the Site Mapper that you control is what image you use for the button, You can use the one supplied by NetObjects Fusion (the one that appears when you create the button), or you can use a custom image. To change the image, double-click Image in the Properties palette and select a new one. If you've forgotten how to add an image, take a look at Chapter 7.

To use the Site Mapper, you need to publish your site. Chapter 18 explains how to publish your site on your own hard drive. This is the easiest way to test the Site Mapper. I want to take a moment to explain how the Site Mapper works from a user standpoint.

When you publish your site, view it in your Web browser, and click the site map button, NetObjects Fusion displays the site map in a separate browser window, as shown in Figure 12-6.

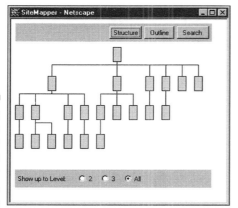

Figure 12-6:
This is the initial view that the Site Mapper provides.

This initial view is the Structure view; it shows your site in a hierarchical format. At the bottom of this window, you can control how many levels of the site are displayed. When you move the mouse pointer over one of the pages, the page changes color and its name pops up next to it.

If you click the Outline button, the view changes to something like the one in Figure 12-7.

Figure 12-7:
People can view your site as an outline.

Some users may find this view more convenient, because it lists all the pages on your site by name.

If you click the Search button, the view changes to the one shown in Figure 12-8.

Search for a page name here

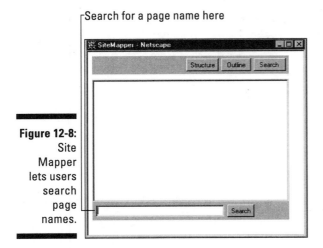

Figure 12-8:
Site
Mapper
lets users
search
page
names.

This view lets you search for a particular page name. When you type in a term and click the Search button, Site Mapper displays a list of all pages that include that term in their name. Note that this search feature does not search page contents; it only searches page names.

Mixing and Mingling with a Message Board

The Message Board component enables you to add a fully functioning, Web-based message board to your site. This lets users post and read messages much as they would with a Usenet newsgroup. You can add only one message board per site with NetObjects Fusion.

Gathering information for the Message Board component

Setting up the parameters for a message board can be a little tricky because you need a considerable amount of information about the server where your site resides. Specifically, before you get started, you should contact your Internet service provider or system administrator and find out the following:

✔ The operating system used by your server. The Message Board component supports Windows, Macintosh, and Unix servers, but it needs to
know which one you're using.

✔ If you're publishing to a Unix server, you need to know the path to the
Perl5 interpreter. This is the program that actually processes the CGI
scripts that the Message Board component generates. (Note that
Macintosh servers require WebStar 2.0 running Perl5, but you don't
need to specify the path for a Mac server.)

✔ The location of your CGI-bin directory.

When NetObjects Fusion publishes the various files necessary to run your
message board, it attempts to configure some elements using the chmod
command. The problem is that some Web servers don't allow the use of this
command. Check this out with your Internet service provider or system
administrator. If NetObjects Fusion can't use the chmod command, you
won't be able to publish a message board.

Creating your message board

Assuming you have all the server information you need and that the server
will accept the chmod command (look under the preceding heading,
"Gathering information for the Message Board component"), then you're
ready to set up your message board. Switch to Page view on the page where
you want to add the message board, and follow these steps:

1. **Click the Message Board button on the Component toolbar.**

   If you don't see the Component toolbar, choose View➪Toolbars➪
   Component tools.

2. **Click the part of the page where you want the button to appear.**

   A button marked Message Board appears where you clicked and the
   Properties palette changes to Message Board Properties, as shown in
   Figure 12-9.

   In the list on the Properties palette, you can skip the Subdirectory
   option. This indicates the subdirectory in which NetObjects Fusion
   stores all your message board stuff. NetObjects Fusion creates the
   directory automatically, so you don't really need to change it — unless
   you want to.

3. **Double-click Page Title in the list on the Properties palette, type a
   new name for your message board in the Message Board field, and
   press the Enter key.**

Figure 12-9:
Make sure
you have
your server
info in hand
before you
get here.

4. **Double-click Publish To until your server type appears in the Message Board field.**

5. **If you're publishing to a Unix server, double-click Perl Path for Unix, type the correct path to the Perl5 interpreter in the Message Board field, and press the Enter key.**

6. **Double-click CGI-bin Directory, type in the correct location of your CGI-bin directory, and press the Enter key.**

To take your message board for a test drive, you have to publish it to your Web server. Because the message board relies on some software that resides on your Web server, publishing it to your own hard drive doesn't do the trick.

When you view your published site and click the Message Board button, the message board appears in a separate browser window, as shown in Figure 12-10.

Don't necessarily assume that just because the message board appears on your screen, everything is working properly. Go ahead and post a message just to make sure.

Making CGI Easy: The Form Handler Component

In Chapter 11, I tell you how to create forms and explain the need for CGI scripts to handle the form output. If your form output needs are relatively simple and you want to avoid hunting around for a programmer to design your CGI scripts, you can use the Form Handler component. This component adds the necessary CGI scripts to your site to either save form output into a text file or have it e-mailed to an e-mail address you specify.

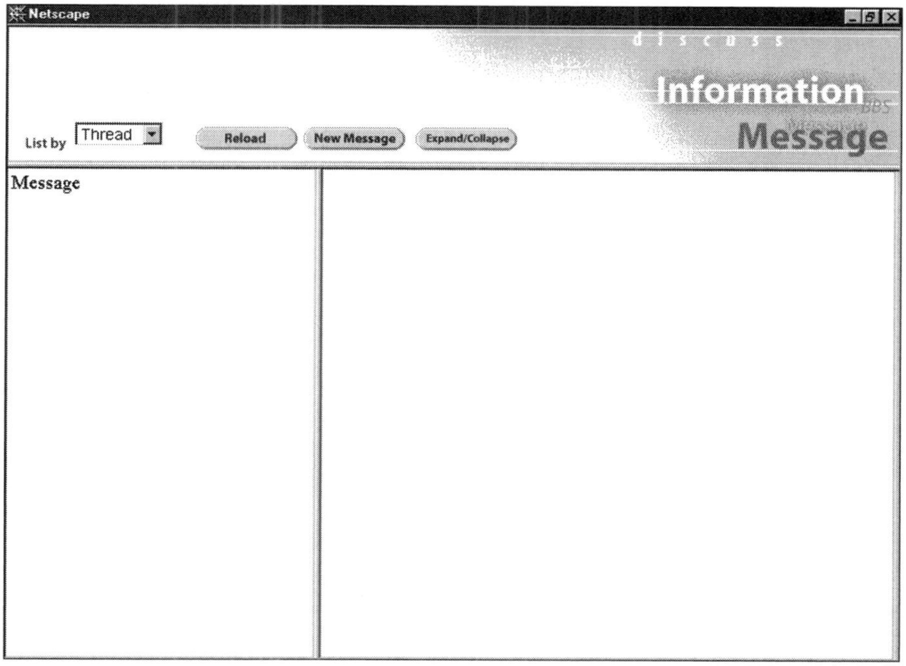

Figure 12-10:
Your
message
board is
ready to go.

Getting ready to use Form Handler

Because Form Handler uses CGI scripts that rely on your Web server for
processing, you need to know a little information about your Web server
before you get started. Specifically, you should gather the following tidbits
from your Internet service provider before you fiddle with Form Handler:

- ✔ The operating system used by your server. The Form Handler component supports Windows, Macintosh, and Unix servers, but needs to
  know which one you're using.

- ✔ If you're publishing to a Unix server, you need to know the path to the
  Perl5 interpreter. This is the program that actually processes the CGI
  scripts generated by the Message Board component. (Note that Mac
  servers require WebStar 2.0 running Perl5, but you don't need to
  specify the path for a Mac server.)

- ✔ The location of your CGI-bin directory.

Furthermore, you need to make a few decisions of your own:

✔ After someone submits his or her form output, the Web browser moves on to some other page. With the Form Handler, you can specify both a Success URL and an Error URL. The Success URL is the page that appears if all information is completed correctly; the Error URL appears if the user makes an error — for example, fails to complete a required field. You need to create separate pages for each of these.

Each of these two pages should say something appropriate for the occasion. For example, the Success URL might congratulate the user for for a job well done, while the Error URL might advise the user to click their browser's Back button and try again.

✔ If you're saving the form output to a text file, you have to pick a name for the file and decide which directory to store that file in.

✔ If you're forwarding the form output via e-mail, you have to decide what e-mail address you want the output forwarded to.

When NetObjects Fusion publishes the various files necessary to run the Form Handler CGI scripts, it attempts to configure some elements using the chmod command. The problem is that some Web servers don't allow the use of this command. Check this out with your Internet service provider or system administrator. If NetObjects Fusion can't use the chmod command, you won't be able to publish the Form Handler.

You can use the Form Handler for only one form per page; the Form Handler doesn't work with multiple forms on the same page.

Using the Form Handler component

To have the Form Handler component take care of your form information, you simply create your Submit button from inside the Form Handler component rather than using the standard Submit Button tool. To go through it a step at a time, make sure that you're in Page view on a page where you previously created a form (check out Chapter 11 if you need to create a form first) and follow these steps:

1. **Click the Form Handler button on the Component toolbar.**

2. **Click the page where you want the Submit button to appear.**

   A Submit button appears where you clicked and the Properties palette changes to Form Handler Properties, as shown in Figure 12-11.

Figure 12-11:
Make sure
you have
your server
info in hand
before you
get here.

3. **If you want to change the text in the Submit button, double-click Button Name, type a new name in the Form Handler field, and press the Enter key.**

4. **Double-click Publish To until the correct server type appears in the Form Handler field.**

   Your choices are Windows, Mac, Unix, and E-mail. If you select E-mail, the list in the Properties palette changes to show your only option: the e-mail address to send form output to. Double-click E-mail, type in the e-mail address, press the Enter key, and you're done.

5. **Double-click Success URL.**

   NetObjects Fusion displays a Link dialog box. This is the same dialog box that appears any time you create a link. Check Chapter 8 for everything you ever wanted to know about creating links, but had too much of a life to ask.

6. **Specify the link, then click the Link button.**

7. **Double-click Error URL.**

   NetObjects Fusion displays another Link dialog box.

8. **Specify the link, and then click the Link button.**

9. **Double-click Output File, type a name for the output file in the Form Handler field, and press the Enter key.**

   This is the file that the Form Handler outputs the form data to. Make sure you use a filename with no spaces and no special punctuation.

10. **If you're publishing to a Unix server, double-click Perl Path for Unix, type the path to the Perl interpreter in the Form Handler field, and press the Enter key.**

11. **Double-click CGI-bin Directory, type the location of your CGI-bin directory in the Form Handler field, and press the Enter key.**

12. **Double-click Storage Directory or Abs Storage Dir. (For whatever reason, NetObjects Fusion uses Abs Storage for the Windows server, but it means the same thing.) Type the name of the directory where you want the output stored in the Form Handler field, and press the Enter key.**

To test the Form Handler, you have to publish your site to your Web server. Because the message board relies on some software that resides on your Web server, publishing it to your own hard drive doesn't help any.

Rolling with the Picture Rollover Component

The DynaButton component allows you to jazz up your pages, but it has one important limitation. It uses only the Primary Button images defined for the current SiteStyle. If you want to create the same effect — a button that changes as the mouse pointer passes over it — you can do so with the Picture Rollover component.

The Picture Rollover component allows you to specify three images: the initial image; the image displayed when the mouse pointer passes over it; and, optionally, a third image that displays when the mouse pointer moves away from the image.

Before you begin these procedures, make sure you've already created the images you need, or know where they reside on your system. Also, make sure that all the images have the same physical dimensions. If they don't, the subsequent images will be scrunched or stretched to the same size as the initial image when they appear in your Web browser.

These procedures assume that you're in Page view on the page where you want to add a Picture Rollover button, that you already know what graphics you're going to use, and that you already know what you're going to link the button to.

To add a Picture Rollover button, follow these procedures.

1. **Click the Picture Rollover button on the Component toolbar.**

2. **Click the page where you want the button to appear.**

   A gray placeholder appears where you clicked and the Properties palette changes to *Picture Rollover Properties,* as shown in Figure 12-12.

Figure 12-12:
Tell
NetObjects
Fusion what
picture to
use and
where the
link is
to lead.

Notice the field on the Properties palette marked Picture Rollover. When you click any of the items in the list below that field, you use the Picture Rollover field to enter a value for that particular item. After you've entered a value, you click one of the two buttons to the right of the field. The check mark accepts your entry and the X cancels it, returning that item to its previous value. As a shortcut, you can simply press the Enter key instead of clicking on the check mark.

 3. **Double-click Initial image in the Properties palette.**

    NetObjects Fusion displays a Picture File Open dialog box just like the one used to place any graphic image on your page. If you need a refresher course on how to place an image, skip back to Chapter 7.

 4. **Select the image you want NetObjects Fusion to display first and click Open.**

    The image appears where the placeholder used to be and the Properties palette changes to offer the Mouse Over Image option and the Mouse Out Image option.

 5. **Double-click Mouse Over Image in the Properties palette.**

    NetObjects Fusion displays another Picture File Open dialog box.

 6. **Select the image you want NetObjects Fusion to display when the visitor's mouse is over the image and click Open.**

    If you want to specify another image to appear when the mouse pointer is no longer over the image, you can do so by double-clicking Mouse Out Image and repeating Step 6. If you don't specify an image for this option, the image will change back to the initial image when the mouse pointer is no longer over it.

 7. **Double-click Link URL.**

    NetObjects Fusion displays a Link dialog box. This is the same dialog box that appears any time you create a link. Check Chapter 8 for a refresher on how to create links.

8. **Specify the link you want the picture to take the visitor to; then click the Link button.**

To test your Picture Rollover button, you need to publish your site. Chapter 18 explains how to publish your site on your own hard drive. This is the easiest way to test your Picture Rollover buttons.

Making Your Images Punch a Time Clock

The Time Based Picture component enables you to load a different image on your page according to the time of day that a user accesses it. You set each image to display at a particular time, and everyone who visits your site sees that image until it's time for the next one. Because this component lets you specify only on-the-hour times, you can specify up to 24 images — one for each hour of the day.

Why would you want to display different images at different times of the day? If you try, I bet you can think of all sorts of reasons. For example, suppose you run a Web site that provides links to local events and activities. You might have one image that links to daytime activities appear during the day, and another that links to evening activities appear in the evening.

Anyhow, the procedures that follow assume that you're already in Page view on the page where you want to add your time-based pictures.

1. **Click the Time Based Picture button on the Component toolbar.**

2. **Click the page where you want the picture to appear.**

   A gray placeholder appears where you clicked and the Properties palette changes to Time Based Picture, as shown in Figure 12-13.

Figure 12-13:
You can tell NetObjects Fusion what pictures to use and where their links lead.

Notice the field on the Properties palette marked Time Based Picture. When you click any of the items in the list below that field, you use the Time Based Picture field to enter a value for that particular item. After you've entered a value, you click one of the two buttons to the right of the field. The check mark accepts your entry and the X cancels it, returning that item to its previous value. As a shortcut, you can simply press the Enter key instead of clicking the check mark.

3. **Double-click Number of Images in the Properties palette, type the number of images you want in the Time Based Picture field, and press the Enter key.**

   NetObjects Fusion displays three options in the list on the Properties palette for each image: Image, URL for Image, and Start Time for Image.

4. **Double-click Image 1.**

   NetObjects Fusion displays a Picture File Open dialog box just like the one used to place any graphic image on your page. If you need a refresher course on how to place an image, skip back to Chapter 7.

5. **Select the image in the dialog box and click Open.**

   The new image replaces the gray placeholder. However, the new image may be stretched or scrunched to fit into the same space as the placeholder. To fix this, choose Edit⇨Undo Resize.

6. **Double-click URL for Image 1.**

   NetObjects Fusion displays a Link dialog box. This is the same dialog box that appears any time you create a link. Check Chapter 8 for a refresher on how to create links.

7. **Specify the link; then click the Link button.**

8. **Double-click Start Time for Image 1 until the time you want appears in the Time Based Picture field.**

9. **Repeat Steps 4 through 8 for each additional image.**

As with all other components, you need to publish your site before you can test your time-based pictures. However, seeing if they all work could take some time — you have to check back at different times of the day to see if the correct picture loads.

Taking a Load Off with the Picture Loader

One interesting thing about the Web is that your pages can include pictures that don't even reside on your Web server. As long as you specify the entire URL to the picture in question, your Web browser will put the picture in the location you specify. The Picture Loader greatly simplifies this task. You just tell Picture Loader where the image is located and it handles the rest.

You should determine the size of the picture to be loaded — measured in pixels — before you use the Picture Loader so that you're sure you allow the right amount of space for it.

To insert a picture that you don't have on your hard drive onto your site, get into Page view on the page where you want to add the Picture Loader placeholder and follow these steps:

1. **Click the Picture Loader button on the Component toolbar.**

2. **Drag the mouse to draw a box where you want the loaded picture to appear.**

   A gray placeholder appears where you specified and the Properties palette changes to Picture Loader Properties, as shown in Figure 12-14.

   In Figure 12-14, the placeholder is 290 pixels wide by 80 pixels high, as the coordinates at the bottom of the screen indicate. By dragging any of the handles on the placeholder, you can adjust its size so that it matches the size of the image that will eventually replace it.

3. **Double-click Image URL in the Properties palette and type the complete URL of the image in the Picture Loader field.**

   When I say *complete,* I mean it. You have to include the whole enchilada, including the http:// part.

You have to publish your site before you can test whether the Picture Loader component works properly. If you plan to publish your site on your own hard drive, make sure your Internet connection is active or your Web browser can't load the picture.

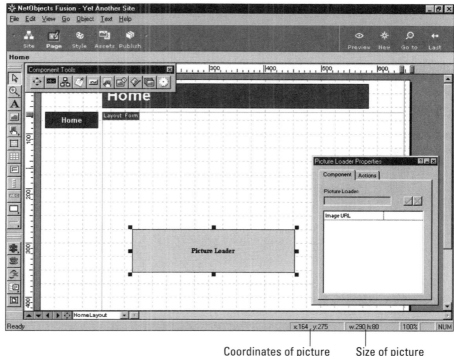

Figure 12-14:
The Picture Loader puts in a placeholder for the picture.

Coordinates of picture   Size of picture

Going a Round with Rotating Pictures

The Rotating Picture component allows you to specify a series of pictures that appear one after another so that the image changes while the user is looking at the page. You control how quickly they rotate by telling NetObjects Fusion how many seconds to allow for each picture. You can pretty much specify as big or small an interval as you want. When I was fiddling around with this, NetObjects Fusion wouldn't accept 10 million seconds, but it did accept 500,000 seconds.

The procedures that follow assume that you're already in Page view on the page where you want to add the rotating pictures. They also assume that the Component toolbar is visible.

1. **Click the Rotating Picture button on the Component toolbar.**

2. **Click the page on which you want the picture to appear.**

   A gray placeholder appears where you clicked and the Properties palette changes to Rotating Picture, as shown in Figure 12-15.

Figure 12-15:
You tell
NetObjects
Fusion how
long to
display
each image.

3. **Double-click Pause Time (Seconds) in the Properties palette, type the interval you want in the Rotating Picture field, and press the Enter key.**

4. **Double-click Number of Images in the Properties palette, type the number of images you want in the Rotating Picture field, and press the Enter key.**

   The Properties palette displays two options for each image: Image and URL for Image.

5. **Double-click Image 1.**

   NetObjects Fusion displays a Picture File Open dialog box just like the one used to place any graphic image on your page. If you need a refresher course on how to place an image, see Chapter 7.

6. **Select the image you want in the dialog box and click Open.**

   The gray placeholder is replaced by the image you selected. However, the new image may be stretched or scrunched to fit into the same space as the placeholder. To fix this, select Undo Resize from the Edit menu.

7. **Double-click URL for Image 1.**

   NetObjects Fusion displays a Link dialog box. This is the same dialog box that appears any time you create a link. Check Chapter 8 for a refresher on how to create links.

8. **Specify the link and then click the Link button.**

9. **Repeat Steps 5 through 8 for each additional image.**

To test your rotating pictures, you need to publish your site. Chapter 18 explains how to publish your site on your own hard drive. This is the easiest way to try out your rotating pictures.

Adding New Components to the Mix

NetObjects intentionally designed NetObjects Fusion's component architecture to be wide open so that users and third-party developers can design their own custom components. The NetObjects Web site (www.netobjects.com) has information about commercial third-party components that are available.

Before you can use a third-party component, you need to install it. To install a new component, make sure you're in Page view on the page where you want to add the new component and follow these steps:

1. **Click the NetObjects Fusion Components button on the Component toolbar (View⇨Toolbars⇨Component tools).**

2. **Click the page where you want the picture to appear.**

   NetObjects Fusion displays an Installed Components dialog box like the one in Figure 12-16. If you had already installed other third-party components, they'd show up in this dialog box.

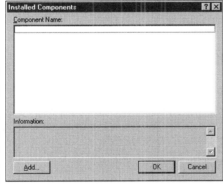

Figure 12-16:
Installed
third-party
components
appear in
this list.

3. **Click the Add button at the bottom of this dialog box.**

   NetObjects Fusion displays an Install Components dialog box like the one in Figure 12-17. Note that a component file ends with an *.nfx* extension, or a *.class* extension if it's Java-based.

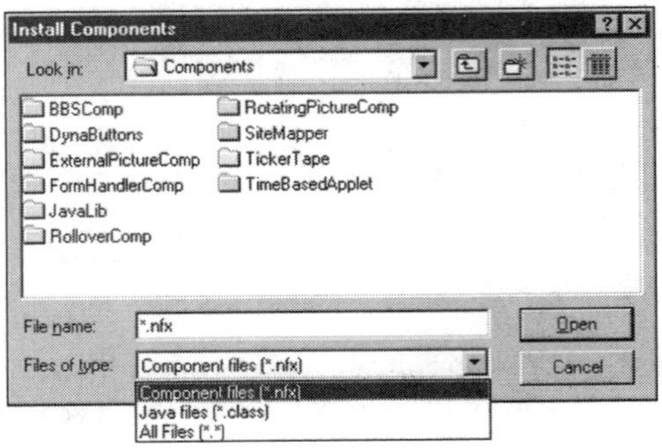

Figure 12-17:
Components
come in two
flavors.

4. **Click the arrow to the right of the Files of Type field and select the correct file type according to the component you want to install.**

5. **Navigate your system to locate the right component file and then click Open.**

   This takes you back to the Installed Components dialog box, with the new component listed.

6. **Click the OK button and use the new component according to its creator's instructions.**

Use the same procedures to reuse your new component on some other page. The only difference is that you get to skip the installation part.

Chapter 13

Fun with Frames and HTML Scripting

*T*he folks at Netscape brought us HTML frames with the introduction of Navigator 2.0. Prior to that, a Web page was a Web page was a Web page. But with *frames,* Web authors were able to split what appeared to be a single Web page into two or more subpages, or frames (thus, the name).

Understanding Frames

Each frame on a page can contain information that's entirely independent from the information in any other frame on the page. Figure 13-1 shows an example of a Web page that's divided into frames.

 On a page that contains frames, the actual Web page indicated in the URL contains very little HTML code. The content for each frame on that page is contained in a separate HTML file. For example, suppose a page named *index.html* contains two frames. The HTML code in *index.html* merely contains a description of how those two frames should be laid out on the page, as well as the name of each HTML file that holds the content for each frame. When your Web browser loads *index.html,* the browser automatically pulls in those other two HTML files and dumps them into their respective frames.

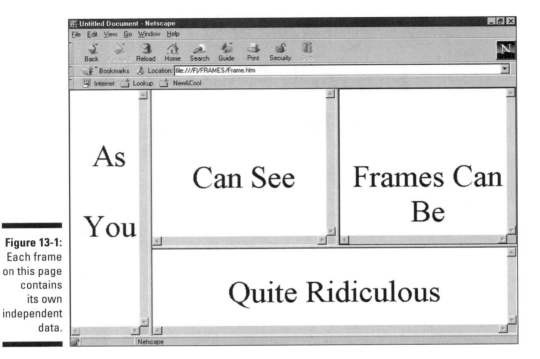

Figure 13-1:
Each frame on this page contains its own independent data.

When frames first appeared on the scene, they presented a couple of problems. For starters, because only the current version of Netscape Navigator supported them, anyone with an different browser was left out in the cold. Even more problematic, nobody seemed to really know what to do with them. At the time, frames seemed like little more than a neat parlor trick. Daring Web authors began to create pages broken up into five or six frames for no apparent reason other than that they could, and most users ended up hating frames.

Today, frames are somewhat more acceptable. For starters, all the major browsers now support frames.

You can utilize frames in your Web page in a number of ways; use them for

- **Banner graphics.** You can use AutoFrames to keep your banner graphic permanently visible on the page. That way, users can always see what page they're on.

- **Stationary navigational aids.** If you put a NavBar (in NetObjects Fusion) in its own frame, you can ensure that the NavBar is always visible, even when a user scrolls to some other part of your page. This is handy for the user and, in my opinion, represents the best implementation of frames.

Creating AutoFrames in NetObjects Fusion

NetObjects Fusion gives you two ways to create frames. The hard way is to start fiddling with the page HTML. Because you can add any HTML code you want, it you can simply create your own frames. My advice: *Don't go there.* I cover adding page and object HTML later in this chapter (collectively called scripting HTML), but I intentionally avoid frames. The HTML coding for frames can become very confusing very quickly. In my opinion, it's not worth the effort, especially when NetObjects Fusion offers you AutoFrames. (If you insist on experimenting with your own frames, I suggest you bone up on the various coding techniques by reading *HTML For Dummies,* 3rd Edition, by Ed Tittel and Steve James, and published by IDG Books Worldwide, Inc.)

By using the AutoFrame feature in NetObjects Fusion, you can have the program automatically convert any of your MasterBorders to frames when your site is published. Because NavBars are normally within the MasterBorder, you can ensure that a page's NavBar is always available to users no matter how far they scroll down through the other content on the page.

Before you begin: Things to keep in mind

Before you start tearing through your Web pages, you need to keep a few things in mind. 'Tis better to think ahead and avoid problems later, no? Ask yourself these questions:

- ✔ **Does my site really need frames?** Many users don't care much for frames. In fact, some ambitious Web authors create both framed and unframed versions of their sites, and give users the option to choose. If you decide that frames are imperative for the presentation of your site, take some time to consider which MasterBorder sides you want to convert to frames. (I explain MasterBorder creation in Chapter 5.)

- ✔ **What types of items really need to be in frames?** In my opinion, the only MasterBorder area that warrants its own frame is whatever side contains a NavBar. By putting the NavBar in its own frame, you keep it visible on the page at all times. If your banner graphic and banner are on different sides of the MasterBorder, you can also put the banner graphic in its own frame. However, this seems like more of a vanity thing than a functionality thing.

- ✔ **How many frames should I have?** Too many frames slows down the loading of your page unnecessarily and also demonstrates a lack of Web authoring skills.

Just because the AutoFrame feature lets you convert each MasterBorder area — top, bottom, left, and right — into a frame doesn't mean that you have to have that many. Each frame must be rectangular in shape. If you convert all four sides of the MasterBorder into frames, you end up with five frames on your page — one for each side of the MasterBorder and one for the Layout area.

Here's one other very important point to keep in mind. AutoFrame settings are a property of the MasterBorder, *not* of the individual page. If you set up AutoFrames on a particular page, any other page that shares the same MasterBorder shares the same AutoFrame settings. If you want AutoFrames on some pages but not others, you may need to create a new MasterBorder for those pages.

Creating a frame with AutoFrame

With the AutoFrame feature, you can have NetObjects Fusion convert any or all of your MasterBorders in frames without you having to type an iota of HTML code. That way, you can spend more time creating great Web pages and no time at all trying to get your frames to work right.

Make sure you're in Page view on a page where you want to create frames. Then follow these steps to create the AutoFrame.

1. **Click the mouse anywhere in the MasterBorder area.**

   The Properties palette changes to *MasterBorder Properties*.

2. **Click the AutoFrames tab on the MasterBorder Properties palette.**

   The MasterBorder Properties palette displays four buttons that you use to control which sides of the MasterBorder become frames, as shown in Figure 13-2.

Figure 13-2: You control each side of the MasterBorder individually.

3. **Click the appropriate button to specify which side of the MasterBorder — left, right, top, or bottom — you want to convert to its own frame.**

   Clicking the button outlines that area of the MasterBorder in a thin red line. It stays that way for easy reference as you're working on your page. The AutoFrame button you clicked also darkens, and a *1* appears next to its label. If you click the wrong button, just click it again to unhighlight it.

I recommend converting only one side of the MasterBorder to a frame so that you can prevent overlap of the frames. If you're interested in converting more than one side, read the the next section.

Take note of the Generate HTML Frame Borders check box on the Properties palette. With this box checked, NetObjects Fusion generates a visible border between the frames on your page. The default value is checked, so if you want visible borders, just leave it that way. Otherwise, uncheck it. Figure 13-3 shows a page with a visible frame border, and Figure 13-4 shows the same page without one.

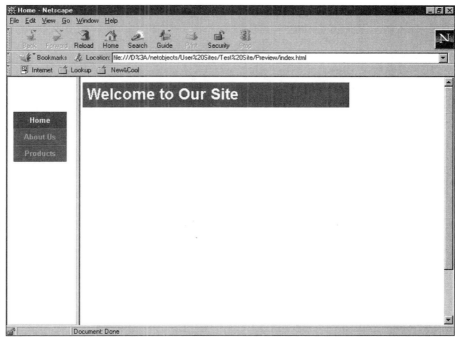

Figure 13-3:
Here's a page with a visible frame border.

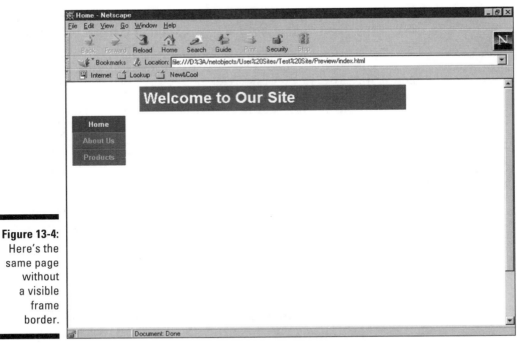

Figure 13-4:
Here's the
same page
without
a visible
frame
border.

Just remember that while you're working on your site in NetObjects Fusion, the MasterBorders behave as normal (see Chapter 5), regardless of how you've set up the AutoFrames. They won't behave like real frames until after you've published your site.

Creating multiple frames with AutoFrames

Using the AutoFrames feature, you can convert any or all of the sides of your MasterBorder to frames. However, at each corner of the page, the different sides overlap. For example, the area in the upper left corner of the page could be included in the top AutoFrame or the left AutoFrame. You determine which frame includes the overlap area by the order in which you click the various buttons on the MasterBorder Properties palette:

1. **Click an AutoFrame button, such as the Left button.**

2. **Click another AutoFrame button, such as the Top button.**

   A number 1 appears under the first button you clicked, and a 2 appears under the second button you clicked. This numbering system shows you which button has priority of the overlap area. The overlap area is included in whichever AutoFrame has the lowest number.

3. Repeat Step 2 as necessary.

If you happen to goof the first time around and get the AutoFrame buttons in the wrong order, just turn them all off by clicking them and start over again.

Modifying Individual Frames

Once you create a frame using AutoFrames, the Frame tab appears on the Properties palette. You can use this tab to adjust the characteristics of each AutoFrame on your page. Just remember that anything you do to a frame on the current page affects all pages that share the same MasterBorder.

To modify frames using the Frame tab, follow these steps:

1. Click the mouse anywhere in the AutoFrame you want to modify.

2. Click the Frame tab in the Properties palette.

The Frame tab is shown in Figure 13-5.

Figure 13-5:
You control individual AutoFrames with the Frame tab.

The following describes the various elements of the Frame tab:

- ✔ The User Scrollable radio buttons control whether or not a scroll bar appears for this particular frame. If you select Yes, the scroll bar always shows up. If you select No, the scroll bar never appears. If you select Auto, the scroll bar appears only if necessary. If you've created an AutoFrame so that your NavBar always appears, there should be no need for scrolling in that frame, and adding a scroll bar would only add clutter to your page. In this instance, I suggest that you set this option to No. Otherwise, use Auto. I can't think of a good reason to insist on a scroll bar when none is needed.

✔ If you check the User Resizable Frame box, users can manually adjust the size of the frame. In my opinion, doing so simply invites the user to mess up the appearance of your finely crafted page. Hence, I suggest that you leave this box unchecked.

✔ The Background area on the Frame tab lets you control the background of the frame independent of the rest of the page. These options work just like the corresponding page controls I discuss in Chapter 5. I recommend that you stick with SiteStyle, which uses the background defined for your current SiteStyle, to maintain the look and feel of your site.

✔ The Table Structure radio buttons control whether any nested tables (tables within tables, which the program uses to control layout) that NetObjects Fusion creates in this frame are organized into rows or columns. This works just like the corresponding page control I talk about in Chapter 5.

Adding HTML to Your Pages

You may have noticed that most every Properties palette includes a button marked HTML. This button also appears in various dialog boxes. These HTML buttons do one of three things:

✔ If you've selected an object on your page, this button lets you add *object HTML,* that is, HTML code associated with that particular object.

✔ If no object is selected, the HTML button lets you add to the *page HTML,* or the HTML associated with the page as a whole.

✔ If you're editing a text box, the HTML button lets you create a custom object within that text box.

All of these are explained later in this chapter.

Adding page HTML

When you click one of these HTML buttons, NetObjects Fusion displays a large Page HTML window, as shown in Figure 13-6. This window allows you to add bits of HTML code that affect only the current page. If you find the need to add some sort of HTML code that NetObjects Fusion doesn't support directly (which I think is not too likely), you can do so here.

The Page HTML window includes three tabs at the top: Between Head Tags, Inside Body Tag, and Beginning of Body. These tags control where NetObjects Fusion puts the code that you type in this window. NetObjects Fusion displays what you type in the Generated HTML field at the bottom of the window.

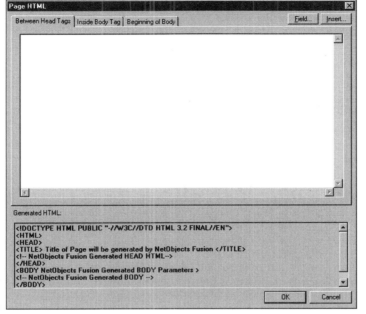

Figure 13-6:
You can
add HTML
that affects
only the
current
page.

At the top of the Page HTML window are the Field and Insert buttons. The Field button allows you to add a variable; I explain variables in Chapter 6. The Insert button allows you to insert HTML code from another source, such as another Web page or a text file.

One of the best uses of this feature is adding *META tags* to help search engines index your Web pages (see Chapter 19 for a discussion of search engines). A META tag is a section of HTML code that doesn't produce any visible results on your page, but helps in some other way. In the case of search engines, you can add keywords and a description of the page content. These META tags help the search engine match your page to requests from users looking for the type of information contained on your page. You should add these META tags to your home page.

To add META tags to aid search engines in identifying your site, make sure the Page HTML window is displayed, and then follow these steps:

1. **Click the Between Head Tags tab.**

2. **Type in the following HTML code, inserting your own information where appropriate, and making sure to include all the quotation marks:**

```
<META NAME="DESCRIPTION" CONTENT="(type a sentence or
     two describing your Web site)"
<META NAME="KEYWORDS" CONTENT="(type as many keywords as
     you want, each separated by a comma)"
```

NetObjects Fusion fills in the code in the Generated HTML field as you type it.

3. Click OK.

When you publish your site, these META tags will be included in your home page.

Adding object HTML

NetObjects Fusion lets you add custom code to the HTML associated with a particular object on your page. This is called *object HTML*. You do this by clicking the HTML button on the Properties palette or in a dialog box associated with that object. The big question is: Why would you want to do this? Adding object HTML is handy when you want to add custom JavaScript functionality to an object, which is entirely beyond the scope of this book. If you'd like to dive headlong into the world of JavaScript, I suggest you read *JavaScript For Dummies,* 2nd Edition, by Emily A. Vander Veer (IDG Books Worldwide, Inc.).

Creating a custom object

When you're editing a text box and you click the HTML button in the Properties palette, you're presented with an Insert HTML dialog box. Typing HTML code into this dialog box allows you to create a *custom object* on your page. A custom object is simply an object created from resources over which NetObjects Fusion has no control. For example, if you read Chapter 8, you know that NetObjects Fusion is somewhat weak in the area of table creation. If you want to add a table that you can't create with the tools provided by NetObjects Fusion, you can create one as a custom object by adding all the necessary HTML code yourself.

Web counters (little numerical tickers that tell you how many people have visited the site) are pretty popular. A number of companies offer free Web tickers as a promotional gimmick. They provide you with all the HTML code you need to use the ticker; it's up to you to put that code on your page. In NetObjects Fusion, you simply create the ticker as a custom object, typing in the code supplied to you by whoever provided the Web counter.

Here are the basic steps for creating a custom object:

1. **Create a new text box on the page where you want the custom object.**

   The width of the text box is especially important here, because you want to leave enough room for the object you create.

2. **Click the HTML button in the Properties palette.**

   An Insert HTML dialog box appears, as shown in Figure 13-7.

Figure 13-7:
Type your
custom
code here.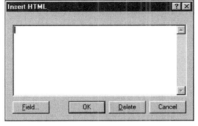

3. **Type the HTML code for your custom object.**

   Note that you can use the Field button to add variables (see Chapter 6) to your code. Also, the Delete button erases all HTML code and closes this dialog box.

4. **Click OK.**

When you're done, don't forget to preview the page. You want to make sure your custom object appears the way you want and fits where you put it.

Chapter 14

Data Publishing Made Easy

*O*ne of Web authoring's biggest challenges has been simplifying the process of publishing existing data. You have information — a catalog, for example — in some database format that needs to go out on your Web site. How can you translate your catalog to a Web site without building a bunch of pages from scratch?

Many tools out there can help you convert spreadsheet information to HTML tables. However, sometimes your data publishing needs are more sophisticated. In the case of a catalog, for example, you probably want to publish each data record (that is, catalog item) as a separate Web page.

NetObjects Fusion is *the* answer to your database publishing needs. Whether you need to publish data from some external source or want to maintain a mini-database within your NetObjects Fusion site, you're covered. Data publishing is one area that truly sets NetObjects Fusion apart from all other Web authoring tools that I've used.

Using NetObjects Fusion's database publishing tools, you create what's called a DataList, a table-like list that describes the various records in your database and provides a link to each *Stacked Page*. A Stacked Page is simply a Web page that contains one record's worth of information.

Using NetObjects Fusion as a Database

When it comes to data publishing, NetObjects Fusion is unique among Web authoring tools in that it enables you to maintain a database of sorts within the confines of your site, with no need for an external database program. You can create and store *internal data* (data that you don't import from another program), whether it's simple text, formatted text, or images. And you don't have to open any program but NetObjects Fusion, which makes publishing your data on the Web a snap.

Suppose you have information for your Web site, such as press releases, that would be convenient to maintain in a database format, but you don't have a database program. You can store this information in a database-like format within your NetObjects Fusion site.

The basic steps to create internal data involve

1. **Creating a Data Object that defines the data.**
2. **Specifying the particulars of the DataList that provides the links to your Stacked Pages.**
3. **Creating a Stacked Page for each record you want to maintain and enter data for each page.**

    A *Stacked Page* is simply a page that contains one record's worth of data (see Figure 14-1).

I break these steps down further in the next few sections.

Creating a Data Object and DataList

The first step in the data publishing process is to define the data that will appear on your Stacked Pages by creating a *Data Object*. A Data Object is the database-like container that NetObjects Fusion uses to store your data.

Before you get started, you should give some thought to exactly what data you're going to publish and what data fields, or individual elements on your Web page, you need to do it. Say, for example, you're adding press releases to your Web site. Because each data field represents a different element of a record, you may need one data field for the headline, one for the body of the press release, and one for any accompanying picture.

The following procedure for creating your Data Object assumes that you're in Page view on the page below the one in which you want your Stacked Pages to appear. For example, if you're creating an archive of company press releases, you should be on the main press page from which all your press releases are linked.

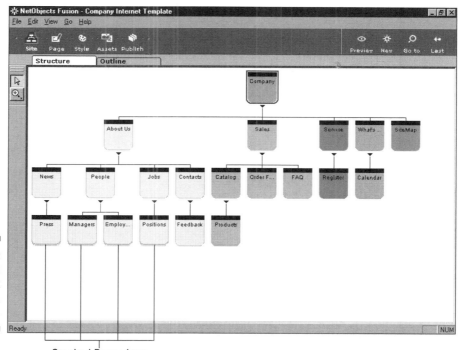

Figure 14-1:
Stacked
Pages look
. . . well,
stacked.

Stacked Pages icon

1. Select the DataList tool from the Advanced Tools toolbar.

Note that the DataList Tool and the New External Data Source tool share the same location on the Advanced Tools toolbar. The button for the DataList tool looks like a drum with a page on top of it; the button for the New External Data Source tool looks like a drum with an arrow pointing at it. These tools are second from the bottom on the Advanced Tools toolbar.

2. Click the mouse on the location in the Layout area where you want your DataList to appear.

The DataList names the records contained in your Stacked Pages. You can move the DataList later if you need to, so don't worry too much about getting the location exactly right.

After you click the mouse, a Data Publishing dialog box appears, just like the one in Figure 14-2.

3. Click the New button to the right of the Data Object field.

A Data Object dialog box appears, as shown in Figure 14-3.

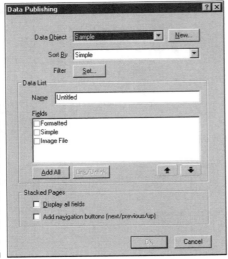

Figure 14-2:
You need
to tell
NetObjects
Fusion a
little about
the data
you plan
to publish.

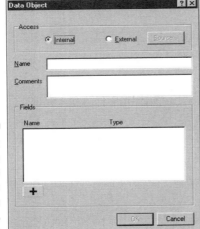

Figure 14-3:
You're
ready to
create a
Data
Object.

4. Type a name for your Data Object in the Name field.

The name can be anything that helps you identify this particular Data Object. This name will appear in the Assets view.

5. Type any comments in the Comments field.

Again, you can type anything you want here. These comments are for your reference only.

6. Click the plus sign (+) button at the bottom of the Fields area.

A Data Field dialog box appears, as shown in Figure 14-4.

Figure 14-4:
You need to
define each
field for
your data.

7. **Type a name for this particular Data Field.**

   Later on, you'll specify which Data Fields are included in the DataList. The name you type here serves as the column header in the DataList.

8. **Select one of the formatting types.**

   Here's a description of each type:

   - *Formatted Text.* Use this type if you want to be able to apply special formatting to individual parts of the text contained in the Data Field. If you are using this data in a press release, for example, choose Formatted Text for the press release body so that you can bold or italicize certain words as desired.

   - *Simple Text.* You can still apply formatting to Simple Text, but any formatting you apply affects *all* the text in the Data Field. For example, you can use Simple Text for the press release headline and then make the headline bold.

   - *Image File.* Use this option for Data Fields that contain graphics.

9. **Click the OK button.**

   The Fields list in the Data Objects dialog box now lists the Data Field you just created. Note that any image file fields you create are listed as External File.

10. **Repeat Steps 6 through 9 for any additional Data Fields you need to create.**

11. **Click the OK button in the Data Object dialog box.**

    Doing so takes you back to the Data Publishing dialog box.

12. **Click the arrow to the right of the Sort By field and select the Data Field by which you want the records sorted.**

    The Sort By field controls the order in which records appear in the DataList. Note that you cannot sort by a Data Field that is marked as Formatted Text.

    Skip the Filter button for now; I explain it later in this chapter in the section "Recycling or Splitting Your Data with Filter."

13. **Type a name for your DataList in the Name field.**

14. **Click the check boxes in the Fields area to specify which Data Fields you want listed in the DataList.**

    If you are going to display a list of press releases, for example, then you may want to include the headline and date, but definitely not the body of the press release.

15. **Use the Link/Unlink button to determine which Data Field(s) serves as the link to the Stacked Page.**

    When you publish or preview your site, you'll be able to click on the field(s) you specify here to go to the appropriate Stacked Page.

16. **Click the Display All Fields check box so that NetObjects Fusion automatically creates the necessary data-entry fields when you create a Stacked Page.**

    If you don't use this option, you'll have to manually add fields to your Stacked Pages later.

17. **Click the Add Navigation Buttons check box if you want NetObjects Fusion to automatically add navigation buttons to assist users in moving through your Stacked Pages.**

18. **Click the OK button.**

    Your page now displays a DataList placeholder. The actual DataList with all its list contents isn't generated until you publish or preview your site. I explain how to customize your DataLists later in this chapter under the heading "Organizing Your DataList."

Stacking the pages and adding data

A Stacked Page is simply a page that contains one record's worth of data. The reason they're called Stacked Pages is that all the pages that relate to a particular DataList appear as a single icon with stacked look when you're in Site view. If you refer back to Figure 14-1, you can see examples of what a Stacked Pages icon looks like: The Press, Managers, and Positions icons all represent Stacked Pages for a company Web site.

When you publish internal data (that is, data stored within your NetObjects Fusion site), you have to create your Stacked Pages manually and then add the data to them. For example, if you want to publish a collection of press releases, you need to create a Stacked Page for each press release and then add the content for each of those pages.

To create your Stacked Pages, first make sure that you're in Page view on the page that contains the DataList, and then follow these steps:

1. **Click the Go to First Child Page button in the navigation bar at the bottom of the screen.**

   Doing so takes you to a template page marked in the banner as Untitled Stacked Page. The template page looks something like the one shown in Figure 14-5. Notice the words Stacked Page 0 of 0 that appear in the gray bar above the banner. This message indicates that you haven't actually created any Stacked Pages yet. You use this template page to adjust the look of your Stacked Pages.

2. **Use any of the techniques that I describe in Chapters 5 and 6 to adjust the look of this template page to your liking.**

   You can change the MasterBorder, adjust the Layout area, and so on, just as you would on any other page.

   The areas marked with red outlines are the actual Data Fields. The regular text boxes are simply labels that NetObjects Fusion creates for you.

3. **After you make any formatting changes, click the Add button in the control bar at the top of the screen.**

   NetObjects Fusion creates your first Stacked Page.

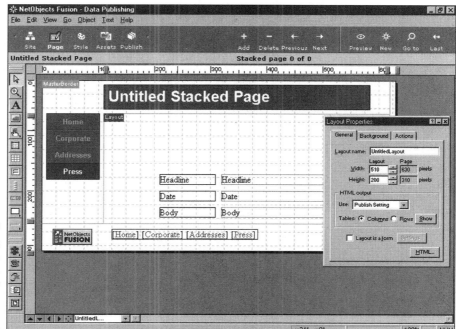

Figure 14-5:
Now you're ready to format your Stacked Pages.

 4. Enter data/images into the various Data Fields by using the techniques that I describe in Chapters 6 and 7.

 5. Repeat Steps 3 and 4 for any additional Stacked Pages you need to create.

   You can navigate back and forth between your Stacked Pages by using the Previous and Next buttons in the button bar at the top of the screen.

You may have noticed that the banner on your Stacked Pages reads `Untitled Stacked Page`. To change the name, switch to the Site view (by clicking the Site button at the top of the page), select the Stacked Page, and click the Custom Names button on the Properties palette. Note that this change affects all the Stacked Pages associated with any given DataList.

If you view the page that contains the DataList, you notice that the DataList still appears to be empty. That's because the contents of the DataList are not determined until you preview or publish your site. If you want a quick look at how the DataList will appear to your site visitors, simply preview the page.

Publishing Data from External Sources

NetObjects Fusion gives you the option to import data from desktop databases and spreadsheets like Access, Excel, and FoxPro, or from Structured Query Language (SQL) data sources. Importing SQL data sources is accomplished through the use of Open Data Base Connectivity (ODBC) drivers. This SQL/ODBC option requires a thorough understanding of SQL databases and ODBC drivers and is outside the scope of this book. If you need to publish data from an SQL database, I suggest you consult your system administrator with your *NetObjects Fusion User Guide* in hand. You may also want to consider picking up a copy of *SQL For Dummies,* 2nd Edition by Allan Taylor (IDG Books Worldwide, Inc.).

This section covers publishing data from a desktop database.

Creating a Data Object and DataList

NetObjects Fusion lets you extract data from some external source, such as a Microsoft Access database. For example, if you maintain an address book in Access, you can publish it on the Web by using the steps that follow in this section. The biggest difference between using an internal and external data source is that when you use an external data source, you don't have to (and in fact can't) manually create your Stacked Pages. Because the data already exists, NetObjects Fusion creates the Stacked Pages for you.

To publish data from an external source, make sure that you're in Page view on the page below the one in which you want your Stacked Pages to appear. For example, if you're creating an online address book, you should be on the page from which all your address book entries are linked. You should have a database program installed on your computer, and you should have used it to create a database that you now want to publish on your Web site.

To publish an external database, follow these steps:

1. **Select the DataList tool from the Advanced Tools toolbar.**

   The DataList tool is the second one from the bottom.

2. **Click the mouse on the location in the Layout area where you want your DataList to appear.**

   The DataList lists the records contained in your Stacked Pages. You can move the DataList later if you need to, so don't worry too much about getting the location exactly right.

   After you click the mouse, a Data Publishing dialog box appears, just like the one in Figure 14-6.

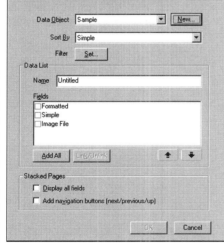

Figure 14-6:
Give
NetObjects
Fusion
some
information
about the
data you
plan to
publish.

3. **Click the New button to the right of the Data Object field.**

   A Data Object dialog box appears, as shown in Figure 14-7.

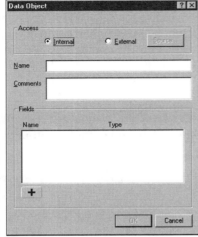

Figure 14-7:
You're
ready to
create
a Data
Object.

4. **Click the External radio button and then the Source button that's next to it.**

   NetObjects Fusion displays a Data Source Type dialog box, as shown in Figure 14-8. Here you have two radio buttons to choose from. The first one is followed by *Microsoft Access* and the second is followed by *ODBC.* The ODBC option is not covered in this book.

Figure 14-8:
NetObjects
Fusion
needs to
know what
type of
data you're
importing.

5. **Click the arrow to the right of Microsoft Access and select a data source from the drop-down list.**

   The contents of this list varies from computer to computer, depending on what database programs are installed on your computer.

6. **After you select a database source, click the Browse button.**

   NetObjects Fusion displays a standard Open dialog box.

7. **Navigate through your system to locate the desired database file and then click Open.**

   If the database you select contains multiple files (or in the case of a spreadsheet, multiple tabs), NetObjects Fusion displays a Select dialog box that lists those files. In this case, simply click the desired file and click OK.

   NetObjects Fusion takes you back to the Data Publishing dialog box, with much of the information already filled in based on the database file you selected.

8. **Click the arrow to the right of the Sort By field and select the Data Field by which you want the records sorted.**

   The Sort By field controls the order in which records appear in the DataList. Note that NetObjects Fusion doesn't allow you to sort by a Data Field that is marked as Formatted Text.

   Skip the Filter button for now. I explain that one later in this chapter under the section "Recycling or Splitting Your Data with Filter."

9. **Type a name for your DataList in the Name field.**

10. **Click the check boxes in the Fields area to specify which Data Fields you want listed in the DataList.**

    If you are going to display a list of press releases, for example, you may want to include the headline and date, but definitely not the body of the press release.

11. **Use the Link/Unlink button to determine which Data Field(s) serves as the link to the Stacked Page.**

    When you publish or preview your site, you'll be able to click on the field(s) you specify here to go to the appropriate Stacked Page.

12. **Click the Display All Fields check box so that NetObjects Fusion automatically creates the necessary data-entry fields (which it generates from your Stacked Pages).**

    If you don't use this option, you'll have to manually add fields to your Stacked Pages later.

13. **Click the Add Navigation Buttons check box if you want NetObjects Fusion to automatically add navigation buttons to assist users in moving through your Stacked Pages.**

14. **Click the OK button.**

    NetObjects Fusion automatically creates a Stacked Page for each record in the database you imported.

Back on the page where you started these steps, you see a DataList place-holder. The actual DataList with all its list contents isn't generated until you publish or preview your site. I explain how to customize your DataLists later in this chapter under the heading "Organizing Your DataList."

Formatting (not smoking) your stack

When you publish *external data* (that is, data stored in some other database program), NetObjects Fusion automatically generates a Stacked Page for each record in the external database. Although NetObjects Fusion creates these Stacked Pages, you have to customize their look.

To customize your Stacked Pages, first make sure that you're on the page that contains your DataList. Then follow these steps:

1. **Click the Go to First Child Page button in the navigation bar at the bottom of the screen.**

    This button takes you to a new page marked in the banner as Untitled Stacked Page. This page looks something like the one shown in Figure 14-9, and it contains the first record from the database you imported.

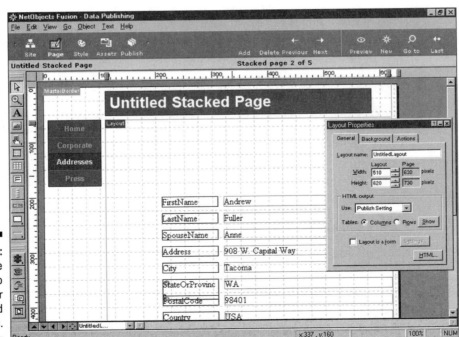

Figure 14-9:
Now's the time to format your Stacked Pages.

2. **Use any of the techniques that I describe in Chapters 5 and 6 to adjust the look of this template page to your liking.**

   You can change the MasterBorder, adjust the Layout area, and so on, just as you would on any other page.

   The areas marked with red outlines are the actual Data Fields. The regular text boxes are simply labels that NetObjects Fusion creates for you. Keep in mind that any formatting changes you make on one Stacked Page affect all the Stacked Pages that relate to your DataList.

   You can navigate back and forth between your Stacked Pages by using the Previous and Next buttons in the button bar at the top of the screen.

You may notice that the banner on your Stacked Pages reads Untitled Stacked Page. To change the name, switch to the Site view (by clicking the Site button at the top of the page), select the Stacked Page, and use the Custom Names button on the Properties palette. Note that this change affects all the Stacked Pages associated with any given DataList.

Also, if you view the page that contains the DataList, you notice that the DataList still appears to be empty. That's because the contents of the DataList are not determined until you preview or publish your site. If you want a quick look at how the DataList will appear to your site's visitors, simply preview the page.

Organizing Your DataList

When you publish your site, NetObjects Fusion generates your DataLists as HTML tables, which means you can adjust things like size and column width in the same way that you do other tables (see Chapter 10 for table details). Furthermore, when you select a DataList in Page view, the Properties palette offers a variety of options.

Resizing a DataList

When you select a DataList in Page view, eight little handles appear around it just as they do around any object you select in NetObjects Fusion. You can resize the DataList by clicking and dragging any one of these handles. You do so to make room for list items that may not fit in the space provided by default.

To adjust column width, move your mouse pointer over any column divider. Doing so turns the mouse pointer into a double arrow. When you see the double arrow, click and drag to the right or left as desired to change relative column widths. Note, however, that doing so does not change the width of the DataList. The point of adjusting the column width is to make sure that you have enough room in each column for the information that's listed in that column. However, because you can't see the contents of the DataList while you're working on it, making sure that you allot enough room can be a little tough. As you make adjustments to your DataList, I suggest that you preview the page in your Web browser to make sure that you're really getting the results you want.

You can delete a DataList just like any other object on your page. However, doing so does not delete any Stacked Pages that were created as a result of the DataList. To delete the Stacked Pages, switch to Site view and delete the Stacked Pages just as you delete any other individual page.

Adjusting DataList properties

When you select a DataList in Page view, the Properties palette offers several options to adjust the DataList, as shown in Figure 14-10. A description of each option follows.

Figure 14-10:
Use these
options to
customize
the look of
your
DataList.

✔ **List Name.** Type in any name that makes the list easier for you to identify.

✔ **Define.** Use this button to redisplay the Data Publishing dialog box so you can make any necessary changes.

✔ **Display Column Titles.** This check box controls whether column titles appear across the top of the DataList.

✔ **Bullet.** These radio buttons determine which graphic appears in front of each item in the DataList. SiteStyle uses whatever image you specify as the DataList Icon in the current Style (see Chapters 3 and 16). Selecting File and then selecting its Browse button enables you to specify any image you want. The None option is self-explanatory.

> ✔ **Cell.** The options in this area control the border, spacing, and padding of the table that contains the DataList when you preview or publish. This works just like it does for any other table (see Chapter 10).
>
> ✔ **Fill Background.** The Fill Background section has two radio buttons that enable you to control the DataList's background color.

Recycling or Splitting Your Data with Filter

One of the great things about NetObjects Fusion is that after you do something, it's done, and you never have to do it again. The same holds true with Data Objects. After you create a Data Object, it becomes an *Asset,* which means that you can it use over and over again to create DataLists anywhere you need to.

The big question is: Why would you want to use the same data from a Data Object in different DataLists? The answer is: You probably wouldn't. This situation is where *filtering* comes into play. By setting up a filter for each DataList, you can make some records appear in one DataList and other records appear in another DataList.

For example, suppose that you maintain an online archive of press releases for your company. These press releases are all listed in a single DataList on your press page. But after a while, you realize that having too many press releases all in one list is quite awkward. One solution is to split them up into two DataLists. By using filters, you can have one list display last year's press releases and the other list display this year's press releases.

If you've been following along, you've probably already created a Data Object. Now you want to create a new DataList that displays only a portion of the total records represented by that Data Object.

To create a filtered DataList, make sure that you're on the page where you want to create the new DataList, and follow these steps:

1. **Select the DataList tool from the Advanced Tools toolbar.**

   The DataList tool is the second one from the bottom.

2. **Click the mouse on the location in the Layout area where you want your DataList to appear.**

   After you click the mouse, a Data Publishing dialog box appears, just like the one in Figure 14-11.

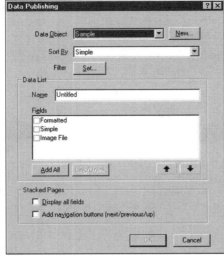

Figure 14-11:
Tell
NetObjects
Fusion about
the data
you want
to publish.

3. **Click the arrow to the right of the Data Object field and select the desired Data Object from the drop-down list that appears.**

   As soon as you make your selection, the information in the Data Publishing dialog box changes to reflect the contents of the Data Object you selected.

4. **Click the Set button that appears next to the word Filter.**

   NetObjects Fusion displays a Query dialog box, as shown in Figure 14-12.

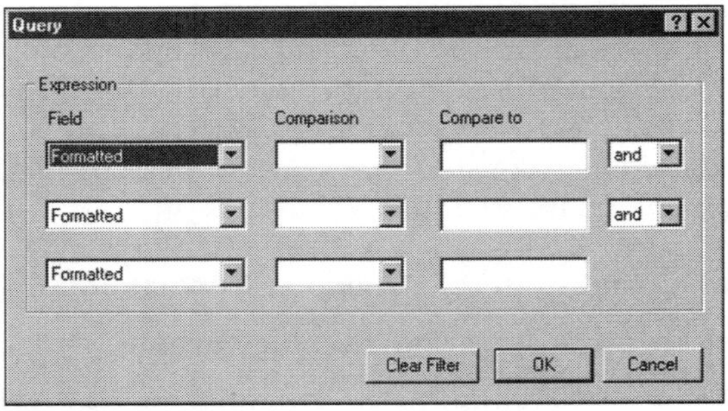

Figure 14-12:
You can
specify
up to three
filtering
criteria.

Here's an explanation of the three elements of each filter criterion:

- The Field drop-down list names all the fields associated with the Data Object you specify.

- The Comparison drop-down list offers three options that vary according to the type of data field you select. If the field you select contains numerical data, your options are equal to, less than, or greater than. If you select a field that contains text information, your options are begins with, contains, or ends with.

- The Compare To field is where you type the text that you want to compare to. For example, if the Data Object you choose includes a Year field and you want to use only records from 1998, then select Year from the Field list, *equals to* from the Comparison list, and type **1998** in the Compare To field.

Notice that the first two criteria also have an extra drop-down list at the end. Your choices here include: *and, or,* or *end.* Select *and* to include records that include all the specified criteria; select *or* if you want to use records that meet at least one of the specified criteria. Select *end* if you're not going to specify any additional criteria.

5. **Set the filtering criteria to meet your specific needs and click OK.**

If you goof, you can click the Clear Filter button to reset all the filters to their original values.

When you click OK, NetObjects Fusion takes you back to the Data Publishing dialog box.

6. **Set the other options in the Data Publishing dialog box according to the procedures that I describe earlier in this chapter under both "Using NetObjects Fusion as a Database" and "Publishing Data from External Sources;" then click OK.**

Make sure that you check the Display All Fields check box so that NetObjects Fusion creates all the fields for you on each Stacked Page.

Back on your page, NetObjects Fusion displays a new DataList that looks just like any other. However, when you preview or publish, the DataList only displays those records indicated by your filtering criteria.

Also, because data has already been entered somewhere else for the Data Object you just used, NetObjects Fusion automatically creates the Stacked Pages for any records that meet your criteria.

Searching for Missing Data Fields

As you work on the layout for your Stacked Pages, you may at some point delete one or more data fields. If you decide you need to get one of those fields back on your Stacked Page, just use the Data Field tool. This tool appears alongside the DataList and New External Data Source tools only when you're on a Stacked Page. When you select the Data Field tool and then click in the Layout area, NetObjects Fusion displays a Data Field dialog box, as shown in Figure 14-13.

Figure 14-13:
Which
field do
you need?

The drop-down list in the Data Field dialog box displays all the fields from the Data Object you're using. Simply select the one you want and click OK.

Use this same procedure if you happened to *not* select the Display All Fields check box in the Data Publishing dialog box. If you leave that check box unchecked, your initial Stacked Page appears with no fields, and you have to add them manually.

Chapter 15

Lights, Camera — Actions!

● ●

In This Chapter

▶ Understanding Dynamic HTML

▶ Defining Actions

▶ Creating an object for an Action

▶ Creating text as an Action trigger

● ●

*H*aving an element on your page that contains some sort of animation is one thing. Actually animating individual page elements and seeing them move around on your screen is quite another. Not too long ago, this second feat couldn't be accomplished at all on the Web. Thanks to recent developments in browser technology, however, animating page elements is now possible. And thanks to NetObjects Fusion, animating page elements is now easy, too.

Exploring the Link Between DHTML and NetObjects Fusion

The 4.*x* browsers (as Microsoft Internet Explorer 4.*x* and Netscape Navigator 4.*x* are collectively called) took a big leap forward in browser technology by creating Dynamic HTML (DHTML). DHTML shakes things up by allowing objects and text on your pages to get active. But because the standards between the 4.*x* browsers differ, NetObjects Fusion is there to please everyone.

NetObjects Fusion generates the right DHTML code to make your pages dynamic. Using DHTML, you can make the elements on your pages do just about anything. For example, you can have objects fly in from off the page and settle in the proper positions. You can let users drag objects around on the page. Your options are virtually limitless.

When the idea for DHTML first popped up, the development community hoped that a standard would develop. Well, if you're familiar with the bitter rivalry between Microsoft and Netscape, the idea that each company has its own concept of DHTML should come as no surprise. Alas, no one has developed a standard, and each company implements DHTML in its own way.

Fortunately, standards aren't a problem with NetObjects Fusion. The folks at NetObjects were clever enough to implement DHTML support in a format they call Everywhere HTML. Using Everywhere HTML, NetObjects Fusion creates the proper DHTML code so that your pages function properly on both Microsoft and Netscape browsers — that means you don't need to worry about which 4.*x* browser your visitors use; they all experience your Web page in the same way.

Actions Speak Louder Than Words

DHTML is implemented in NetObjects Fusion using what the program calls Actions. An *Action* is simply a routine that you define and associate with a specific element on your Web page. Any time you see the Actions tab on the Properties palette, you can define an Action for the selected element.

You can see an example of an Action in the Business Presentation template that comes with NetObjects Fusion: One page has different slices of a pie chart flying into place from different corners of the page as the page loads. If you've never seen DHTML in action before, this looks pretty amazing, yet it's very simple to set up in NetObjects Fusion. Chapter 3 gives you the scoop on templates.

As exciting as Actions are, the concept is a bit difficult to get your mind around because Actions can be used in many different ways and for many different purposes. In fact, I could probably write a whole book about Actions and still not cover every possibility — or even come close, for that matter.

The only real way to appreciate the potential of Actions is to experiment. Set some time aside to fiddle around with them and see what kind of results you can produce. In the meantime, here are a couple of points to remember as you begin your trek through the wild world of Actions:

✔ Actions are supported only by 4.*x* browsers, which means that you need a 4.*x* browser to preview them and that visitors to your site who have earlier browser versions can't experience the amazing effects you create using Actions.

✔ Actions rely on Cascading Style Sheet (CSS) layering and positioning, which means that you either have to publish your site using the CSS and Layers option (if you want the whole site to be 4.*x* browser–specific) or publish just the pages that contain Actions using the CSS and Layers option (if you want the rest of your site to be compatible with earlier browsers). Chapter 18 covers publishing options.

✔ Complex tables (which NetObjects Fusion uses in its two other output options, Nested Tables and Regular Tables) typically take longer to load than pages with no tables, so the CSS and Layers option produces more-efficient HTML code. If you use Actions on some pages, this last point may give you reason to publish the entire site using the CSS and Layers option.

Creating an Action

The best way for you to understand Actions is to create one. You can use either text or objects in your Actions, or you can combine Actions with text and objects to create some really cool effects.

If you've ever worked in a presentation program like Microsoft PowerPoint, you know that one of the cool effects is making individual bullet points (such as accompanying text) glide onto the page at a click of the mouse. That movement effect is pretty easy to duplicate as an Action. Follow the specific instructions after the basic steps to create this effect.

To get you in touch with the power of Actions, I show you how to create this Action on your Web site.

Creating an element to use with an Action

Before you can create an Action, you need an object to attach it to. This can be either an existing element on your page or a new element that you create specifically for the object.

To create a cool, clickable bullet that sends text flying across your screen, use the Draw tools to create a shape to serve as a bullet character. (Chapter 7 tells you all you need to know about creating cool graphics in NetObjects Fusion.) Then create a line of text and position it next to your bullet character. When you're finished, your screen should look something like the one in Figure 15-1.

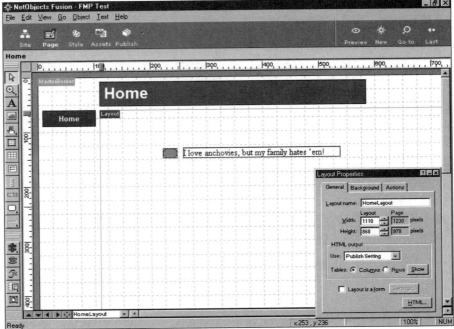

Figure 15-1:
Creating
an object
to which
to attach
an Action.

Creating an Action

The Action defines exactly how the object behaves. It defines how the object moves (does it fly across the screen, appear from nowhere, or some other effect?) and what triggers this movement (a mouse click, a page loading, or some other trigger). To demonstrate how Actions work, I show you how to make the text from Figure 15-1 fly across the screen when you click on the bullet character. You can use this as a springboard to create gobs of cool effects by just changing a few settings.

To create an Action that makes a bullet fly across your Web page, follow these steps:

1. **Select the element on your page that you want to use with your Action.**

   To create a nifty bullet effect, select a bullet element like the one illustrated in Figure 15-1.

   To determine if you can create an Action from any element on a page, just click it; if you see the Actions tab on the Properties palette, you can define an Action for that element. No matter what element you select, clicking the Actions tab displays a Properties palette like the one in Figure 15-2.

Figure 15-2:
You use the same techniques to define any Action for any element.

2. **Click the Actions tab on the Properties palette.**

   The Actions tab contains the following elements:

   - *The Object ID field,* into which you can type a new name for the selected object to help you identify it more easily later on. This is the same name that appears in the Object Tree.

   - *The Object Initially Visible in Browser check box,* which if deselected, makes the object invisible to the user when the page first loads. Presumably, if you elect to make an object invisible, you'll later define some sort of Action that makes it visible at some point. Surprise!

   - A list of any Actions that have already been defined for this object. If you're just starting out, the list should be empty.

3. **In the Object ID field, you can type a new name for the selected object to help you identify it more easily later.**

   This is the same name that appears in the Object Tree. For this example, **Bullet1** will suffice, but you could also pick **niftybullet** or **Fred** if one of them turns you on. Note that you can't use any spaces in the name.

4. **Either check or uncheck the Object Initially Visible in Browser check box.**

   The default setting is for this check box to be selected. In this example, you want this box checked.

5. **Click the plus sign (+) button near the bottom of the Properties palette.**

   This Action displays the Set Action dialog box, as shown in Figure 15-3.

6. **In the Set Action dialog box, fill in the Name field.**

   This just allows you to call up the Action from the list. Try to give the Action a name that tells you what the Action does at a glance like **Fly Out**. There are no space/punctuation restrictions for this field.

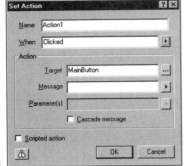

Figure 15-3:
Putting an
Action into
action.

7. **Click the arrow to the right of the When field to select when you want the Action to take place.**

   This event is sometimes referred to as the *trigger*. When you click the arrow to the right of the When field, you're presented with several options. Each one of these options offers its own submenu.

   - *Mouse:* Clicked, Mouse Down, Mouse Up, Mouse Over, Mouse Out
   - *Object:* Hidden, Shown, Error, Loaded
   - *Page:* Page Loaded, Page Exiting
   - *Transition:* Transition Started, Transition Ended
   - *Motion:* Motion Started, Motion Ended
   - *Drag:* Drag Started, Drag Ended
   - *Custom:* Edit

   Take a moment on your own to explore them. Chances are, the ones you use most are Mouse⇨Clicked, which means that the Action takes place when the user clicks on the selected object, and Page⇨Page Loaded, which means that the Action takes place when the page loads.

   For our bullet example, the default of Mouse⇨Clicked is fine.

 8. **Click the button next to the Target field and select your text from the Object Tree.**

   The Target field indicates what element on the page is to be affected by the Action. When you click on the button to the right of the Target field, NetObjects Fusion displays the Object Tree. To select the target object, click on it in the Object Tree and then click the OK button.

   To select the text box you created earlier like the one in Figure 15-1, you probably need to look for something called Text1, which is the default. If you gave the text another name, look for that instead.

9. **Click the arrow to the right of the Message field to select a specific Action to take place.**

The Message field presents several options for you to choose from. Each one of these options offers its own submenu. I find myself using the Object and Motion messages more often than the others. The transition messages also make for some interesting effects. The message field offers the following options:

- *Object:* Hide, Show, Bring Forward, Bring Backward, Bring to Front, Bring to Back, Save Position, Restore Position, Delay, Set Image, Use Image

- *Transition:* Wipe, Peek, Iris

- *Motion:* Fly, Move To, Move By

- *Drag:* Start Drag, End Drag, Constrain Drag, Set Collision Detection, Clear Collision Detection

- *Get Property:* Get Top, Get Left, Get Position, Get Z-Index, Get Clip Top, Get Clip Bottom, Get Clip Left, Get Clip Right, Get Src, Get Low Src

- *Set Property:* Set Top, Set Left, Set Position, Set Z-Index, Set Clip Top, Set Clip Bottom, Set Clip Left, Set Clip Right, Set Src Set Low Src

- *Custom:* Edit

For this example, choose Motion⇨Fly.

10. **Select an option from the Parameters field.**

Each message offers a unique set of parameters. For example, if you select Motion⇨Fly as the message, you need to specify where you want the target object to fly. In this case, if you click on the arrow to the right of the Parameters field, you can specify whether you want the target object to fly to its current position from off the screen or off of the screen from its current position. You can also select the path for the target object — top, bottom, either side, or any of the four corners of the screen.

To create a bullet that has text shooting out the side, like the bullet example, select In From Right.

11. **Decide whether you want to select the Cascade Message check box.**

If the target object contains other objects, this option passes the same message to the objects contained in the target object. For example, if your target object is the entire Layout Region and you select the Cascade Message check box, NetObjects Fusion passes the same message to all objects in the Layout Region.

For the bullet example, leave this check box deselected.

12. Skip over the Scripted Action check box unless you're a JavaScript-savvy individual.

You can use this check box to define your own Actions instead of using one of the built-in Message Parameter combinations in NetObjects Fusion. However, that kind of customization is beyond the scope of this book.

Oh, yes — the Set Action dialog box has one more button at the bottom. It looks like a little "alert" symbol. Click that button and you're taken to the page in the NetObjects Fusion help file that explains some of the problems you're likely to encounter if you try to publish your Actionized pages using Regular Tables or Nested Tables. If you stick with the CSS and Layers output option, you shouldn't run into too many problems.

13. Click OK.

That's all you have to do to create an Action. Notice that a little pink circle with an arrow in it appears on your character. This indicates that an Action is defined for that object.

To finish up our flying bullet example, you only need to make the object invisible when the user first opens this page. (You actually could have done this earlier, but the set of steps as they are written here will apply more generally to any Action you want to define.)

14. Select the bullet text you created in the heading "Creating an action from an object."

15. Click the Action tab on the Properties palette.

16. Deselect the Object Initially Visible in Browser check box.

When you preview this page (using your 4.x browser, of course), you should see only the bullet character when the page first loads. Click the bullet character and out slides the text. Pretty awesome, huh?

Defining text as an Action

You can define an Action for an object pretty easily. But suppose you want a segment of text to serve as the clickable trigger for an Action — for example, Click Here to See the Pie Implode. No problem. Just follow these steps:

1. Highlight the portion of text you want to serve as the trigger.

2. Click the Link button on the Properties palette.

The standard Link dialog box appears. Check out Chapter 8 for the ins and outs of this dialog box.

3. **Click the Smart Link tab.**

4. **Click *Blank* in the Link Types list, and then click the Actions button at the bottom of the dialog box.**

   Selecting the Blank option tells NetObjects Fusion that you're not really creating a hyperlink (that is, a link to another page). Clicking the Actions button displays an Actions dialog box that functions identically as the Actions tab on the Properties palette.

5. **Define the Action; when you're done, click OK.**

   Take a look at the previous section if you need some help with this part.

6. **When you return to the Link dialog box, click the Link button.**

Voila! That's all there is to it.

Part IV
Other Views You Can Use

The 5th Wave   By Rich Tennant

THE MODERN JAMES BOND

The name is bond.com, JAMES bond.com.

In this part . . .

NetObjects Fusion is big on site management and offers several *views* in which you can accomplish all your site management tasks.

The Site view allows you to tweak your SiteStyles to your heart's content and even lets you create new ones. You say you don't have any graphics with which to create new SiteStyles? Don't worry. Check out the CD at the back of the book for a few examples.

One thing that makes NetObjects Fusion so powerful is that after you create any sort of page element, it becomes an Asset. That means that you can reuse it again and again without repeating the steps you initially used to create it. You can manage all your site Assets on a grand scale using the Assets view.

NetObjects Fusion also makes short order of publishing your site by using the Publish view. You tell NetObjects Fusion how and where you want the site published. NetObjects Fusion handles the rest without any need for any other program. As Mary Poppins always said, "Spit-spot!"

This part closes with some issues you should consider to keep your Web site cool and current.

Chapter 16

Now You're Stylin' with the Style View

I realize that *Wired* magazine has become a pop icon of the cyber age, but quite frankly, that's one magazine that really bugs me. Don't get me wrong. Some of the writing is top-notch. It's the chaotic layout that gets to me. You just never know quite what to expect from one page to the next. I much prefer a clean, consistent layout that allows me to read the content with maximum ease.

Likewise, I prefer a clean, consistent look on a Web site. Each page should be neat and should look like it belongs with the rest of the Web site. When I come across a site that appears to adhere to the *Wired* guidebook of design — with different colors and fonts on every page, and no continuity whatsoever — I'm never sure if the site's author was trying to be artsy or if he was simply out of his mind.

To help you maintain a consistent look throughout your site, NetObjects Fusion offers what it calls SiteStyles, or simply Styles.

Acquiring a Sense of Style

A *Style* is a collection of related graphics and color schemes, each of which serves a specific purpose on your Web page. To be precise, each Style consists of the following graphic elements:

- **Background.** A Style background can be either a solid color or a picture of some sort.

- **Banner.** The Banner is the large graphic that appears across the top of your Web page. It usually contains the name of the page.

- **Primary Button.** This is the image that you use as buttons in your NavBars. (I cover NavBars in Chapter 8.) The Primary Button is actually a set of two buttons, one for regular and one for highlighted. The highlighted button indicates the current Web page.

- **Secondary Button.** This is an alternate button set that you can use at will instead of the Primary Button.

- **Line Picture.** Instead of using boring, HTML-generated horizontal rules, you can choose to replace your rules with this picture. I talk about Rules in Chapter 7.

- **DataList Icon.** This graphic functions as a bullet character when you publish a DataList. I cover DataLists in Chapter 15.

- **Normal Text Color.** This option controls the color of normal text on your Web page.

- **Regular Link Color.** This option controls the color of linked text before the linked-to page has been visited.

- **Visited Link Color.** This option controls the color of linked text after the linked-to page has been visited.

You select, modify, and create Styles from the Style view. To demonstrate how to manipulate SiteStyles, I explain in this chapter how to create a new one. You can use these same basic techniques to manipulate an existing SiteStyle.

Creating Your Own Style

When you create a new SiteStyle, NetObjects Fusion copies the images you select for various elements of the Style into its Styles folder. Therefore, you don't have to worry about your images' locations when you're starting out;

NetObjects Fusion moves them to the right place for you. You can use any graphic format supported by NetObjects Fusion (see Chapter 7), but you'll save yourself a little time if the graphics you use for your Styles are already in GIF or JPEG format.

The CD at the back of this book includes graphic elements for several SiteStyles that I developed with the help of the graphics department at IDG Books Worldwide. If you've run the installer program on the CD, you can use these Style elements in the procedures that follow.

To create a new SiteStyle, follow these steps:

1. **Click the Style button on the button bar at the top of the screen to go to the Style view.**

   NetObjects Fusion displays a list of available SiteStyles, as in Figure 16-1.

2. **Click the New button on the right side of the button bar at the top of the screen.**

   NetObjects Fusion displays a New Style dialog box into which you type your new Style's name. NetObjects Fusion uses that name to create a new subfolder in its Styles folder. As you designate graphics for the various elements of your new Style, NetObjects Fusion copies those elements into this folder.

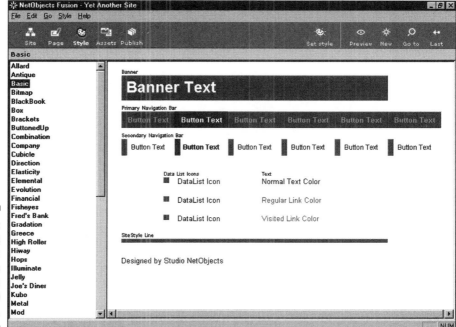

Figure 16-1: NetObjects Fusion comes with more than 50 SiteStyles.

3. Enter a name for your Style and click OK.

NetObjects Fusion creates a new blank Style and displays the new Style name in the list on the left side of the screen, as you see in Figure 16-2.

As you can see, creating a new Style is easy. Now it's time for the tricky part — setting the variables for each SiteStyle element.

Working from the background up

I find it easiest to start at the back of a SiteStyle and work my way forward. What I mean is that I specify the background first, and then work on the other elements. Keep in mind that you have two choices for backgrounds: a solid color or a graphic image.

To set the variables for your new SiteStyle background, follow these steps:

1. Double-click anywhere on the right side of the screen where the SiteStyle elements appear, except on one of those elements.

NetObjects Fusion displays a Background Style dialog box like the one Figure 16-3 shows. If you don't want to specify any background, you can click the None radio button and then click OK. However, if you do that,

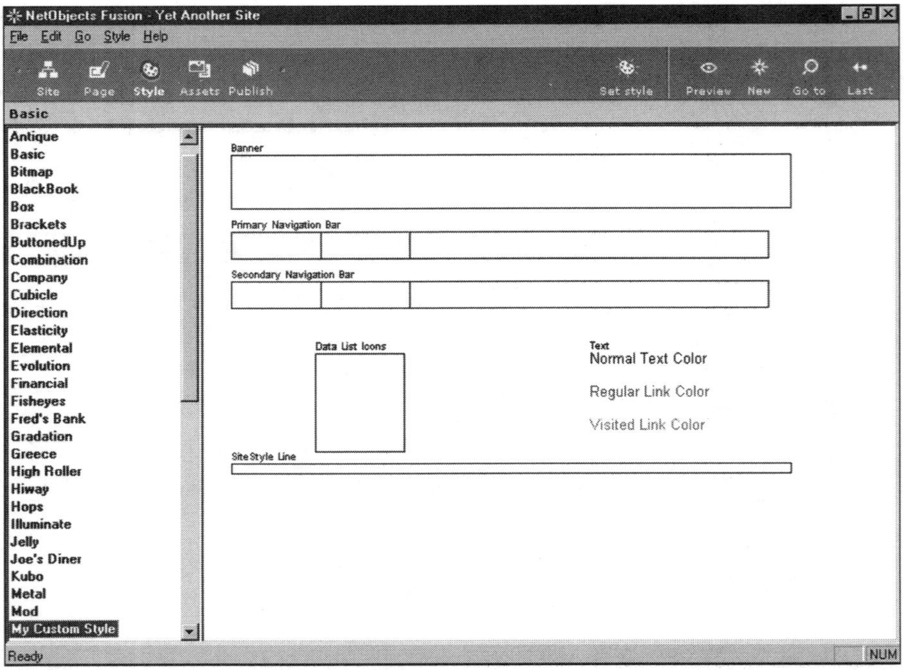

Figure 16-2:
You've created a Style, but there's not much to it yet.

the background will show up in whatever color your visitors specify as a default in their respective Web browsers, which probably won't produce the results you want. I urge you to select one of the other two options.

If you want to use a solid color, continue with Step 2. If you want to use a graphic, continue with Step 4.

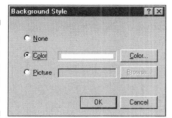

Figure 16-3:
You have
three
background
options.

2. **Click the Color button in the dialog box.**

   NetObjects Fusion displays a Color Picker palette from which you can select a color for your background.

3. **Click the desired color in the color palette and then click OK.**

   NetObjects Fusion displays the new color in the Background Style dialog box. Click the OK button and you're done. NetObjects Fusion displays the new color in the Style view background.

4. **Click the Picture radio button and then the Browse button.**

   NetObjects Fusion displays a Picture File Open dialog box. Before you continue, take a closer look at this dialog box. Notice that it has two tabs: Folder (which you're on now) and Image Assets. Once you place a graphic on any Web page in your site, it becomes an Asset. (I discuss Assets in Chapter 17.) The next time you need that graphic, you can click on the Image Assets tab and select the graphic from the resulting list. This saves you the trouble of having to navigate your system to find the graphic, as you're about to do.

5. **If the image you want to insert is not a GIF, JPEG, or PNG, click the Files of Type field and select the correct file format.**

6. **Navigate through your system to locate the desired graphic file.**

7. **When the desired file name appears in the dialog box, click the file name once and then click Open.**

   If you inserted a GIF or JPEG, you're almost done. If you inserted a PNG, BMP, PCX, or PICT, NetObjects Fusion warns you that the original file format isn't recognized by most Web browsers and asks you whether you want to convert the file and store it as a GIF or JPEG. About the only time you'd choose not to convert the image is if you're intentionally using a PNG file and want to keep it in that format.

After you select an image and click Open, NetObjects Fusion takes you back to the Background Style dialog box, which now displays the path and name of the file you selected. Click the OK button and you're done. NetObjects Fusion displays the new image in the Style view background.

If you need to modify the background settings for your new Style or for a preexisting Style, just double-click anywhere in the Style's background on the right side of the screen and try again.

Adding a top-notch banner on every page

A *banner* is an image that appears at the top of every page in your site and usually contains the name of the page. Because a banner includes both a graphic and text, you can control both of the components from the Style view.

To set up a new banner, follow these steps:

1. **Double-click the Banner placeholder on the right side of the screen.**

   NetObjects Fusion displays a Banner dialog box, shown in Figure 16-4.

2. **Click on the Browse button.**

Figure 16-4:
You control which graphic you use and how you display text on that graphic.

NetObjects Fusion displays a Picture File Open dialog box. This dialog box works just like the one in the procedure for adding a background graphic.

3. **If the image you want to insert is not a GIF, JPEG, or PNG, click the Files of Type field and select the correct file format.**

4. **Navigate your system to locate the graphic file you want.**

5. **When the desired filename appears in the dialog box, click the filename once and then click Open.**

   If you insert a PNG, BMP, PCX, or PICT, NetObjects Fusion warns you that the original file format isn't recognized by most Web browsers and asks you whether you want to convert the file and store it as a GIF or JPEG. It's a good idea to store it as a GIF or JPEG.

   After you select an image and click Open, NetObjects Fusion takes you back to the Banner dialog box, which now displays the path and name of the file you selected.

6. **Click the Text Settings button in the dialog box.**

   NetObjects Fusion displays a Text Settings dialog box (see Figure 16-5).

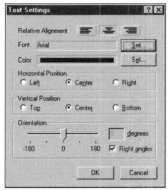

Figure 16-5:
You have precise control over how text appears on your banner.

Here's a rundown on the various parts of the Text Settings dialog box.

- *The Relative Alignment buttons* control how the lines of text line up with each other if your banner text uses more than one line.

- *The Set button* to the right of the Font field displays a list of all the fonts available on your system. You can select any font you want without concern for what fonts your visitors have, because during the publishing stage, NetObjects Fusion makes the banner text part of the graphic.

- *The Set button* to the right of the Color field displays a color palette from which you can select a new color for your banner text.

- *The Horizontal Position* radio buttons control the horizontal position of the text in relation to the banner graphic — in other words, where the text as a whole is positioned (right, left, or center) within the graphic. Note that this is entirely different from the Relative Alignment buttons described earlier.

- *The Vertical Position radio buttons* control the vertical position of the text in relation to the banner graphic — in other words, where the text as a whole is positioned (top, bottom, or middle) within the graphic.

- *The Orientation settings* let you rotate your banner text by a specified number of degrees. If you leave the Right Angles check box checked, you can only specify 90-degree increments. You can change the rotation by typing a number in the Degrees field or by using the slider.

7. **Set the text options to your liking and then click OK.**

   This takes you back to the Banner dialog box.

8. **Click OK in the Banner dialog box.**

   NetObjects Fusion displays the new banner according to your specifications, including sample text.

If you need to further modify the settings, just double-click the banner and adjust the settings again.

Placing buttons here, there, and everywhere

As I explain in Chapter 8, a NavBar consists of two graphics. One graphic indicates the current page, and one copy of the other graphic represents each of the other pages available from that NavBar. That means that to set up a NavBar in the Style view, you need to define the variables for two different graphics.

NetObjects Fusion doesn't lock you into just one NavBar per Style. You can also set up a secondary NavBar that you can use anywhere you want. (I explain how in Chapter 8.) For example, you may want to use the primary NavBar for any NavBars you place in the MasterBorder, and the secondary NavBar for any NavBars you place on individual pages.

Here's how to set up the NavBars for any given SiteStyle:

1. **In Style view, double-click the Primary Navigation Bar.**

   NetObjects Fusion displays a Primary Button dialog box, as shown in Figure 16-6.

Figure 16-6:
You adjust
the settings
for each
NavBar
button
individually.

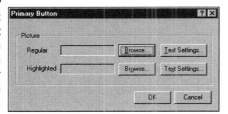

   The Highlighted field controls the button that displays for the currently showing page; the Regular area controls the button that displays for the other pages in the NavBar.

2. **Click the Browse button to the right of the Regular field.**

   NetObjects Fusion displays a Picture File Open dialog box. While looking at this dialog box, notice the two tabs: Folder and Image Assets. Once you insert a graphic into your Web site, that graphic becomes an Asset. (See Chapter 17 for more about Assets.) The next time you need that graphic, click the Image Assets tab and select the graphic from the resulting list. You can avoid navigating your system to find the graphic again.

3. **If the image you want to insert is not a GIF, JPEG, or PNG, click the Files of Type field and select the correct file format.**

4. **Navigate your system to locate the desired graphic file.**

5. **When the desired file name appears in the dialog box, click the filename once, and then click Open.**

   If you inserted a PNG, BMP, PCX, or PICT, NetObjects Fusion warns you that the original file format isn't recognized by most Web browsers and asks you whether you want to convert the file and store it as a GIF or JPEG (which is a good idea).

   After you select an image and click Open, NetObjects Fusion takes you back to the Primary Button dialog box, which now displays the path and name of the file you selected.

6. **Click the Text Settings button to the right of the Regular field.**

   NetObjects Fusion displays a Text Settings dialog box, shown in Figure 16-7.

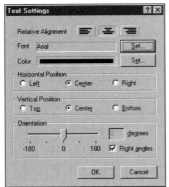

Figure 16-7:
You have
precise
control over
how text
appears
with your
NavBar
buttons.

The Text Settings dialog box here is exactly the same as the one I describe in the section "Adding a top-notch banner on every page" preceding in this chapter. Check in that section for an explanation of your text-settings options.

7. **Set the text options to your liking and then click OK.**

   Clicking OK takes you back to the Primary Button dialog box.

8. **Repeat Steps 2 through 7 for the highlighted button.**

   When you're done with the Primary Button dialog box, click OK to finish up. NetObjects Fusion displays your new buttons in Style view.

9. **Double-click the Secondary Navigation Bar.**

10. **Repeat Steps 2 through 8 for the secondary buttons.**

When you're through, you should have specified the settings for four different buttons — two primary and two secondary. To modify any button, start by double-clicking on the appropriate NavBar.

Raging bullets

When you create a DataList, which is part of the data publishing process I discuss in Chapter 14, you use the DataList Icon as a bullet character in front of each List entry. In your published site, the DataList looks just like any other bulleted list.

Because this graphic is used as the bullet character for a single line of text, you generally want to keep it pretty small.

To specify the DataList Icon for a SiteStyle, follow these steps:

1. **Double-click the DataList Icon on the right side of the screen.**

   NetObjects Fusion displays a Picture File Open dialog box with two tabs: Folder and Image Assets. After you insert a graphic into your Web site, that graphic becomes an Asset. (See Chapter 17 for more about Assets.)

2. **If the image you want to insert is not a GIF, JPEG, or PNG, click the Files of Type field and select the appropriate file format.**

3. **Navigate your system to locate the desired graphic file.**

4. **Click the filename once, and then click Open.**

   If you inserted a PNG, BMP, PCX, or PICT, NetObjects Fusion warns you that the original file format isn't recognized by most Web browsers and asks you whether you want to convert the file and store it as a GIF or JPEG. Converting the file is a good idea.

NetObjects Fusion displays a sample DataList using the image you specified. To choose a new DataList icon, just double-click on the current one.

Laying down some rules for your graphics

Standard HTML code provides a means by which you can create simple horizontal rules in your Web pages without adding a real graphic. However, an HTML rule is terribly boring, and the clever programmers at NetObjects agree. So they've included as an element of each SiteStyle something called a SiteStyle Line. This is a graphic that you can use in place of simple HTML rules. The truth is, you can use any graphic you want for a SiteStyle Line, but if you use one that doesn't have the same basic dimensions of a line (long and narrow), you're in for some pretty wacky results.

To specify the SiteStyle Line for a SiteStyle, follow these steps:

1. **Double-click the SiteStyle Line on the right side of the screen.**

   NetObjects Fusion displays a Picture File Open dialog box with two tabs: Folder and Image Assets. After you insert a graphic into your Web site, that graphic becomes an Asset. (Chapter 17 covers Assets.) The next time you need that graphic, click the Image Assets tab and select the graphic from the resulting list. This way you avoid having to navigate your system to find the graphic again.

2. **If the image you want to insert is not a GIF, JPEG, or PNG, click the Files of Type field and select the appropriate file format.**

3. **Navigate your system to locate the desired graphic file.**

4. **Click the filename once and then click Open.**

    If you inserted a PNG, BMP, PCX, or PICT, NetObjects Fusion warns you that the original file format isn't recognized by most Web browsers and asks you whether you want to convert the file and store it as a GIF or JPEG. Converting it is a good idea.

NetObjects Fusion displays the image you specified. To choose a new graphic for the SiteStyle line, just double-click on the current one.

Taking a crayon to your text

In addition to specifying various graphics for use in the SiteStyle, you also have control over the color of various types of text. Specifically, you can set the color for normal text, regular links, and visited links. In the steps that follow, I explain how to set the color for normal text. You can use the same basic procedures for changing the color of the two types of links; just double-click on the type of link you want to change.

To change the color of normal text, follow these steps.

1. **Double-click the words "Normal Text Color" on the right side of the screen.**

    NetObjects Fusion displays a Color Picker palette from which you can select a color for your background.

2. **Click the desired color in the color palette.**

3. **Click the OK button.**

    NetObjects Fusion displays the words *Normal Text Color* in the color you specified.

Managing Styles Like Armani

Suppose you create a new SiteStyle while working on one site and it looks so cool that you decide to use it on another site. When you open any given site and switch to Style view, NetObjects Fusion displays the same list of Styles that was there the last time you worked on the site. To add a Style that you've created since, you have a couple of options.

When you create a new Style, NetObjects Fusion automatically creates a text file with an SSF extension in the same directory as your Style elements. This file contains all the particulars of that Style — graphic files, text settings, and so on.

If you're in Style view and you want to add a single Style to the list of available Styles for this site, you can select Add Style to List from the Style menu. Doing so displays a standard Open dialog box. Simply navigate your way to the folder that contains the Style you want to add, click the SSF file in that folder, and then click Open. NetObjects Fusion adds that Style to the list.

If you create several Styles and want to add them all to your current list, you can select Update Styles List from the Style menu — but I wouldn't do it if I were you! NetObjects Fusion will indeed update the list, but due to a bug in the original shipping version of NetObjects Fusion 3.0, doing this also crashes the program. Perhaps this bug will be history by the time you read this, but just to play it safe, I suggest that you add your Styles one at a time.

Unfortunately, probably due to the same bug, selecting Remove Style From List produces similar results. This option removes the selected Style from that site's Style list, but in the original shipping version of NetObjects Fusion 3.0, it also crashes the program. The reason that it's so important to avoid these crashes is that if NetObjects Fusion doesn't have the opportunity to properly close your site, you may lose recent changes. Yikes!

Chapter 17

Manage Your Assets
Like a Wall Street Tycoon

. . . .

In This Chapter

▶ Understanding assets

▶ Managing file assets

▶ Delving into data assets

▶ Learning to love link assets

▶ Getting the most from variable assets

▶ Validating your assets

. . . .

*O*ne of the most powerful features of NetObjects Fusion is its ability to tame the site management beast. *Assets* are among the most versatile site management tools that NetObjects Fusion provides. NetObjects Fusion stores most everything that you add to your Web page as an *asset,* meaning that you can control each element in your entire site individually. The Assets view in NetObjects Fusion lets you view, modify, and add all instances of any asset in your site in a single step. Using the Assets view, site-wide changes to variables, links, data objects, and files are a snap.

Suppose, for example, that you've been using a particular version of your company's logo on every page in your site only to discover that the marketing department wants you to use some newer version. In most Web authoring programs, you have to go into each page on your site and fiddle with the HTML code to reflect the new filename. NetObjects Fusion provides a much simpler solution. Just edit that particular Asset in the Asset view to reflect the new filename, and NetObjects Fusion instantly updates all the Web pages in your site the moment you're done. That's what I call site management power!

The Basics of Asset Management

Assets enable you to manage various types of data across your entire site. NetObjects Fusion organizes your Assets into these data types:

- ✔ **Files.** These are external files, such as graphic images or multimedia files, that you've used to create your site. (Chapters 7 and 9 provide information on creating and manipulating files.)

- ✔ **Links.** These include all of your external links. (See Chapter 8 for more on working with external links.)

- ✔ **Data Objects.** These are the Data Objects you create for data publishing purposes. (Check out Chapter 14 for more on data objects and data publishing.)

- ✔ **Variables.** These are predefined text entries that you can add to any page. (Beam yourself to Chapter 6 for the scoop on creating and defining variables.)

NetObjects Fusion handles each of these data types a little differently (I discuss how to manage the various types of assets in the following sections of this chapter), but all the various assets follow some general guidelines.

Checking out your assets

No matter which kind of asset you want to manage, your first step is to click the Assets button in the control bar. After you click the Assets button, you see a tabbed dialog box like the one shown in Figure 17-1.

The Assets view defaults to the Files list, which displays all your image and other media files. To view any of your other Assets, simply click the appropriate tab — Links, Data Objects, or Variables.

Note that each column in the list has its own header (for example, Name, Type, In Use, Location, and so on). If you have a rather lengthy list, you may want to sort it according to one of these headers. To do this, just click the desired header. For example, if you want to sort the list by file size, click directly on the Size header.

You can always tell how the list is sorted because all the information in that particular column appears in bold type.

You can also change the width of a any column of the Assets view that's not to your liking. To do this, position the mouse pointer between the header of the column you want to change and the one next to it. Doing so changes the

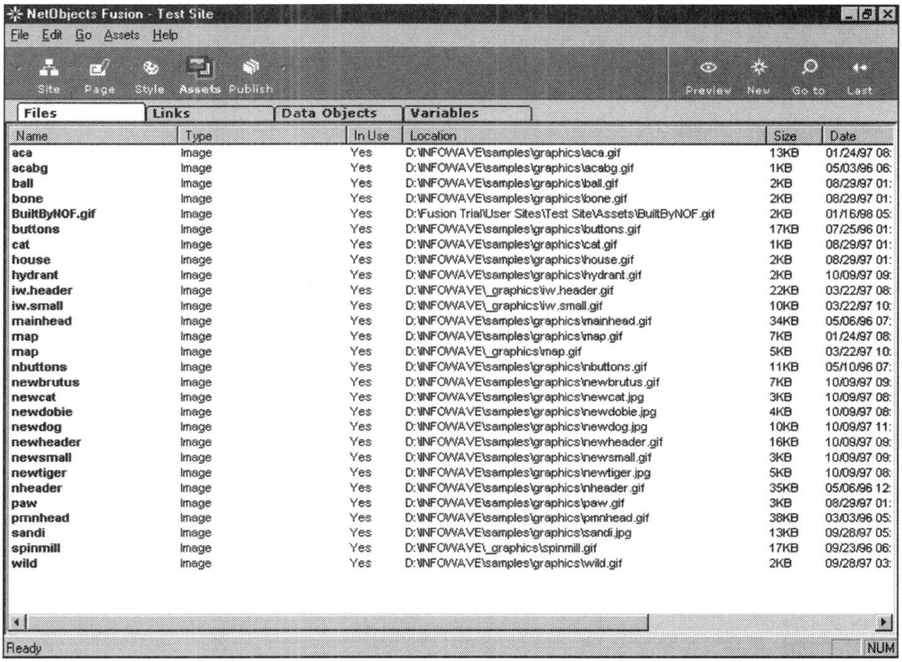

Figure 17-1:
The Assets
view puts
you in
control of
files, links,
data
objects, and
variables.

pointer into a heavy crosshair with arrows sticking out of either side. Now hold down the mouse button and drag either right or left. Depending on which way you drag, one column becomes wider and the other becomes narrower.

Deleting assets

Although creating a new Asset varies from type to type (see later in this chapter), deleting any item from the Assets view requires only one step. To delete an asset from the Asset view, just click it once and then press the Delete key. Deleting an asset from the Asset view doesn't delete it from every Web page throughout your site — only from the Asset view. Here are some additional considerations, depending on which type of Asset you attempt to delete:

✔ If you delete an Asset from the Files list and that Asset appears on any page, the Asset will reappear in the list the next time you go to the Assets view. To permanently delete it, you first need to remove that Asset from every page on which it occurs.

✔ Deleting an asset currently being used displays a warning that deleting it may leave the site in an inconsistent state.

✔ If you delete a particular image from all the pages on which it appears, that image remains in the Assets view with a label reading `not in use`.

✔ NetObjects Fusion does not allow you to delete a Links Asset that is in use anywhere in your site. To permanently delete it, you first need to remove that Asset from every page on which it occurs.

✔ If you delete a Variables Asset, the text on any page where that Variable appeared will change to `<Undefined User Variable: (variable name)>`. To delete this placeholder from the page, you must delete the text box that contains it. (See Chapter 6 for more information on deleting variables.)

✔ You can delete all unused file Assets by choosing Assets⇨Delete All Unused File Assets when you're on the Files tab. This is handy for clearing some of the excess baggage from the Files tab's file list.

Organizing File Assets

The ability to create a new File Asset before you actually use it can be very handy. For example, if you're just starting on your new site and know that you're going to be using the company logo all over the place, you can add it as an Asset first. Then the logo will be ready for instant use any time you need it.

The steps for creating or modifying a File Asset are essentially the same. Before you begin, make sure you're in the Assets view on the Files tab and then follow these steps.

1. **To create a new File Asset, click the New button in the control bar; to modify an existing Asset, double-click it.**

   You see a File dialog box like the one shown in Figure 17-2. If you're modifying an existing Asset, the information is already filled in.

2. **If you want to specify a name for the Asset that will make it easier for you to identify, type a new name in the Name field.**

   If you don't specify a name, NetObjects Fusion uses the name of the file you specify.

3. **Click the Browse button and navigate your computer to locate the desired file.**

   Identifying the file brings you back to the File dialog box.

4. **If you want NetObjects Fusion to publish the Asset even if you haven't used it on any pages, check the Always Publish Asset check box.**

   This comes in handy if you want to publish a file that's referenced in some other page that wasn't created in NetObjects Fusion.

Figure 17-2:
You can change some characteristics of a Files Asset.

If you're modifying an existing Asset, the Pages list shows all pages on which the Asset appears. You can go right to any one of these pages by clicking on it and then clicking the Go To button.

5. Click the OK button.

Managing Link Assets

No matter how consistent you try to make your own site, the rest of the Web is always changing. If you link to a particular page on some other site, the URL for that page can change without your knowledge. Likewise, people's e-mail addresses change from time to time. When that happens, you need to make some minor repairs on the Asset view's Links tab. You can also use the procedures that follow to create a Link Asset for later use on your site.

Before you begin, make sure you're in the Assets view on the Links tab and then follow these steps.

1. To create a new Link Asset, click the New button in the control bar; to modify an existing Asset, double-click it.

You see a Link dialog box like the one shown in Figure 17-3. If you're modifying an existing Asset, the information is already filled in.

2. If you want to specify a name for the Asset that will make it easier for you to identify, type a new name in the Name field.

If you don't specify a name, NetObjects Fusion uses the address you specify in the next step as the Asset name.

Figure 17-3:
Fixing any
outdated
link is easy.

3. Type the complete Internet address in the L̲ink To field.

4. Click OK.

If you're a little rusty on links, you may want to refer back to Chapter 8.

Dealing with Data Object Assets

I find it easiest to create a Data Object as I'm creating a DataList, steps for which I provide in Chapter 14. However, you may want to create your Data Object ahead of time if, for example, you plan to create several filtered DataLists from a single Data Object.

When you double-click any Data Object on the Asset view's Data Objects tab, a Data Object box like the one in Figure 17-4 appears. Data publishing is a fairly complex operation with which you need to be familiar before fiddling with your Data Object Assets. Check out Chapter 14 for additional details about data publishing in NetObjects Fusion.

Getting Value from Variable Assets

Variables are one of my favorite NetObjects Fusion features, because they let you add boilerplate (standard, repeating) text anywhere you want in your site (see Chapter 6). If you ever need to change that boilerplate wording, all it takes is one trip to the Variables tab to modify every occurrence of that wording. You can also create new variables for use later in your site.

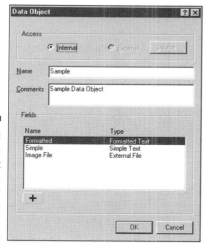

Figure 17-4:
Use the
Data Object
dialog box
to get your
Data Object
into shape.

Before you start, make sure you're in the Assets view on the Variables tab, then follow these steps.

1. **To create a new Variable Asset, click the New button in the control bar; to modify an existing Asset, double-click on it.**

   You're presented with a New Variable or Edit Variable dialog box as appropriate, just like the one shown in Figure 17-5. If you're modifying an existing variable, the information is already filled in on the Edit Variable dialog box.

Figure 17-5:
It's time to
modify that
boilerplate
text.

2. **Type a new name in the Variable Name field.**

   NetObjects Fusion doesn't let you leave the dialog box until you fill in the name field.

3. **Type the complete text for the variable in the Value box.**

4. **Click OK.**

Verifying Your Assets

While NetObjects Fusion does a great job of managing the various elements that make up your site, you can't very well expect the program to keep track of elements over which it has no direct control. For example, when you add an image file from somewhere on your hard drive, NetObjects Fusion remembers its location so it can retrieve a copy whenever necessary. But what happens if you move that file and forget to let NetObjects know? The short answer is, it doesn't know, unless you tell it to check.

This problem of assets changing while NetObjects Fusion is looking the other way isn't confined to your hard drive, either. No matter how consistent you try to make your own site, the rest of the Web is always changing. If you link to a particular page on some other site, the URL for that page can change without your even knowing it. Likewise, people's e-mail addresses change from time to time.

Luckily for you, NetObjects Fusion can verify both the locations of File Assets and the validity of all your external links.

✔ To verify your File Assets, make sure you're on the Assets view Files tab and choose Assets⇨Verify All File Assets. NetObjects Fusion goes through each File Asset to verify the file's location. If one comes up missing, the program displays a dialog box showing the name of the file and a Browse button. Use the Browse button to indicate the new location of the file. When you're done, the Verify Status column in the Asset view's file list shows the date and time that each Asset was verified.

✔ To verify your Link Assets, make sure you're on the Assets view Links tab and that your Internet connection is active. Then choose Assets⇨ Verify All Links. NetObjects Fusion goes out onto the Internet and verifies each link. As it's doing this, you see a status box that shows the percentage complete. When the status box disappears, the verification is complete. The Verify Status column in the Asset view's link list shows whether or not the verification was successful for each link and the date and time the last verification was attempted. It's up to you to investigate any links that NetObjects Fusion was unable to verify.

Chapter 18

Finally! Get That Darned Thing Online!

. . . .

In This Chapter

▶ Looking at the Publish view

▶ Giving NetObjects Fusion the setup information it needs

▶ Setting up publishing for local, global, and multiple locations

▶ Publishing your site — finally!

. . . .

*I*n the early days of Web pages, when simple text editors were the order of the day and even later when the first WYSIWYG (what-you-see-is-what-you-get) HTML editors hit the store shelves, moving your site off your hard disk to the World Wide Web could be pretty complicated. You needed a separate File Transfer Protocol (FTP) program to handle uploading the files, and you had to be very careful to make sure that after you uploaded the files, the files were organized in folders on the Web server in exactly the same way they were on your hard disk. (That was essential if you wanted your relative links to work.)

Today, Web authoring programs like NetObjects Fusion handle all the file uploading for you. You don't need a separate FTP program and, more importantly, you don't need to know where to place different files. NetObjects Fusion takes care of all this stuff for you.

One thing that makes publishing a NetObjects Fusion Web site different from publishing any other site is that prior to publishing your site, NetObjects Fusion saves your files in its own efficient format that only NetObjects Fusion can read. During the publishing process, NetObjects Fusion goes through the site and creates the HTML code. So until you publish your site, nobody except other NetObjects Fusion users can see your masterpiece.

This chapter covers everything you need to know to get your NetObjects Fusion site onto the Web where it belongs.

The Publish View Exposed

The Publish view handles all your publishing tasks. To get to the Publish view, just click the Publish button on the button bar across the top of your screen. When you do, NetObjects Fusion displays a list of all the elements that make up your Web site. It looks something like the one in Figure 18-1.

Here's an overview of the various columns in this list:

✔ The Directory Structure column shows the basic directory structure of your entire site. As with the Windows Explorer in Windows 95, you can click a folder in the Directory Structure column to display its contents on the right side of the screen.

✔ The Name column displays the filename of each element. If you want to make a last-minute name change, just triple-click the current name to go into an edit mode. Next, change the name to whatever you want.

✔ The Type column indicates the file type, such as HTML, image, and so on.

✔ The Attributes column indicates whether the element has any of two special attributes. For example, if you rename an element used in your site, NetObjects Fusion marks it with a *C* for customized. The site you see in Figure 18-1 was imported from an existing HTML site, so many

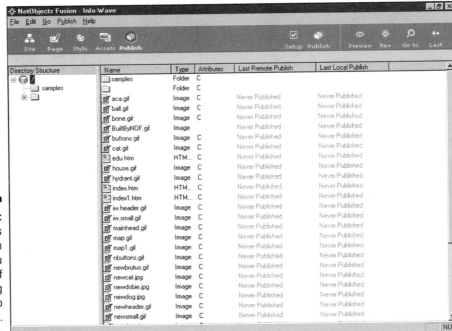

Figure 18-1: NetObjects Fusion shows you a list of everything it plans to publish.

files have a *C* mark. The other attribute marker is *R*, which stands for read-only. These are usually files that NetObjects Fusion has generated automatically, such as a SiteMap page, and therefore you can't change them manually.

✔ The Last Remote Publish column displays the date that each element was last published on a remote server — that is, somewhere other than on your own computer. If this is your first time publishing, the column reads `Never Published`.

✔ The Last Local Publish column displays the date that each element was last published on your own computer. If this is your first time publishing, the column reads `Never Published`.

Setting the Stage

Before you can publish your Web site, NetObjects Fusion needs to know a few details about exactly how you want the program to handle certain aspects of the publishing operation. Specifically, NetObjects Fusion needs to know

✔ How you want the directory structure managed on the published site

✔ Whether you want the site published by using nested tables, standard tables, or CSS (Cascading Style Sheet) positioning

✔ Where you want the site published

Don't worry if all this doesn't make complete sense. I explain everything you need to know on the pages that follow.

Organizing your site: Structural choices

NetObjects Fusion gives you three choices for organizing the files that make up your published site. Here's a description of each.

✔ **By Site Section.** This option makes NetObjects Fusion put all the files from each section of your site into a separate folder.

✔ **By Asset Type.** This option causes NetObjects Fusion to put all your HTML files in one folder and all your other files in a separate folder.

✔ **Flat.** This option puts all your files in the same folder.

Which option you choose has absolutely no effect on the end user. You base your choice solely on what you expect to find more convenient if you ever have to connect to your Web server via an FTP program and manipulate some of the files manually (like that time you accidentally deleted the company logo from your hard drive and needed to retrieve a copy from the Web server).

My personal preference is to structure the site according to asset type. For me, it's easier if I know that upon connecting to my Web server, all my graphics are in one place. You, on the other hand, may find it more convenient to structure the site by site section (which is also the option recommended by NetObjects). I generally wouldn't recommend the flat option, because on a large site, you can have tons of files to wade through just to find the one you want. Use this option only if your ISP requires it for some reason.

Here's how to set the site structure for your published site.

1. **Click the Publish button on the button bar across the top of your screen to get to the Publish view.**

2. **In Publish view, click the Setup button on the button bar at the top of the screen.**

   After you click the Setup button, NetObjects Fusion displays a Publish Setup dialog box like the one shown in Figure 18-2. This dialog box defaults to the Directory Structure tab.

Figure 18-2: NetObjects Fusion offers several options to control your site structure.

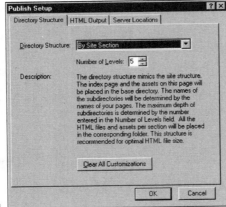

3. **Click the down arrow to the right of the Directory Structure field to display the list of options.**

4. **Click the desired option.**

   If you selected By Site Section, you can use the Number of Levels field to control the maximum number of subdirectories NetObjects Fusion creates in publishing your site. Generally speaking, you can just accept the default value of 5.

If you want to remove all customizations for your site (that is, return all files to their original names), you can do so by clicking Clear All Customizations button. Because this operation has no undo option, I suggest that you leave it alone.

5. **Click the OK button.**

Before your very eyes, the Publish view changes to reflect the site structure that you specified.

Outputting HTML for compatibility

NetObjects Fusion maintains the precise layout of elements on your Web pages by outputting the HTML code in one of three ways:

✔ **Nested Tables.** By using this method, NetObjects Fusion creates as many nested HTML tables as necessary to preserve the positioning of elements on your page. This method is compatible with both Navigator 2.01 and later and Internet Explorer 2.1 and later. Therefore, it offers the greatest balance of browser compatibility and layout preservation.

✔ **Regular Tables.** Some older browsers don't support nested tables. If you want to include compatibility for those browsers, you should select the Regular Tables option. However, because NetObjects Fusion won't create any nested tables, your layout may vary considerably from what you intended.

✔ **CSS and Layers.** Cascading Style Sheet (CSS) positioning is a new feature that only 4.*x* and later browsers support. It uses specific coordinates to control the positioning of objects. CSS and Layers is the only output option that supports Actions or overlapping objects on a page. However, using this option excludes anyone who uses a 3.*x* or earlier browser.

My recommendation is to stick with nested tables until 4.*x* browsers become more prevalent. CCS positioning is more precise, but publishing your site in this format excludes many people. However, if you're publishing your site for an intranet and you're sure that everyone in your company is using a 4.*x* browser, go ahead and use CSS positioning.

You also have three other minor options to control the output of your page:

✔ You can have NetObjects Fusion generate HTML comments for your pages. These comments identify different parts of the page (such as head, body, and so forth), and you may find them useful if you ever need to examine the HTML code for a particular page.

✔ You can have NetObjects Fusion convert high ASCII (nonstandard) characters to standard characters. Normally, you want NetObjects Fusion to do this task. However, you can leave this option off if you're publishing something like foreign-language characters.

✔ You can also control whether NetObjects Fusion generates straight quotes, curly quotes, or newspaper quotes. For greatest compatibility, I recommend sticking with straight quotes.

To set the output options for your site, follow these steps.

1. **In Publish view, click the Setup button on the button bar at the top of the screen, and then click the HTML Output tab in the resulting dialog box.**

   NetObjects Fusion displays several options, as you see in Figure 18-3.

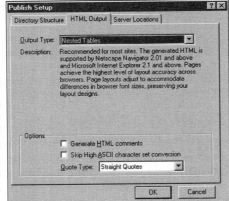

Figure 18-3:
Go here to control how NetObjects Fusion generates your HTML.

2. **Click the down arrow to the right of the Output Type field to display the list of options.**

3. **Click the desired option: Nested Tables, Regular Tables, or CSS and Layers.**

4. **Click any desired check boxes in the Options area.**

   Check earlier in this section for explanations of these options.

5. **Click OK.**

Where to, Buddy?

Perhaps the most important information NetObjects Fusion needs to know about your site is where to publish it. NetObjects Fusion can publish your site locally (on your hard drive or another computer that's on your immediate network) or remotely (on a Web server that you connect to over the Internet).

Normally, you'll want to publish your site locally so you can test it on your own system and then publish remotely for the rest of the world. The steps are a little different for each.

NetObjects Fusion also offers a couple of options that you can set for each possible location:

✔ You can have NetObjects Fusion automatically change the name of the main page in each folder to *index, default, home,* or any name of your choosing.

✔ You can have NetObjects Fusion use any one of the following extensions for your HTML files: *html, htm,* or *shtml.* (Some servers use the *shtml* extension to indicate secured (encrypted) form pages.) ***Note:*** You can also specify any other extension of your choosing.

✔ You can have NetObjects Fusion convert any spaces or other unallowable characters in your file names to underscores. I highly recommend this.

Testing locally

To set up your site for publishing locally (so that you can test it), follow these steps:

1. **In the Publish view, click the Setup button on the button bar at the top of the screen, and then click the Server Locations tab in the resulting Publish Setup dialog box.**

   NetObjects Fusion displays two choices, as you see in Figure 18-4.

2. **Click My Computer and then click the Edit button.**

   A Location Properties dialog box appears, as shown in Figure 18-5.

3. **If desired, change the Server Name to something that better describes the server.**

4. **If desired, click the Browse button to navigate your computer and select an alternative folder for local publishing.**

   The default, Local Publish, is a subfolder of the folder in which your site's NetObjects Fusion files reside.

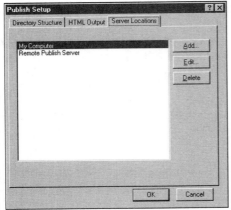

Figure 18-4:
You can
publish your
site in
different
locations.

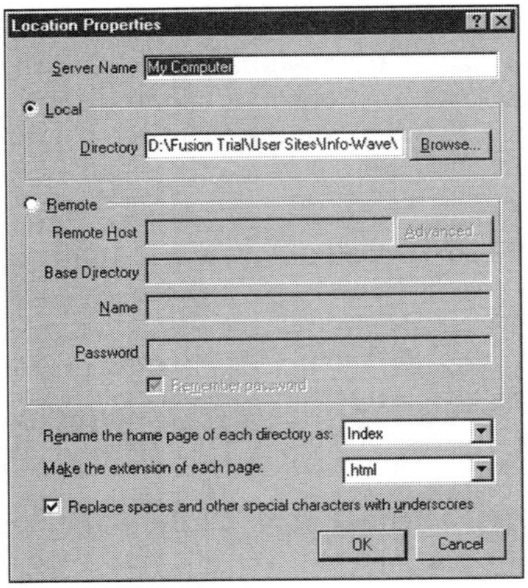

Figure 18-5:
You need
to tell
NetObjects
Fusion
where
to go.

5. If you want, change the name of each main page by using the Rename Home Page of Each Directory As field.

You can select one of the common names from the pop-up list or type any name you want in this field.

6. If you want, change the default extension for your HTML files by using the Make the Extension of Each Page field.

You can select one of the common extensions from the pop-up list or type any extension you want in this field. If you type your own, just remember to start it with a period.

The reason I don't include the Replace Spaces and Other Special Characters With Underscores check box in the steps is that I believe you should *always* leave it checked. That's because out on the Web, URLs aren't allowed to contain spaces and other special characters.

7. Click the OK button.

Doing so takes you back to the previous dialog box.

8. Click the OK button again.

Publishing globally

Setting up your site for remote publishing requires a little more information than doing it for local publishing. Chances are, you'll need to get this information from your system administrator or your ISP, as appropriate. Specifically, you need:

- ✔ The name of the remote server to which you upload your files. This is something similar to `ftp.myserver.com`.

- ✔ The name of the directory into which your files should be placed. This is called the *target* or *base* directory.

  Figuring out the target directory can be tricky, because some ISPs set up a virtual server for you. For example, to upload my site, I connect to `ftp.info-wave.com` (my domain name) instead of `ftp.sandiego.com` (my ISP's domain name). This being the case, I don't need to enter any directory name. Make sure that you check on this when you talk to your system administrator or ISP.

- ✔ The username and password to connect to your Web server via FTP. If you don't know this information, find out now and then keep it in a safe place.

To set up your site for publishing on a remote server, follow these steps.

1. In the Publish view, click the Setup button on the button bar at the top of the screen, and then click the Server Locations tab in the resulting Publish Setup dialog box.

NetObjects Fusion displays two choices: My Computer and Remote Publish Server.

2. Click Remote Publish Server and then click the Edit button.

A Location Properties dialog box appears, as you see in Figure 18-6.

3. If you want, change the Server Name to one of your liking.

4. Type the name of the remote server in the Remote Host field.

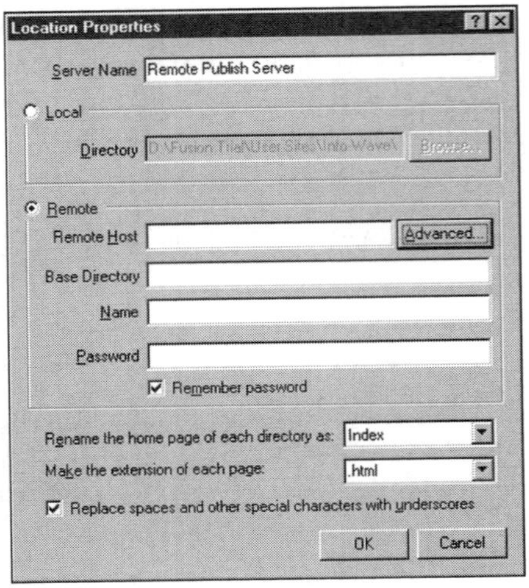

Figure 18-6: NetObjects Fusion needs some instructions to get your site where it's going.

What about that "Advanced" button?

The Location Properties dialog box includes an Advanced button next to the Remote Host field. Click this button and you're presented with an Advanced Settings dialog box that allows you to adjust the default Server Port, permission settings, and aliases for your Web server. Here's a brief description of each:

✔ Each piece of server software (for example, Web, gopher, e-mail, and so on) running on a given server uses a different port. The most common port for Web server software is 21, which is the default in the Advanced Settings dialog box. However, if your Web server uses some other port, you need to enter the port number here.

✔ Depending on the setup of your Web server, you may need to enter a different set of permissions, represented by alphanumeric characters, for the server to properly access your site.

✔ If you're using CGI scripts that reside somewhere else on the Web server, you may need to provide information to create an *alias* to the location of those scripts. An alias is like a Windows 95 shortcut, providing a pointer to the proper location.

✔ NetObjects Fusion also lets you set up other aliases if you want to store certain portions of your site elsewhere on the server, while having them appear as a normal part of the site. However, besides creating and identifying the aliases in the Advanced Settings dialog box, additional setup is required on the server.

If your Web server uses all standard settings, you will likely never need to use this dialog box. If you're not sure, consult with your ISP or system administrator.

5. **If necessary, type the name of the target directory in the Base Directory field.**

   If you do need to enter a directory name, you *don't* need to use a slash unless you're specifying a subdirectory. For example, if the target directory is named `myfiles`, just type **myfiles**. However, if the target directory is a subdirectory of `myfiles` named `test`, type **myfiles/test**. You may want to specify a subdirectory to publish your site remotely for testing.

6. **Type your username in the Name field.**

7. **Type your password in the Password field.**

   I recommend that you leave the Remember Password check box checked so that you don't have to retype it each time you upload your site.

8. **If desired, change the name of each main page by using the Rename Home Page of Each Directory As field.**

   You can either select one of the common names from the pop-up list or type any name you want in this field. (This choice is largely a matter of personal preference.)

9. **If desired, change the default extension for your HTML files by using the Make the Extension of Each Page field.**

   You can either select one of the common extensions from the pop-up list or type any extension you want in this field. If you type your own, just remember to start it with a period.

The reason I don't include the Replace Spaces and Other Special Characters with Underscores check box in the steps is that I believe you should *always* leave it checked. That's because out on the Web, URLs aren't allowed to contain spaces and other special characters.

10. **Click the OK button.**

    Doing so takes you back to the previous dialog box.

11. **Click the OK button.**

Publishing to multiple locations

You can use the same basic procedures that I describe in the last two sections to create additional locations to publish your site. So, why would you want to publish to more than one location? One possibility is that you want to publish a *mirror site*. A mirror site is simply an exact duplicate of another site, published on a different server.

If your site is extremely popular, all that activity may be too much for one server to handle. The idea behind publishing a mirror site is that hopefully some people will access the original site and others will access the mirror, thereby spreading the burden of serving your site over multiple servers.

Here's another reason why you may want to publish to more than one site. After you publish the site locally, on your own hard drive, and put it through its paces, you may want to publish locally on your company's LAN to allow your fellow employees to give it a try.

Creating additional locations is easy. In Publish view, click the Setup button and then click the Server Locations tab. Click the Add button and a blank Location Properties dialog box (like the ones shown in Figures 18-5 and 18-6) appears. Fill in the appropriate information, click OK, and you're ready to go. When you publish your site (see the next section), just choose whichever location you want to publish to. In the case of a mirror site, you have to publish twice — once for each location.

So Publish It Already

After you have all the settings right, publishing your site is the easy part. It just takes a couple of mouse-clicks:

1. **In the Publish view, click the Publish button next to the Setup button.**

   Doing so displays the Publish Site dialog box like the one in Figure 18-7.

Figure 18-7: Publishing your site takes just a couple of clicks.

2. **Click the arrow to the right of the Location field to display a list of locations you've already set up.**

3. **Click the location you want.**

   If you suddenly realize that you need to make a change to the specified location, you can do so by clicking the Edit button.

4. **If you've already published your site to the specified location, click the Publish Changed Assets Only check box if you want.**

   Checking this box causes NetObjects Fusion to publish only the parts of your site that have changed, thereby cutting down on the upload time. However, I personally like to play it safe and upload the entire site every time.

5. Click the OK button.

If you forget to enter any important information during the setup process, NetObjects Fusion displays a warning, like the one in Figure 18-8, that tells you what's missing.

Figure 18-8:
Oops! You
need to
recheck
those
settings.

If all your settings are correct, NetObjects Fusion displays a status bar, like the one shown in Figure 18-9, to show its progress.

Figure 18-9:
Watch
NetObjects
Fusion go!

When you finish, NetObjects Fusion automatically starts your default Web browser so you can see your handiwork as it now looks to the rest of the world.

Chapter 19

You Published It; Now Keep Up with Upkeep

So . . . you've created a truly awesome Web site. It's packed with useful and important information. It has just the right amount of multimedia sizzle. In short, it's a masterpiece. You're done, right? Wrong: The fun has just begun.

The Information Is a Changin'

Publishing on the Web is different from any other sort of publishing. Consider books — this one, for example. It's taken months to get this book from my hard drive to your hands. The writing took plenty of time on my part, and all the production stuff took plenty of time on IDG's part. Furthermore, IDG puts a tremendous amount of time and money into marketing, sales, and publicity for every *...For Dummies* title. It took a gargantuan effort by many talented people just to get this book on the bookstore shelf where you could find it when you needed it.

Making your site a current affair

What would happen if NetObjects decided to issue a new NetObjects Fusion release tomorrow? Would you wake up, open this book, and expect to see the pages changed to reflect the new changes in the software? Not unless you tied one on the night before. It wouldn't take IDG and me as long to get out a revision, but it would still take a few months. And you, understanding the process to some degree, would be willing to live with that. On the other hand, if you connected to the NetObjects Web site (at www.netobjects.com), you'd expect to see up-to-the-minute information, and rightly so. (Incidentally, if you do connect to the NetObjects Web site, you will indeed find current information; the company is very good about keeping its users informed.)

Why is the expectation of currency so much higher for online information? That's an easy question to answer. Publishing on the Web is a much more streamlined process than publishing on paper, both in terms of time and money. Time-wise, the limiting factor in Web publishing is organizing the information. After you have everything together and know exactly what you want to publish, the actual publishing takes very little time. Likewise, the cost to publish your Web site depends only on the dollar value you place on your time.

In short, Web publishing is cheap and easy. For this reason, people who visit your Web site expect to be greeted by current information. They know, as you do, that having outdated information on your Web site is inexcusable. It's a simple equation: Old information equals a lazy Web publisher.

Getting rid of bad habits

If you're used to dealing in print media, say as a member of your company's marketing department, you've probably learned some bad habits. The company comes out with an enhancement to one product or another and you think, "Gee, I'll have to update that brochure when I get a chance." You can get away with that sort of thinking because the expectation for current information is much lower in print media. It's not uncommon for a salesperson to hand a prospective client a brochure and offer as an addendum a statement such as, "Hey, we've added such-and-such feature since the brochure was printed." That's no big deal.

On the other hand, in my capacity as editor of *ComputorEdge* magazine, I received a new product announcement from a fairly major manufacturer of office equipment. (The name of the company has been omitted to protect the guilty.) I found this particular device quite interesting and the accompanying press release assured me that I could find additional information about the product on the company's Web site.

Without hesitation, I fired up Netscape Navigator and plunked in the company's URL. Now, fast-forward about an hour. Despite using every trick in the book to dig through this company's Web site, I couldn't find a single mention of the product I was looking for.

If I had been browsing through a paper catalog, I would have thought, "Oh well, the company hasn't printed a new catalog." No biggie. But knowing how easy it is to update a Web page and, further, having the press release directed me to the Web site, I felt deflated like a tire with a slow leak (in fact, you could say I was a little *ticked*).

Since that day, I've received other press releases from the same company, some of possible interest to *ComputorEdge* readers. Nevertheless, each one has been promptly transferred from envelope to trash can faster than you can say *lousy service*. After that first episode, it's hard for me to take this company seriously. If that's the kind of service they give the press when trying to promote their products, I can only guess about the kind of service they'd offer to my readers. Sure, one magazine isn't going to affect their bottom line. On the other hand, I'd find it hard to believe that I'm the only press person who experienced this problem.

By now, the point I'm driving at is probably obvious. Keep your Web site as updated as humanly possible! As information relevant to your Web site changes, make updating your Web site a top priority — especially if, as in the case of the bonehead equipment manufacturer, you publish information directing people to your Web site for current information. One slipup in this area is enough to make people question the credibility of your site. Several goofs and the public will dismiss your entire site as utterly useless, regardless of what other good stuff you have online.

I recognize that keeping your Web site current isn't always as easy as I make it sound. I've seen plenty of companies where the people who should know about new developments are actually the last to find out about them. I don't much care for buzzwords like *proactive*, but that one is really applicable here. If you rely on others to get the information for your Web site, make sure they understand how important it is for you to stay on top of changes. Keep after them and they'll soon realize that it's easier to keep you in the loop than tolerate your constant nagging.

Change for the sake of change? You bet!

But what if you really don't need to make any changes? Should you just leave the site alone? I think not.

When you pick up a book, you can check inside the front cover and see when it was published. This lets you know how current the information is. Likewise, I think every Web site should include a *last modified* date at the bottom of the home page.

Even if you don't have any changes to make, I suggest that you still go in and change that *last modified* date every couple of weeks. This way, visitors to your site know that the information on your site is the most current as of a recent date. They don't have to wonder if perhaps somebody just forgot to update the Web site.

If people visit your site and discover a six-month-old revision date, they may surmise one of the following:

- ✔ Your company is a dud that hasn't produced any relevant work in the past six months.
- ✔ The information on the site is not the most current information about the company.
- ✔ They've encountered a ripple in the space/time continuum.

Worst of all, they have no way to be sure which of these, if any, is true. If you at least update that revision date on a regular basis, visitors to your site will be assured that they're viewing current information.

 Changing your site's revision date when nothing has really changed may sound sneaky at first — but it's not. You're not saying, "On this date, we updated all the information on this site." Instead, you're saying, "On this date, this was the most current information available." And that's a valid and useful statement to make.

Doin' is learnin'

One more good reason to change your site every now and then: It's fun and educational. Shortly after I acquired my first shareware HTML editor, I published the first version of my site. When I figured out how to work with image maps, up went a new version of my site that used image maps. Later on, I became intrigued by frames. You can guess the result. Since switching to NetObjects Fusion, I've been delighted by how easily I can change the look and feel of a site by simply changing its Style, and I've done so several times.

Understandably, if you're working in a corporate environment, you may not have free rein of the company's Web site. Nevertheless, as new Web technologies are introduced, examine them carefully to see which ones may be appropriate for your site. Experiment with the ones that seem like they might work, and implement the ones that really do. You'll have a better site for your effort, and you'll also enhance your own skills should you need to later take them to a new environment.

If You Build It, They Won't Come — Yet

In the movie *Field of Dreams,* no sooner did Kevin Costner complete the building of his baseball field than a steady stream of cars appeared on the road leading to his farm. Wouldn't it be grand if Web sites worked the same way? You build the site, publish it, and *bam!* thousands of hits are pelting your site.

Unfortunately, Web development is not a Hollywood movie. Perhaps the single most important thing you can do, aside from developing the site, is publicizing it. Web surfers don't find new sites by ESP. It's your job to get the word out.

Desperately seeking search engines

It should come as no surprise that the best place to publicize your new cyberventure is in cyberspace. Most Web surfers find their way around the Web by using one *search engine* or another. For the uninitiated, a search engine is a Web site that allows you to type in a word or words that relate to the sites you're looking for. One mouse-click, and the search engine displays a list of sites that may relate to your topic of interest.

If this is how people typically find new Web sites, it stands to reason that you want your site listed on as many search engines as possible. The good news is that these search engines have strong motivation to include your site. The more sites they list, the more useful search engines are, and (hopefully) the more people will use them. Usage is important to these guys because they get most of their revenue from banner advertising — those sometimes annoying advertisements you often see on commercial sites.

Because of their desire to draw in as many people as possible, virtually all search engines make it easy to add your site to their list — or at least initiate the process. This is where it becomes important to distinguish different types of search engines.

You can break search engines down into two broad categories:

- **Indexes.** You have to register your Web page with this type of search engine before someone manually adds your Web page to the site's index. Yahoo! is a good example of an indexed search engine. I can't tell you exactly what criteria Yahoo! uses, because it hasn't added some perfectly acceptable sites, while it's a snap to find sex-oriented and white supremacist sites through Yahoo! Figure 19-1 shows the Yahoo! "add URL" page.

- **Spiders.** A spider-driven site attempts to compile a listing of every single page on the World Wide Web. To do this, it employs automated software agents that actually go out on the Web looking for new sites to index. AltaVista (www.altavista.digital.com) is such a search engine. You may find that AltaVista eventually lists your site even if you don't take the time to manually add it. On the other hand, adding your site in this manner speeds up the whole process; the instant you're done, other people can find your site. Figure 19-2 shows the AltaVista "add URL" page.

Regardless of which type of search engine you visit, adding your site requires essentially the same steps. Somewhere on the home page for any given search engine, you're likely to find a button marked something like Add URL.

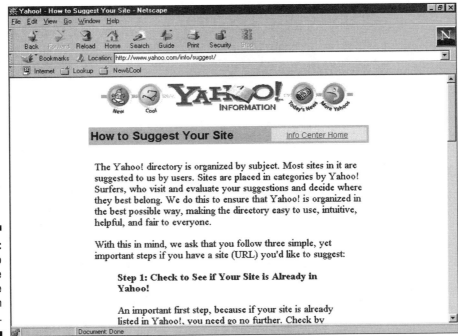

Figure 19-1:
There's no guarantee you'll be listed with Yahoo!.

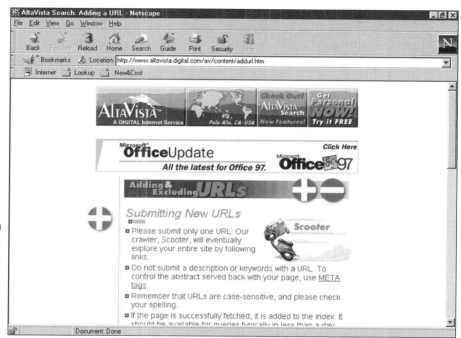

Figure 19-2:
An
AltaVista
submission
is active
instantly.

Clicking this button takes you to an online form, where you type in the Web address you want to register, as well as other information about your site. The exact information you need to supply varies from search engine to search engine. After you complete the form, click the Submit button and you're on your way to having your site added to that search engine. Not sure which search engines to register with? Table 19-1 lists some of the ones I find most useful.

Table 19-1	Search Engines Where You Can Add Your Site
Name	**URL**
Yahoo!	www.yahoo.com
AltaVista	www.altavista.digital.com
Lycos	www.lycos.com
Excite	www.excite.com
WebCrawler	www.webcrawler.com
Infoseek	www.infoseek.com
HotBot	www.hotbot.com
Magellan	www.mckinley.com
MetaCrawler	www.metacrawler.com

Keep in mind that hundreds of search engines exist on the Web, many of them dedicated to very specific topics. Perhaps a search engine exists that focuses specifically on your field of endeavor. If so, you can probably find it by using one of the general search engines listed in the previous table.

If you show mine, I'll show yours

Suppose for a moment that you use your Web site to sell pet supplies online. I'll admit that this isn't likely to be *the* growth industry for the 21st century, but just suppose. And suppose further that you're one of the leading resellers for the immensely popular Super Studly Dog line of dog food products. Finally, suppose that Super Studly Dog has its own Web site. Does this mean (a) absolutely nothing, (b) a potential opportunity, or (c) I've completely lost my mind? If you answered *b,* you're right.

Someone visiting the Super Studly Dog Web site is likely doing so because they're interested in buying Super Studly Dog products. So it's not a great leap to surmise that they'd be interested in finding an online outlet to buy those products. And because Super Studly Dog is in business to sell product, chances are they'd be more than happy to direct visitors to your site.

The point here is that if your site has some tangential relationship with the subject matter on another site, contact the owner of that site to see if you can trade links. In the previous example, you'd offer to put a link to the Super Studly Dog site on your home page in exchange for their putting a link to your site on theirs. These simple link exchanges benefit both parties involved and, best of all, don't cost either party a dime.

If you're not sure about the existence of sites related to your site, visit your favorite search engine (see earlier in this chapter).

The paper chase

Exciting as the World Wide Web may seem, the truth is that *most* people still get *most* of their information from printed material. Depending on the nature of your enterprise, you may generate a lot of printed material. You may issue press releases, run advertisements in various newspapers and magazines, write letters, and hand out your business card at professional get-togethers.

Each time your company's name appears in print — no matter where it is — that's an opportunity to spread the word about your Web site. Here's a quick checklist to help make sure you're taking advantage of every printed opportunity to promote your cyber presence.

✔ Change all company letterhead to include the company Web site's URL. This information is roughly equivalent to phone and fax numbers, and you should present it in the same manner.

✔ Reprint everyone's business cards to include the company's URL.

✔ Issue a press release to announce the launch of your Web site.

✔ Make sure you include your URL in the boilerplate blurb at the end of all subsequent press releases. Also state that digital copies of press releases are available on the site (and then make sure they really are).

✔ Modify any print advertising to include your URL.

✔ If your company produces a packaged product, make sure to include your Web address on the packaging.

✔ Include your URL in the signature line on all your e-mail. (OK, that's not really print related, but it could be. I know plenty of people who print e-mail as soon as they receive it, but don't even get me started on that.)

Putting the word out on the street

No, I don't expect you to run from group to group at your next cocktail party announcing, "Hey, I got a Web site! Hey, I got a Web site!" What you should do, however, is keep in mind exactly what information is on your Web site, and if in conversation you discover that someone could benefit from the information, tell them your URL. Or better yet, give them your business card, which already has the URL printed on it.

You have to be careful not to come off as rude when you're promoting your site, though. From time to time, I encounter one PR lackey or another who refuses to answer a simple question, instead directing me to the all-knowing company Web site. If you know the short answer, give it. If it looks like the person needs the long answer, then suggest the Web site.

Be Snoopy, Charlie Brown

Consider the area of endeavor commonly known as *competitive intelligence*, which involves the gathering of as much information as (legally) possible about one's competitors. This may sound a little 007-esque at first, but it's really just a matter of practicality. If your competitor puts out information for the whole world to see, you have every right to use that information to your advantage.

You want your company to maintain its competitive edge, and you want your Web site to maintain its competitive edge, too. If your competitors have Web sites, don't hesitate to visit them often. This is a good way to keep track of what they're doing both online and off. If they offer a useful online service, perhaps you should consider something similar.

Again, there's nothing wrong with this. It's just smart business. Chances are that your competitors are already making regular rounds through *your* site. Hey, it's a dog-eat-dog world out there in cyberspace.

A Site for More Eyes

In creating your Web site, you naturally make every effort to accommodate the wants and needs of as many potential cyber visitors as possible. Nevertheless, it's a very big world out there, and it's impossible to create a site that makes everyone happy.

For example, create a site that uses frames and you've excluded anyone without a frames-enabled Web browser. Create a site that has large graphics or video files and you're likely to offend anyone with a slow modem connection. Add Shockwave multimedia and you can kiss anyone without the Shockwave plug-in good-bye. Publish your site only in English and you may close the door to potential customers in other parts of the world.

In a perfect world, where you had unlimited time to spend customizing your site, you'd ideally have both low-bandwidth (not much in terms of graphics) and high-bandwidth (loaded with whatever multimedia you want) versions of your site in as many different languages as there are countries in which you'd like to do business. Oh, yeah — and you'd have a frames-enabled and a no-frames version of each.

While this scenario is highly impractical, you may want to consider offering at least one alternative version of your site. This obviously takes some extra work on your part, but it may be worth the trouble. You need to evaluate this alternative audience and decide if it's big enough and important enough to address with an alternative version of your site. Here are a few for-instances to help you with the decision.

> ✔ **If you've designed a site with frames, you may want to offer a no-frames alternative.** While the average user probably doesn't think twice about accessing a site that uses frames, I've met plenty of technical people who *hate* them. According to these folks, frames add very little in terms of functionality and overcomplicate the otherwise simple task of browsing the Web. If you consider this group a major portion of your audience, give them a version they can view.

✔ **If you plan to offer mega-high-bandwidth content on your site, I urge you to offer a low-bandwidth option.** Millions of users don't have the time or the bandwidth to download monster multimedia files. It's understandable that game companies, Web developers, and other media companies love to strut their stuff online — and with cable modems, satellite links, and DSL becoming more common — a growing audience can easily download a 2MB video file. However, most of the world still gets online with a modem.

✔ **If you really want to make an impression in a foreign market, offer a version of your site in that market's native tongue.** Sure, English is unquestionably the language of the business community worldwide. If you're interested in expanding into a global presence in your industry, chances are you'll find potential customers all over the world who can make sense of your English-language Web site. However, just because these people *can* understand your Web site, don't assume that they necessarily *want to*. Most people would rather conduct business in their native tongue. If you make different-language versions of your Web site while your competitors ignore the opportunity, you may have an important competitive advantage.

The good news is that you shouldn't have to start from scratch to create an alternative version of your site. Just save a copy of your original site and change the stuff that needs to be changed. You can even buy translation software to assist with any foreign-language translation. One caution: If you employ software for this purpose, I strongly suggest that you hire a qualified language expert to verify the results. These programs aren't perfect, and one little goof could cause a lot of embarrassment.

After you created your alternative site, just create a link to it from your home page. Nothin' to it.

NetObjects Fusion Online Support

As you dig deeper into the amazing powers of NetObjects Fusion, you're likely to discover that one of your most valuable resources is the support area of the NetObjects Web site (www.netobjects.com). This is an invaluable tool for anyone who wants to get the most out of NetObjects Fusion. To encourage you to make regular use of this important resource, I thought a guided tour might be in order. Remember, though, that the descriptions here reflect the state of the NetObjects site as of this writing. As with anything on the Internet, the NetObjects site is subject to change without notice. (In this case, though, I'm confident it will only get better.)

The base of all knowledge

Wouldn't it be great if you could call a company's tech support number and speak with a highly skilled expert with intimate knowledge of every aspect of the program? That *would* be great, but it's not a very realistic expectation. While the support staff at NetObjects is extremely competent, you can't expect any one of them to know every answer to every question.

One of the most valuable tools at the disposal of the tech support staff is NetObjects' Support Knowledgebase. This is a database compilation of known problems and questions, as well as their solutions. If you have a question, chances are you're not the first one. By checking the Knowledgebase, the support staff can learn whether someone has already answered your question and, if so, what the answer is.

Even better, NetObjects allows users like you to access the Knowledgebase directly via the company's Web site. If you have a question, you can search the Knowledgebase yourself and find exactly the answer you need.

What's more, if you register on the NetObjects site, the company will e-mail you your own user name and password. This lets you submit your questions via the Knowledgebase and have them answered by NetObjects Fusion support staff. If you have a unique question, it will likely end up as part of the Knowledgebase for the benefit of all those after you who have the same question.

In the news

Ever wonder how your peers have chosen to address a particular problem or situation? Wonder no more. NetObjects operates its own news server that acts as home for a wide variety of NetObjects Fusion–related newsgroups. Of particular interest are the newsgroups that relate to NetObjects Fusion 3.0; here are the ones the NetObjects news server currently offers:

- **Announcements.** Up-to-date announcements about NetObjects products.
- **Successes.** You're invited to post your URL in this newsgroup so others can see your handiwork.
- **Installation and Configuration.** Here you can exchange information with fellow NetObjects Fusion users regarding getting the program up and running.
- **Web Design.** Do you have specific questions related to Web design? This is the place to ask.

- **Components.** NetObjects Fusion's Components can be tricky. Plus, other companies make Components that you can add to your site. Check here for the latest tips and information.

- **Publishing.** If you're having trouble getting your site from your computer to its server, chances are you can resolve that problem with a trip to this newsgroup.

- **Databases.** Publishing an external database can be a big project. The information here will help.

- **Rich Media.** Feeling jangled by Java? Aggravated by ActiveX? Stymied by Shockwave? Check here for some relief.

- **General NetObjects Fusion 3.0 Discussion.** Just as the name suggests.

- **New Sites.** Like the Success newsgroup, a place to announce your awesome site.

Accessing these newsgroups can be a little tricky. The problem is that your newsreader is probably configured to connect to a specific news server — most likely the one run by your company or ISP. However, to participate in any NetObjects newsgroup, you need to connect to the NetObjects news server (currently `news.netobjects.com`). And before you access any of these newgroups, you'll probably have to reconfigure your newsreader for the NetObjects server. Incidentally, I sidestep the whole issue by running two different newsreaders on my system. I have one configured to use my regular news server and the other configured to log on to the NetObjects news server.

Docs that make house calls

NetObjects offers a wide array of online documentation, all available through the company's Web site. The documentation is broken down into three broad categories:

- **Usage Notes.** This area is described as "background and tutorials that go beyond product manuals to help you make the most of NetObjects products." I couldn't have said it better myself.

- **Technical FAQs.** Here you'll find answers to common questions in standard FAQ format.

- **Manuals and Tutorials.** NetObjects puts its full user documentation online, include each product's readme file, the *Getting Started Guide*, and the complete *User Guide*.

Odds and ends

The NetObjects Web site also offers the following support tools.

- ✔ An area to report possible software bugs, as well as view a list of known existing bugs.
- ✔ Information about training classes offered nationwide by NetObjects.
- ✔ A list of NetObjects Fusion user groups around the country.
- ✔ A list of books about NetObjects Fusion. (Of course, you already own the only book you'll ever need.)

Part V
The Part of Tens

In this part . . .

The beginning of this book concentrates on how to get the most out of NetObjects Fusion. For the most part, I stray from that idea here by providing advice that I feel is essential for any Web developer, regardless of the program used. This advice is based on my years of experience creating my own Web sites, examining Web sites created by other people, and listening to the complaints or praises of other folks in the computer biz who did or didn't like a particular site.

Chapter 20

Ten Design Tips for Any Aspiring Web Author

In This Chapter

▶ Avoiding graphical excess and multimedia overkill

▶ Editing your copy for maximum effect

▶ Avoiding lame layouts

▶ Getting around your site

*W*hen people order a pizza, they don't much care whether the pizza parlor uses a gas or electric oven, whether the cheese comes from California or Wisconsin, or whether the pepperoni is cut by hand or with an electric slicer. All they want is a pizza that tastes good.

The same holds true for your Web site. It doesn't directly matter to your visitors that you use NetObjects Fusion. For all they care, you could use the Notepad application that comes with Windows. The only thing that really does matter to your online guests is that your Web site is both useable and useful. How it gets that way is of concern only to you.

No matter what tools you use to create your site, you should follow a few basic design principles. Even if you should someday outgrow NetObjects Fusion (which I believe is for all intents and purposes impossible), you can apply these same design tips to whatever program you happen to move on to.

Keep Layouts and Elements Consistent

I know I've mentioned it here and there throughout this book, but I want to be as crystal clear as Jack Nicholson in *A Few Good Men*. If you want to gain respect professionally and not anger your visitors, make every effort to give your entire Web site a consistent look and feel.

A consistent look is a professional look. Long before I was a Web publisher, I was a desktop publisher. You and I take desktop publishing for granted now, but a few years ago, it was quite a big deal. For a relatively small investment, this exciting class of software put the power of professional typography in the hands of mere mortals. This, my friend, was both the greatest and the most frightening aspect of desktop publishing.

What do you think you get when you combine a good desktop publishing package, a few hundred fonts, several thousand pieces of clip art on a CD-ROM, and a novice desktop publishing person? Nine times out of ten, the answer is a *mess*.

Novice desktop publishers seem to use the resources at their disposal for the same reason the guy climbed Mount Everest — because they're there. It's almost as if these people have a secret contest going to see how many fonts they can use in a single document and how many boring documents they can "spice up" with cheesy clip art. The result is invariably a typesetting pile of junk.

Maybe you think that creating a unique masterpiece for every page on your Web site will wow your visitors. It won't. Just as too many different typefaces are a sure sign of an amateur desktop publisher, too many different page styles on a Web site are a sure sign of an amateur Web author. If you're going to do that, you may as well stamp *Amateur* on your forehead, press your face against your scanner, and zap that picture onto your home page.

Another reason to keep a consistent look and feel is that doing so makes your site run more efficiently as a whole by taking up less bandwidth and hard-drive space.

Consider background images, for example. All current Web browsers, like Netscape Navigator and Microsoft Internet Explorer, use what's called a *disk cache*. This is just a fancy name for a folder on your hard drive. When your Web browser loads a particular image from a Web site, it stores a copy of that image in its cache folder. If it should happen to need that same image for a subsequent Web page, it loads the image from this cache folder instead of taking the time to redownload it from the Web site.

If you use a background image on your home page and someone visits your site, that background image is one of the images that gets stored in that person's browser cache. If you use that same background image on all your subsequent pages, that person will never have to download another background image as they explore your site; the browser will simply load it from the cache folder.

However, if you're foolish and inconsiderate enough to use a different background image for each and every page, your visitors will have to waste their time downloading a new background image for each and every page. After a while, they're bound to grow tired of this excessiveness and click their way to some other part of cyberspace, possibly never to return to your site.

Yet another reason to keep a consistent look and feel is that over time, people will come to associate a particular look with your site and, by extension, your company.

In a previous life, I worked as the marketing communications manager for a software company that also sold hardware products from large corporations like IBM and Data General. As such, it wasn't uncommon for me to use the logos of these companies in our print advertisements.

What initially amazed me was how picky these companies are about their logos. Size, position, and precise colors were all major concerns. Why? Because these companies know that giving their logos a consistent look and feel increases the chances that the logo will be instantly recognized by anyone who happens to see it. Take a lesson from the big boys and make your site consistent.

Avoid Graphical Gluttony

As you can read in Chapter 7, you know just how easy it is to add graphics to a Web page. Just click, click, click, and *Bam!* There they are. Man, you may be tempted to fill your page with all kinds of fun and clever graphics. Putting graphics on the Web isn't like developing printed materials where you have to factor in printing costs. A Web page loaded to the hilt with photos and icons won't cost you any more than one with no graphics at all. However, if you decide to go overboard on the graphics, you or your visitors will have to pay
some way.

I've been on the Web long enough and talked to enough fellow Web surfers to know that when most people log on to the Web, they're interested in finding useful information, not pretty pictures. In fact, that's what the whole online explosion is really about: instant global access to *information*. After all, it's called the Information Superhighway, not the Awesome Graphics Superhighway, right?

You should probably be more graphically judicious with your Web site than you would be with, say, a printed brochure. A brochure is a pretty passive thing. You give it to someone. Maybe they glance through it once just long enough to be impressed by the fancy layout. Maybe a little later they have time to skim through the copy. However, it may very well end up in the circular file before it's ever read cover to cover.

On the other hand, visiting a Web site is a very active endeavor. People usually come to your Web site with a specific purpose in mind. And that purpose is most often to gather information.

Keeping in mind that your visitors are looking for something particular, your graphical goal should be to add graphics that enhance the information on your site, not obscure it. You don't want to avoid graphics completely; that makes for a boring site. But you don't want to overdo the graphics to the point that they become a burden on your visitors, either. The trick is to find a happy medium that allows you to tastefully frame your information with attractive graphics.

Of course, sometimes a heavier dose of graphics is in order. For example, suppose you're designing the Web site for an art gallery. Naturally, you'll want to include photographs of the art. The important thing to remember is that in this particular instance, the graphic *is* the information: The artwork is the focus of the entire site.

As for how much graphics is too much, that's a matter better left to you and your design teacher. However, Web graphics also carry with them practical considerations. In other words, how long are people willing to wait for your page and all its graphics to load before they click their browser's Stop button and head elsewhere?

As a general rule, I'd say that any individual graphic should be no larger than 60K; the smaller, the better. And your page should only have one of these fatties at the most. Your other graphics should be in the under-20K range.

Granted, NetObjects Fusion adds a lot of graphics to your page for you. The good news is that NetObjects Fusion optimizes these graphics to be as small as possible. Plus, the graphics that NetObjects Fusion creates are generally functional graphics, serving as links, icons, and so forth. You just need to remember that when you're adding your own graphics, they're in addition to whatever NetObjects Fusion has already added for you.

Avoid Multimedia Mayhem

If you should be careful about how many graphics you put on your Web site, you should be downright compulsive about how much multimedia you use. If your Web page were a pizza, multimedia would be a lot like a double dose of anchovy. Maybe you think you're providing people with something extra special by adding it, but in real life, not all that many people actually want it.

Multimedia isn't necessarily a bad thing; it's just multimedia files are generally huge. And like it or not, most Web surfers today still connect to the Internet using a 28.8-Kbps modem. Furthermore, even with one of today's fast 56-Kbps modems, the prospect of having to wait for a 2MB video file to download isn't any more appealing.

Should you avoid multimedia completely? Well, no, not necessarily. I don't use any multimedia on my personal Web site, but that's because I can't think of any way in which multimedia would enhance my site. I suppose I could add a little talking head of me rambling on about my writing, but that would be more of an ego trip for me than a useful feature for anyone who happens to visit my site.

That brings me back to the same thing I wrote earlier in this chapter about graphics. If multimedia can enhance your Web site so as to make it more useful and useable, go for it. When multimedia becomes the information, or at least part of the information, it has value.

For example, suppose you're selling some sort of educational video on your Web site. It only makes sense to offer a short clip online so people can see exactly what they're getting in exchange for their hard-earned money. Likewise, if you're selling some sort of mechanical device, an animation showing its operation could prove very useful to potential buyers. I think you get the picture.

If you do decide to add multimedia to your Web site, don't just spring it on your visitors without warning. For example, don't include some huge multimedia element on your home page. Maybe some people will want to experience it, but many others won't wait around for the page to load before they click ahead to the next site on their cyber itinerary.

Instead, using the online video shop as an example, provide a link that says something like "Click here for a video clip." Then have that link lead to a separate page that includes the video clip. That way, people who want to see the video clip can do so, while those who don't care to see it aren't burdened with it.

Plug Your Visitors in to the Right Plug-Ins

If you choose to add multimedia to your Web site, chances are that your cyber visitors will need some sort of browser plug-in to experience that multimedia element. For example, when you add a Shockwave element, as described in Chapter 9, your visitors won't be able to get "shocked" if they haven't installed the correct Shockwave plug-in for their particular Web browser. A plug-in is simply a miniprogram that somehow extends the functionality of a Web browser.

Sure, Shockwave has become somewhat of a common format for online multimedia, but you can't just assume that every person who visits your site has the Shockwave plug-in installed on his or her browser. What you need to do is provide a link on your home page that enables visitors to download any plug-ins they need to properly experience your site. You can do this in two ways.

The first, and in my opinion the best, way to go is to obtain copies of the plug-ins and store them right on your Web server. Because plug-ins are usually considered freeware — software that you can give away at will — you're not likely to run into any copyright issues. This way, you never have to worry about someone else's server being down when a visitor needs to download the plug-in.

The second, easier approach is to simply provide a link to another site where the plug-in is available. For example, Shockwave is a product of a company called Macromedia, and the latest version of the Shockwave plug-in is always available on the Macromedia Web site, located at www.macromedia.com. If you use Shockwave elements on your site, you can provide a direct link to the Macromedia site for your plug-in–deficient visitors.

One other thing you need to consider: The Web is supposed to be a platform-neutral environment. In other words, at least in theory, everyone who visits your site should have the same experience, regardless of whether they're using Windows, Macintosh, Unix, or some other more obscure operating system. So when you're providing links for plug-ins, you should provide as many different versions of that plug-in as possible.

You may need to provide one link for the Windows version of the plug-in, one link for the Mac version, and one link for the Unix version, assuming all these versions exist. Even within Windows, you may find it necessary to provide one link for Windows 95 users and another for Windows 3.*x* users, depending on the plug-in. The bottom line is that you want to provide for as many different types of users as possible (assuming your site isn't something like Bob's Win95-Only Webstravaganza).

Be a Crowd Pleaser

Most of my objections to multimedia and heavy graphics center on the current lack of bandwidth on most people's systems. In other words, add too much stuff and you're going to bog down somebody's computer and make for a very unpleasant visit to your Web site. That's bad. However, depending on the exact nature of your Web site, you may be designing for a very specific and narrow audience. If so, the needs and capabilities of that audience may be very different from the public at large.

For example, suppose you're developing your site for your company's intranet. That means very few, if any, of the visitors to your site will get there through a modem connection. Instead, they're going to be accessing your Web pages over a high-speed local area network. Therefore, they can load your Web site over the network just about as quickly as they could load it if the whole thing were on their own hard drive. This being the case, you don't need to be nearly as concerned with bandwidth issues as someone designing a site that's going to be open to the general public.

I happen to live in the San Diego area, which as a whole is a very high-tech place to live. I've read reports showing that San Diego has both the highest per capita base of home computers and the highest per capita base of home modem users in the country. Now that both of the major cable television carriers in the area offer cable modem service, I suspect that San Diego now also has the highest per capita base of cable modem users. (For anyone unfamiliar with the term, *cable modem service* is Internet access delivered over cable TV lines. The advantage is that cable modem service is about a hundred times faster than a standard modem connection.)

What this means is that if I happen to be developing a Web site geared toward San Diego's cable modem users, I, too, can ignore many of the bandwidth concerns I posed previously in this chapter.

When you're evaluating your audience, the speed of their connection is only one consideration. You must also try to think of exactly who they are. For example, if you're designing a site for a highly technical or academic audience, they may be even less interested in graphical elements than the average Joe; a site made up mostly of text may do just fine in this situation.

Likewise, a site designed for a more artistic crowd might call for a little extra dose of graphics or multimedia. If that's the type of thing your audience is looking for when they visit your site, they'll probably be willing to spend the extra time to download those elements.

In short, put yourself in your typical visitor's shoes (or more aptly, in front of your typical visitor's computer) and decide exactly how you'd want the site to be. Design from that perspective.

Don't Get Too Wordy

As a writer, I'd love to be able to write volume after volume and be assured that every person on the planet would take the time to savor each word I created. Unfortunately, I need to get real. As much as it pains me to say so, we live in a *USA Today* society where people are unwilling to read more than a few sentences to get the information they need.

If you put more than a few sentences on your home page, you're making a big mistake. No matter how important you think it is to make sure that every visitor reads the complete history of your company back to the day the company founder dropped out of grad school to tinker in his garage, most Web surfers will see it and simply read it as "more than I want to know." Believe me, I sympathize with you.

That's not to say that your company history has no place on your Web site. On the contrary, it should be tucked away neatly under some heading like Corporate Info or Corporate Background. It just doesn't belong on your home page.

In general, you can apply the same rule to copy that you apply to multimedia. If you have some lengthy dissertation that absolutely has to be housed somewhere on your Web site, make it an option, not a requirement. Provide a link to that page so that people who want to take the time to read it can, while those who are in a hurry can bypass it if they want to.

Be a Merciless Editor

I've heard the Web referred to as the great equalizer. That's because it allows Joe's Discount Computers and Betty's Custom Software to stand side by side with IBM and Microsoft out there in cyberspace. It gives you and me access to the same global audience as the Big Bills (Clinton and Gates). The Internet is truly a marvelous and wonderful thing.

Before you shed too many tears on the pages of this book, let me tell you about the flip site of that coin. That fact that companies like IBM and Microsoft do business of one sort or another on the Web has raised the expectations of the people who use the Web. In other words, if you run the Web site for Betty's Custom Software, your visitors are going to expect to see a site every bit as professional as that of a major corporation. One of the fastest ways to stamp "loser" across the top of your home page is with substandard copy. That could mean spelling, punctuation, and grammar errors, copy that's grammatically correct but just poorly written, or both.

It's been my observation that there are three types of writers in this world: those who can write well; those who think they can write well, but can't; and those who know they can't write well.

If you find yourself in the first group, you have it made, at least in terms of providing good copy for your Web site. Even if you're in the last group, you're not too bad off. At least you recognize your shortcomings in this area and know enough to hire a professional, or perhaps enlist the assistance of a friend who has that certain flare for writing.

It's that middle group that presents the biggest problem. When I worked in the banking industry, I had a manager who had convinced himself that he was *the* premier writer in the entire company. The truth was, he stank. But there was no point in trying to tell him that. It would be like trying to tell someone set on entering the Miss America Pageant that she looked like Jo-Jo the Dog-Faced Boy. Trust me, if you believe that you're a good writer, your friends (and especially your employees) aren't going to tell you otherwise, whether it's true or not.

If you have even the tiniest doubt in your ability to produce top-notch copy for your Web site, I strongly urge you to seek out someone who is willing and able to give you an honest assessment of your skills. This doesn't necessarily have to be someone who is familiar with your project, or even with your particular field. If you know someone who is an avid reader of fiction, that's probably a good place to start. This type of person can usually spot substandard writing in a heartbeat. If you don't personally know anyone who fits the bill, you may want to consider enlisting the assistance of a professional.

Finally, no matter who writes your copy, don't forget to proofread your copy *and* use your spell-checker. Your spell-checker can catch tiny errors that your eyes gloss over, but proofreading can catch errors that the spell-checker couldn't spot in a million years. This isn't an either/or proposition; you have to do both. Everybody makes a mistake now and then — I've spotted a typo or two on some major corporate Web sites — but if your Web site consistently includes careless errors, people soon begin to wonder whether Web development is the only thing your company is careless about.

Just Say No to Scrolling

Study after study has shown that Web surfers hate to scroll through a page to find the information they need. What I mean by scrolling is using the standard scroll bar on the right side of the browser window to view portions of a Web page that are too far down on the page to fit on the initial screen. For example, to see the entire contents of the page shown in Figure 20-1, you'd have to scroll down quite a bit.

Hmm. Let's see. If you want to make sure that people see all your important information, and you know that people don't like to scroll down on a Web page, the conclusion is obvious: Make sure all the important stuff fits on that first screen. That's a darned good rule to follow whenever you can. Just one problem: The size of that first screen can vary from computer to computer.

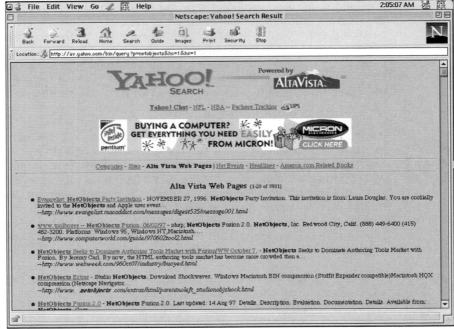

Figure 20-1:
This page
just doesn't
fit on one
screen.

The reason for this screen-size variance is that different monitors can be set to different resolutions. For example, older 14-inch monitors can only display 640 x 480 pixels (a *pixel* is one dot of information on your screen). Newer 14-inch monitors, as well as larger monitors, can handle 800 x 600 displays, and the largest monitors can handle 1,024 x 768 or even higher than that. With a higher resolution, the elements on a Web page appear smaller, but you can see more of the page. For example, Figure 20-2 shows the same screen from the previous figure, but at a lower resolution.

So how big is one screen's worth of Web content? This all goes back to evaluating your audience. If you want to satisfy the lowest common denominator, your "full screen" should fit on a 640 x 480 display. However, if your site appeals to a more advanced user, you may be able to assume that your typical visitor will have at least an 800 x 600 display. Likewise, if you're designing a site for the company intranet and you know that everyone in the building has a 20-inch monitor, you can go even higher than that. It's up to you to make your best guess. And if you get too many complaints from people about having to scroll a lot, you can always go back and modify your layout.

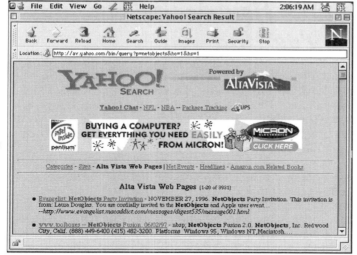

Figure 20-2:
This is an even worse fit than the previous figure.

Make It Easy to Move Around

Making sure that your site contains all the essential information that it should is your top priority; however, making sure that all that information is easily accessible runs an extremely close second. Most Web surfers are willing to do only so much digging to find the buried treasures on your Web site. Thank the Web gods for NetObjects Fusion.

By providing you with the tools to create NavBars and Site Maps, NetObjects Fusion makes it easy for you to make your site easy to use. I cover the how-to aspects of these things in Chapters 8 and 12, but I want to urge you here to make good use of them. I think you'd have to try very, very hard to include too many navigational aids on your site.

The best way to approach this issue is, again, from the perspective of your typical visitor. Look at a particular page and think, I'm here now; what are some of the pages I'd probably want to hit after this one? Go from there. The easier you make your site to use, the more inclined people will be to visit your site again and again. Providing a site that's both usable and useful is really what Web authoring is all about.

Nobody Cares How Many Previous Visitors You've Had

I'll admit it. I hate Web counters — those little number tickers that say "You are visitor 00083162 to this site." This is a personal bias, to be sure, but I think it's justified. Think about it for a second. What value does this information have? The only reason that I can think of to add a Web counter to your site is to brag about how many other people have already been there. But is that something that's really worth bragging about?

I've seen a number of small businesses that are unwilling to take a personal check unless the number on the check is greater than 500 or so. I suppose the thinking here is that someone with a newer account is more likely to bounce a check than someone who has had their checking account for some time. That may be true, but does the check number really tell the merchant what he or she wants to know? Hardly. As a service to their customers, most banks let you choose the starting number for your checks when you open a new account. That means it's pretty meaningless for a merchant to enforce such a rule. I could use check 1042 and it could very well be the first check I ever wrote from that account.

The same is true for Web counters. You don't have to be a brain surgeon to realize that whoever put that Web counter there could have started it at any number he or she wanted. Sure, I may be visitor 00083162, but that counter may have started at 00083160. A high number on a Web counter does not impress me. Instead, it makes me think that someone is *trying* to impress me, and that makes me wonder why. Even if that Web counter displays an accurate number, so what? If 83,000 people already visited the site, it may very well be that 82,999 of them didn't like the site and never came back.

Maybe it seems as if I'm getting a little too uptight about Web counters, but keep in mind that for the Web counter to work, there has to be some sort of program running in the background that advances the counter. Each time somebody visits that site, this program has to do its thing to advance the counter and display the proper number on the Web page. Depending on the speed of the program, a Web counter can add a noticeable amount to the time it takes to load that page — all for something that serves no purpose. And that simply goes against my philosophy of effective Web design.

The bottom line is that your page should be judged on content, not on how many people have been there. If I find a page useful, I'll be back even if I turn out to be visitors 10, 11, and 12. Likewise, the fact that millions have come before me won't do anything to bring me back to a page I find useless.

Chapter 21

Ten Elements Every Web Site Should Include

*T*housands of great Web sites are out there; some of which I've had the pleasure of visiting myself. To get five stars in my little black Web book, a site needs to be unique. Yet, for all their uniqueness, I've found that many of the exceptional sites share some common features and characteristics. I've spent hours and hours poring over these similarities — okay, so it was halftime during a Chargers game — and have reduced them to my top 10 list of elements every Web site should include.

Providing Contact Information

No matter how spectacular a job you do at creating your Web site, you will have a difficult time creating a site that can answer every single question that somebody may have. You need to give your visitors a way to contact a real, live person for additional information.

I'm not just talking about an e-mail link. Your Web site should include the company address and phone and fax numbers, as well as the names of key people who can answer questions about specific topics addressed on the site. Unfortunately, some companies ignore this rule.

A while ago, I needed to find some information about Sony's Mavica line of digital cameras. Naturally, I went to the Sony Web site. I found plenty of information, but after I had explored every possible page on the site, I still had some unanswered questions.

Much to my amazement, I was unable to find even the name of the press contact for this product, much less an e-mail address. To make matters worse, I couldn't find a general phone number to dial. At that point, I had expended all the energy I cared to, so I put the whole thing on hold.

Weeks later, I was at Fall COMDEX in Las Vegas and stumbled across the Sony booth. Sure enough, I found the person I needed to talk to. It struck me as outrageous that I had to travel all the way to Las Vegas to talk in person to somebody I should have been able to track down by e-mail or phone through the Sony Web site. I still like Sony's products, but the bad memory of its Web site still lingers. The lesson here: Provide all the necessary information, such as e-mail addresses and phone numbers, on your Web pages so that your visitors can reach you.

If you're going to provide e-mail addresses on your Web site, do what you can to make sure you have somebody who is available to respond to those e-mail inquiries. As the site's developer, you only have so much control over the actions of others in your company; however, try to implement a company-wide policy on answering customers' questions.

Several months ago, I was researching smart cards for an article I was writing for a financial trade publication. Again, I turned to the Web; this time I visited the site of MasterCard International, a leader in the field. This site had a great-looking press area and even an e-mail address to which press inquiries could be directed. I had some questions, so I e-mailed my inquiry to the specified address.

Guess what? Nobody ever responded to my e-mail, and I wrote the article without mention of MasterCard. The lesson here: Respond to your customers' queries or risk losing customers and valuable publicity.

Polling the Court of Public Opinion

In Chapter 20, I talk about the need to approach your Web development efforts from the perspective of your typical visitors. Well, this role-playing takes you only so far. You need a way to pick the brains of your visitors and find out what they really want from your site.

The best way I know to do this is by using an online form (see Chapter 11). It doesn't have to be anything fancy — just a place where somebody can type in a few comments and click a Submit button.

You may be tempted to take the easy way out and put a simple e-mail link on your Web site, but I think a form is better for a couple of reasons. First of all, a form is easier for the user. A form is all handled within the browser, with no need to run some external e-mail program. The easier you make it for people to offer their opinions, the more likely they are to do so. Plus, forms give you the ability to ask specific questions and probe specific areas of concern.

Forms also give you greater control than e-mail. Depending on how sophisticated you want to get, you can automatically store the comments you receive in some sort of database.

Giving Ample Notice with Copyrights

Copyrights are a big issue on the Internet. Some online extremists believe that any and all information posted on the Internet should be free game, exempt from any copyright laws.

As much as these zanies may wish, any material you publish on the World Wide Web is protected by the same copyright laws that govern any other type of media, such as printed materials or television broadcasts.

On the other hand, plenty of material on the Internet has been released into the public domain by its authors, meaning that it's free for the taking. To make sure that your valuable Web material isn't confused with this public domain rabble, you should include a specific copyright notice on every page on your Web site. This way, nobody can claim that they "borrowed" your copyrighted material because, oops, they thought it was in the public domain.

You don't need anything too fancy, just something that clearly states your position on the matter. For example, here's one that I've used in the past:

```
C1997, (company name), all rights reserved; this page or
any part thereof may not be duplicated without express
written permission of the copyright owner.
```

This disclaimer is pretty clear and can give visitors to your site ample warning.

Taking Credit for Your Work

If you find yourself in the business of creating Web sites for other companies, be sure to ask your customers if you can include a link from their site to yours. A small button at the bottom of the customer's home page is sufficient. Some companies may scoff at the idea, wanting to preserve the purity of their sites. Others are more than willing to help you out. Just remember that although these links are nice perks, you probably don't want the issue to be a deal breaker.

Linking to the Outside World

People are going to visit your site looking for information. If they are researching information on your site, chances are they may be interested in related information on other Web sites, as well. To provide a little extra assistance to these folks, I suggest that you devote a page on your site to links to related sites. These links provide a higher level of services to your visitors without adding any additional cost to your site.

You do, however, need to exercise a certain amount of caution when you link to the outside world. For starters, when you link to another site, you accept the responsibility of making sure that the link is valid when someone tries to use it. The Web is a very transitory medium: It's not uncommon for a Web site to be here today and gone tomorrow.

Unfortunately, if someone clicks a link you've provided and it turns out to be invalid, it reflects poorly on you. For this reason, you should check your external links at least monthly, if not more often, to make sure they work.

When you provide a link to another site, your visitors take this as some sort of endorsement, whether or not that's your intention. Before you add a link to any external site, make sure that you visit that site personally and verify the quality of the content. A user who arrives at a second-rate site via your site is likely to have some doubts about you.

Finally, you don't want to inadvertently steer people to your competitors. A company I worked with once included a link to a particular related site, only to notice later that this other site included a prominent link to one of the company's competitors. Needless to say, this link disappeared in a hurry. You should watch out for the same sort of thing.

Giving Away Free Stuff

One of the best ways to attract people to your storefront, whether it is online or on Main Street, is to give something away for nothing. But what can you give away online? The truth is, you can give away just about anything. You just may not want to. For example, a while back I read about a seed company in Florida that almost went broke giving away free seeds through its Web site. That's not the fate you want for your company.

The best things to give away for free are things that you get for free (or almost free) and that can be delivered online. That pretty much narrows the field to either application software or some sort of informational document.

If you're in the software business, a demo version of your product makes for a logical download. It fulfills the "something-for-nothing" requirement and, assuming the product is good, encourages the recipient to come back and spend a buck.

Online software is another possibility. For example, if you're developing a site for a mortgage broker, an online loan calculator makes a nice match. Even if you don't have any software of your own to offer, providing direct links to related shareware and freeware can be the next best thing.

You may want to consider starting an online newsletter. If your company already publishes a print newsletter, you've already won half the battle. You just need to convert the print newsletter to digital format.

Whatever you do, don't publish your newsletter on your Web site and assume that people will return to view each new issue. Instead, take subscriptions, free as they may be, and e-mail each new issue to each subscriber. Doing so carries two benefits:

- **You can gather valuable demographic information.** You can get good demographic information about your customers and potential customers through the subscription process. Most people don't mind answering a few questions to get a free newsletter subscription.

- **You remind your customers about your business.** By e-mailing your newsletter, you're assured that your company's name is put in front of each subscriber every time a new issue comes out. If you simply post each issue on your Web site, you just have to hope and pray that people return to read it — and unfortunately they probably won't.

Meeting the Press

If your company mails out regular press releases, make sure to post them immediately to the virtual press room on your Web site. (If your company doesn't do press releases, someone at your company needs to start as soon as possible.) Journalists are turning more and more to the Web for current information. The easier you make it for a reporter to mention your company's name, the more likely the reporter is to mention it. That's just good PR sense.

Make sure you put the company's Web address on the printed press releases, too. As a writer, I can tell you from firsthand experience that I invariably look for online versions of the interesting press releases I receive so that I don't have to retype any information I may want to use later.

One last thing: On your press releases page, make sure you organize your press releases from newest to oldest. Every once in a while, I come across a company that does the oldest-to-newest thing. Throwing the newest press releases at the bottom of the page may be easier, but it makes life more difficult for reporters. You want to make it as easy as possible for reporters to give you good exposure.

Mastering Your Domain

If you work for a large company, there's a good chance that the Web server that's home to your site is housed on company premises and maintained by company employees. On the other hand, if you work for a smaller company, you may have to outsource your Web hosting to an Internet Service Provider (ISP). In that case, you have the option either to use your ISP's domain for your Web address (for example, www.YourISP.com/YourCompany) or to register and use your own domain name (for example, www.YourCompany.com). Sure, it's easier and cheaper to use your ISP's domain name, but having your own domain name is still a better idea because

- ✔ **It's pretty cheap.** Registering your name with InterNIC, the organization responsible for such things, only costs $50 a year. Check www.internic.org for more information.

- ✔ **It looks first-rate.** In this day and age, thousands of individuals have registered their own domain names. If you don't have your own domain name, you're going to look like a second-tier player, no matter what business you're in.

✔ **Your address is shorter and easier to remember.** With today's Web browsers, a visitor need only type the `YourCompany` part to get to your Web site. If you rely on your ISP's domain name, people have to remember and type in the entire address.

Register your own domain name and make everyone's life better.

Date-Stamping Your Site

When I visit a Web site wearing my computer journalist hat, one thing I always wonder about is how current the information is. The Web page may declare a particular press release to be the latest news, but I have no way to be sure — unless, of course, that page has a date on it. Maybe it was the latest news six months ago, but that doesn't help me out much today. On the other hand, someone else visiting your site may very well need to know what happened six months ago.

 I know it means a little extra effort on your part, but I strongly suggest that you include a modification date on each and every page on your site. A modification date eliminates any possible confusion as to the timeliness of the information.

Modification dates are often overlooked even by big companies. The lesson here: Don't be a date-forgetter.

What's New?

Along the same line of adding the date the page was last modified, I believe that every company site should have a What's New page that serves as a catch-all for, well, what's new. Granted, a lot of what's new is going to be in the form of press releases, but not all of it.

For example, if your site includes tips and tricks for using your products, a new tip or trick might not warrant a press release, but you still want to have it on the What's New page. A page like this puts *all* the latest information in one convenient location for anyone who happens to stop by.

Part VI
Appendixes

The 5th Wave   By Rich Tennant

"He found a dog site over an hour ago and has been in a staring contest ever since."

In this part . . .

So you've created an awesome Web site, but still haven't found a home for it. Believe me, you're in for a lot of mumbo jumbo when you go out shopping for an Internet Service Provider. Many ISPs will tell you quite convincingly that you need to spend more than you really do and that you should be satisfied with what you get, even if it's not what you wanted to start out with. Before you make your final decision on an ISP, see the advice I offer in Appendix A.

If you desire to find out about the software on the CD — I, for one, am inclined to install first and ask questions later — make sure you check out Appendix B.

Appendix A
Finding a Home for Your Site

* *

In This Appendix

▶ Registering your own domain name

▶ Local versus national ISPs

▶ Evaluating cost and spotting bogus charges

▶ Evaluating a particular ISP: access, bandwidth, and extra benefits

▶ Switching ISPs

* *

*N*etObjects Fusion makes designing a Web site easy. The controls are easy to understand, and you can use the help files and this book to make your site-design projects even easier. However, when it comes time to find a permanent home (not that *anything* on the Web is truly permanent) for your site, you may find yourself on your own. If you've designed your site for your employer — or for some other company, for that matter — it's an easy call. You upload the site to whatever Web server the company tells you to. On the other hand, if you've designed a site for your own use, you're in charge of finding Web space for it. (Whoever commissions the site is responsible for finding it a home.)

You could take the easy way out and sign up with the first Internet Service Provider (ISP) you find in the phone book. But with all the time and energy you spent to make your site just right, I have to believe that you want to find the right home for it — one that's warm, loving, caring . . . okay, I'm getting a little off the track here. My point is that ISPs vary widely in the cost, quality, and services they offer. While the CD in the back of this book includes sign-up software for MindSpring — one of the top national ISPs — you may find that the free Web space included with your MindSpring account doesn't offer enough space or doesn't meet your needs for some other reason.

You and your site can benefit from investing some time exploring several different ISPs. You can use this appendix as your guide.

What's in a (Domain) Name?

Before you even go shopping for an ISP, you need to decide whether you want your site to use its own *domain name*. A domain name is the unique Internet name used to identify you or your company. For example, the domain name for my company is info-wave.com. Each domain name includes the unique part that identifies you, plus a suffix. Table A-1 shows a list of possible domain name suffixes for U.S. domains.

Table A-1	Domain Name Possibilities
Suffix	*Use*
.com	The most common suffix; used by companies
.net	Used by companies and individuals; most common among Internet related businesses
.org	Used by nonprofit and noncommercial organizations
.gov	Used by government agencies

The important thing to keep in mind is that your domain name includes the suffix. For example, even though info-wave.com is registered to my company, some other company could come along and register info-wave.net.

Owning your domain name

Having your own domain name, instead of relying on your ISP's domain name, is important for two reasons. First, it makes your Web address much simpler to remember. For example, to visit my company's Web site, you type in **http://www.info-wave.com**. On the other hand, if I relied on my ISP's domain name for access to my site, the Web address would be something like www.sandiego.com/users/~info-wave.

The second reason to use your own domain name is that you get to keep your domain name forever. If you rely on your ISP for a domain name, what happens if you decide to switch to a different ISP? Your Web address changes, too. Any stationery you printed with your Web address goes in the trash and people who have bookmarked your site can suddenly no longer find you. That's not good. No matter what ISPs come and go, and no matter how many times you switch ISPs, if you have your own domain name, that domain name is yours. You can take it with you anywhere you want and never have to be at anyone's mercy — except maybe InterNIC.

Back in the old days of the Web, having your own domain name meant having to operate your own Web server. Today, nearly all ISPs offer what's called *virtual domain hosting*. This means that the ISP can host your domain name and make it appear to the people who visit your site that you indeed operate your own server.

Registering your domain name

To claim ownership to a domain name, you need to register it. Today in the United States, all domain names are registered by a company called InterNIC. Recently other companies who'd like to break InterNIC's monopoly on domain names and add suffixes (like .xxx for adult sites or .shop for online shopping malls) have shown up and tried to claim their piece of the action. However, for the time being, InterNIC is the only game in town. You can check to see if the domain name you want is registered already by visiting the InterNIC Web site at `www.internic.com`.

The current cost to register a domain name with InterNIC is $100 for the first two years and $50 for each year thereafter. To register a domain name, you simply complete an e-mail–based form available from InterNIC and send it in. The computer system at InterNIC automatically finishes the registration process, spitting you back a rejection notice if there was a problem or a bill if everything went okay. If you don't pay the bill in a certain amount of time, your domain name gets tossed back in the "unused" hopper.

Some ISPs can help you register your domain name. If you have an ISP help you out with this, make sure that your domain name is really registered to you and *not* to the ISP. I've heard of some unscrupulous ISPs who have registered domain name ownership to themselves instead of to their clients. Then when the client decides to move to another ISP, he or she doesn't have the right — at least in the eyes of InterNIC — to take that domain name along.

Choosing between Local and National ISPs

When you go shopping for an ISP, you have no shortage of options. You can narrow your search somewhat by deciding first whether you want to go with a big national provider like MindSpring or a smaller local firm.

For personal accounts, national ISPs are fine. They have local numbers all over the country and are set up to handle your personal affairs no matter where you are. On the other hand, when it comes to a business site, I prefer the smaller, local providers. Local providers don't have the volume that the big guys do, so telephone support is generally more accessible. And if you ever need to meet face to face with your ISP, they're only a couple of miles away. Plus, local ISPs are more tuned in to the local scene and may be able to offer valuable advice in making your site a local success. Finally, the smaller local outfit may cut you a better deal.

How Much Should You Pay?

If you've looked around much for a personal Internet account, you know that prices seem pretty consistent from one ISP to the next. For about $20 a month, you can find unlimited Internet access and maybe 5MB of disk space for a personal Web page. Some ISPs go as low as $9 a month if you pay for a year up front.

At these low prices, a small local company isn't making a ton of money on personal accounts. In retail-ese, this is known as a loss-leader — a low-priced, high-profile product that draws people in and popularizes the business. Many of these local ISPs make their real bread and butter from business accounts. If you're looking for a place to house your business-related Web site, make sure you check the ISP's business rates.

While most ISPs offer personal accounts in the $20 range, prices for business accounts are all over the map. For example, when my partner and I first registered info-wave.com, we went with a very popular ISP in town. We were paying more than $200 a month for Internet service and because we hadn't shopped around, we didn't think much of it. The ISP provided an itemized list of where all our money was going.

Later on, I became good friends with the president of another reputable, local ISP. When I told him what we were paying, he was shocked. He explained that for approximately the same services, his company only charged about $75 a month. Needless to say, we switched ISPs in a heartbeat and have been with that company ever since.

Money for nothing: After the initial setup

The reason my first ISP cost so much was that they charged for just about everything — even automated tasks that were performed by their computers. For example, my first ISP charged approximately $50 a month for domain name hosting. The truth of the matter is that once the ISP has set up the domain name hosting, keeping it active doesn't take any extra ongoing effort on the part of the ISP. Any monthly fee you pay for domain name hosting is just gravy for the ISP. Although it's reasonable to expect some sort of setup charge, I think a high monthly charge is just a plain rip-off.

Many ISPs also impose *traffic* charges. *Traffic* refers to the amount of information, measured in megabytes, that outside users request from your Web site. Many ISPs allot you so much traffic per month, and then charge you extra if you go over. For example, if someone loads a page from your site that contains 1MB of information (a rather large page, I realize), they've just used up 1MB of your monthly allotment.

A monthly traffic limit is just an arbitrary number determined by the ISP. Your ISP's expenses don't go up in any measurable amount when your site goes over its limit by, for example, 10MB. But you can bet your pepperoni your ISP will charge you for that 10MB. You'd need to have an incredibly popular site to create a major impact on your ISP's system. Your best bet is to find an ISP that doesn't nail you for any traffic charges.

The bottom line on cost: What to expect for your money

You need to figure out ahead of time exactly what services you need and don't need. Then compare prices from several ISPs. For me, right now I pay about $75 a month. I get space for my Web site, virtual domain name hosting, and two access accounts — one for me and one for my partner. I have a good working relationship with my ISP and I can count on support pretty much whenever I need it.

If you're developing a big commercial site and you need extras like credit card authorization, shopping cart software, and secure forms, you probably have to pay more than I do.

Easy Remote Access to Your ISP

Depending on your situation, you may want to consider how easy it is to access your Internet account when you're not sitting at your primary computer. A number of considerations fall under this heading:

   ✔ **Access via toll-free number.** If you do a lot of out-of-town travel and need regular access to your account while you're on the road with your laptop, you may want to look for an ISP that offers a toll-free dial-up number. Because your ISP has to pay for the time you're connected using the toll-free number, you can expect them to pass that expense along to you on your next bill. However, unless your ISP is trying to make a hefty profit on the toll-free number, you'll normally find that dialing the toll-free number is less expensive than dialing long distance to one of your ISP's regular phone numbers.

✔ **FTP access between non-ISP members.** You should also make sure that the ISP offers adequate FTP access to your account. I once designed a Web site for a company, only to discover that the company's ISP didn't allow FTP access from anyone not connected through that ISP. Even though my client had provided me with all the necessary password information, I was unable to upload the completed site to their ISP's Web server from my account with a different ISP. After about two months of assurances that the problem would be fixed within the week, my client finally switched ISPs and haven't had a problem since.

✔ **Telnet access.** Make sure that your ISP offers *telnet* access and that you know, at least in general terms, how to use it. Telnet lets you access your account in a text-based terminal mode from any Internet-connected computer on the planet. Using telnet is a kind of clunky way to access your account, but it can prove quite valuable if you've exhausted all other means.

Deciding Which Extras You Need

Internet service is just like any other product. No two companies offer the same services for the same price. If you find two ISPs that offer similar packages at a similar price, you may need to look at the little extras that may or may not be of interest to you.

For example, many ISPs offer predesigned CGI scripts that you can access and incorporate into your Web site without the need to hire a CGI programmer or know any CGI programming yourself. My ISP takes this one step further by providing a fill-in-the-blank form that customers can use to generate the HTML code for their own mailto form (a *mailto form* being one where the form data is e-mailed directly to you). You type in basic information and check some boxes to specify how you want your form to behave. A few seconds after you click the Submit button, a new page appears that displays exactly the HTML code you need to enter on your form. I've found this quite handy on a number of occasions.

Another feature you may find handy and which many ISPs offer, is an *FTP dropbox.* This is simply a directory on the ISP's server where you can place files for others to download or others can place files for you to download. For example, if you created a Web site for a printing shop, you could set up an FTP dropbox where customers can upload printing jobs.

Checking References

If you know people who have their own Web site, check with them to see what they think of their ISP. Make sure you don't just ask who they use, but what they think of the service. You may find that some people stick with the same ISP even though they're not satisfied. The reason? They don't want to hassle with switching over to another ISP (and risk getting disappointed a second time).

Suppose you don't know anyone with a Web site of his or her own. Then what? Every ISP has its own Web site, and every ISP I've ever seen has included on its site a list of all its Web clients, complete with links to the client sites. Check out the sites of some of the companies that do business with each ISP. Chances are good that you can find e-mail links to the people at each company who are responsible for that site. Drop them an e-mail note to see what they think of their ISP. While someone who is happy with their ISP may not take the time to respond — unless they're *extremely* happy or happen to be the cousin of the owner — a dissatisfied customer often takes the time to warn others.

Doing the Bandwidth Boogie

Many ISPs boast of their multiple T1 or T3 phone lines, the implication being that people will be able to access your site much more quickly than with some other ISP. I suppose that in general terms it's true that the more high-speed phone lines, the better. However, it's only part of the picture. Keep in mind that no matter how much bandwidth a particular ISP offers, it has to be shared with everyone using that ISP and therefore may give you even slower access times.

Suppose, for example, that you're considering two ISPs, and ISP A has more T1 lines than ISP B. At first glance, you'd expect ISP A to provide faster access to your site than ISP B. However, this may not be the case — if ISP A is so busy that those T1 lines are always jam-packed with traffic and ISP B typically carries a lighter load relative to its available bandwidth, users will get faster response from Web sites that are hosted by ISP B.

The best way to determine response time is to check it for yourself. Visit other Web sites hosted by each ISP you're considering and see if you're satisfied with the response times from those sites. Make sure that you do your exploring during peak business hours. If you go poking around at 2 a.m., even the lamest ISP is likely to clock in with a reasonable response time.

Oops! I Signed with the Wrong ISP

Even after you've completed the most diligent of searches, you may find yourself with an ISP that doesn't live up to your expectations for one reason or another. Don't worry. As long as you're using your own domain name — let me repeat that: *as long as you're using your own domain name* — this is not a major problem.

If you're using your ISP's domain name and you switch, you may encounter several problems. First, if someone uses a search engine, finds a link to your old Web address, and discovers the link is dead, they may think your venture is dead, too. You'll have to spend plenty of time resubmitting to search engines. Also, if you've had your Web address printed on any stationery, you'll have a nice, big pile of stuff for the recycle box.

Here are the steps to follow if you ever need to switch ISPs:

1. **Contact the new ISP and let them know that you're switching over.**

2. **Set up an account with the new ISP.**

3. **Upload your site to the new ISP so it's ready when the domain name switches over.**

4. **E-mail a change form to InterNIC, available from the InterNIC Web site.**

   As long as you complete the change form correctly, your domain name should get switched over in about 48 hours.

5. **Cancel your account with your old ISP.**

This may seem like a bit of a hassle, but in the long run, it's worth it to be with an ISP that makes you happy.

Appendix B

About the CD

System Requirements

Make sure that your computer meets the minimum system requirements listed below. If your computer doesn't match up to most of these requirements, you may have problems using the contents of the CD.

- ✔ A PC with a 90-MHz Pentium processor or higher.

- ✔ Microsoft Windows 95 or Windows NT 3.51 or later.

- ✔ At least 32MB of total RAM installed on your computer. This is the minimum requirement for running NetObjects Fusion 3.0.

- ✔ At least 106MB of hard drive space available to install all the software from this CD. (You need less space if you don't install every program.)

- ✔ A CD-ROM drive — double-speed (2x) or faster.

- ✔ A monitor capable of displaying at least 256 colors at 600 x 800 resolution.

- ✔ TCP/IP compliance for Internet connectivity.

If you need more information on the basics, check out *PCs For Dummies,* 4th Edition, by Dan Gookin; or *Windows 95 For Dummies* by Andy Rathbone (both published by IDG Books Worldwide, Inc.).

Using the CD with Microsoft Windows

To install the items from the CD to your hard drive, follow these steps:

1. **Insert the CD into your computer's CD-ROM drive.**

2. **Click Start➪Run.**

3. **In the dialog box that appears, type** D:\SETUP.EXE.

   Replace *D* with the proper drive letter if your CD-ROM drive uses a different letter. (If you don't know the letter, see how your CD-ROM drive is listed under My Computer.)

4. **Click OK.**

   A license agreement window appears.

5. **Read through the license agreement, nod your head, and then click the Accept button if you want to use the CD — after you click Accept, you'll never be bothered by the License Agreement window again.**

   The CD interface Welcome screen appears. The interface is a little program that shows you what's on the CD and coordinates installing the programs and running the demos. The interface basically enables you to click a button or two to make things happen.

6. **Click anywhere on the Welcome screen to enter the interface.**

   Now you are getting to the action. This next screen lists categories for the software on the CD.

7. **To view the items within a category, just click the category's name.**

   A list of programs in the category appears.

8. **For more information about a program, click the program's name.**

   Be sure to read the information that appears. Sometimes a program has its own system requirements or requires you to do a few tricks on your computer before you can install or run the program, and this screen tells you what you might need to do, if necessary.

9. **If you don't want to install the program, click the Go Back button to return to the previous screen.**

   You can always return to the previous screen by clicking the Go Back button. This feature allows you to browse the different categories and products and decide what you want to install.

10. **To install a program, click the appropriate Install button.**

    The CD interface drops to the background while the CD installs the program you chose.

11. **To install other items, repeat Steps 7–10.**

12. **When you've finished installing programs, click the Quit button to close the interface.**

You can eject the CD now. Carefully place it back in the plastic jacket of the book for safekeeping.

In order to run some of the programs on the *NetObjects Fusion 3 For Dummies* CD-ROM, you may need to keep the CD inside your CD-ROM drive. This is a Good Thing. Otherwise, the installed program would have required you to install a very large chunk of the program to your hard drive, which may have kept you from installing other software.

What You'll Find

Here's a summary of the software on this CD arranged by category. The CD interface helps you install software easily. (If you have no idea what I'm talking about when I say "CD interface," flip back a page or two to find the section, "Using the CD with Microsoft Windows.")

Web Tools category

NetObjects Fusion 3.0 Demo Version, from NetObjects

If you decided to buy this book before buying Fusion 3.0 just to get your feet wet, this demo version gives you the chance to play with the real thing before you commit your hard-earned money. The trial version is good for 30 days from the date you install it.

Microsoft Internet Explorer, from Microsoft

Internet Explorer is one of the two big cheeses in Web browsers. For best results, you should preview your Fusion Web sites in both IE and Netscape Navigator.

IMPORTANT NOTE: This software, if run under Windows NT 4.0, requires Service Pack 3 to run. If you do not have Service Pack 3, please visit the Microsoft Web site at www.microsoft.com. After installing it, continue the installation and follow the prompts on your screen to install the NT version of Internet Explorer.

Netscape Navigator, from Netscape Communications

The other big cheese in Web browsers. Make sure you preview your Fusion Web sites in both Navigator and Internet Explorer.

MindSpring Internet Access, from MindSpring Enterprises

In case you don't have a connection to the information superhighway, the CD includes sign-on software for MindSpring Internet Access, an Internet Service Provider.

This product only works with Windows 95.

After you are signed on, one of the first places you can check out is the RampUP Web site at www.mindspring.com/.

You need a credit card to sign up with MindSpring Internet Access.

If you already have an Internet Service Provider, please note that MindSpring Internet Access software makes changes to your computer's current Internet configuration and may replace your current settings. These changes may stop you from being able to access the Internet through your current provider.

Media Development category

Adobe Photoshop 4.0 Trial Version, from Adobe Systems

Photoshop is the premier tool for creating and editing still images, but it ain't cheap. You can try before you buy with this version, but you won't be able to save or print your work. Also, the trial version doesn't include all of the image filters you find in the full version.

DDClip Free 2.22, from SoftLab Nsk

This is the freeware version of DDClip, a great tool for editing both audio and video on your PC. If you like this program, you can download a trial version with more features, or purchase the full version with even more features than that, from the SoftLab Nsk Web site. The URL for the Web site is www.softlab-nsk.com.

Shockwave, from Macromedia

If you're going to add Shockwave multimedia elements to your Web page, you need to make sure whatever Web browser you're using supports either the Shockwave browser plug-in or ActiveX control, both of which are included here. These add-ons are freeware.

Elements for new SiteStyles, by John San Filippo and his friends in the IDG Books art department

NetObjects Fusion ships with plenty of Styles, but I wanted to provide you with a few of my own. Unfortunately, if I had to make my living as a graphic artist, I'd be living in a cardboard box. Thanks to the talents of the IDG Books art department, we were able to convert my ideas to graphic elements that you can use to create new Styles in NetObjects Fusion.

If You've Got Problems (Of the CD Kind)

I tried my best to compile programs that work on most computers with the minimum system requirements. Alas, your computer may differ, and some programs may not work properly for some reason.

The two likeliest problems are that you don't have enough memory (RAM) for the programs you want to use, or you have other programs running that are affecting installation or running of a program. If you get error messages like `Not enough memory` or `Setup cannot continue`, try one or more of these methods and then try using the software again:

- ✔ **Turn off any anti-virus software that you have on your computer.** Installers sometimes mimic virus activity and may make your computer incorrectly believe that it is being infected by a virus.

- ✔ **Close all running programs.** The more programs you're running, the less memory is available to other programs. Installers also typically update files and programs; if you keep other programs running, installation may not work properly.

- ✔ **Close the CD interface and run demos or installations directly from Windows Explorer.** The interface itself can tie up system memory, or even conflict with certain kinds of interactive demos. Use Windows Explorer to browse the files on the CD and launch installers or demos.

- ✔ **Have your local computer store add more RAM to your computer.** This may seem like a drastic step, but memory is pretty cheap these days. Adding more memory can really help the speed of your computer and enable more programs to run at the same time.

If you still have trouble installing the items from the CD, please call the IDG Books Worldwide Customer Service phone number: 800-762-2974 (outside the U.S.: 317-596-5430).

Index

• F •

(continued)

(continued)

• Q •

• R •

• *U* •

• *V* •

(continued)

• *Y* •

• *Z* •

Notes

Notes

IDG Books Worldwide, Inc., End-User License Agreement

READ THIS. You should carefully read these terms and conditions before opening the software packet(s) included with this book ("Book"). This is a license agreement ("Agreement") between you and IDG Books Worldwide, Inc. ("IDGB"). By opening the accompanying software packet(s), you acknowledge that you have read and accept the following terms and conditions. If you do not agree and do not want to be bound by such terms and conditions, promptly return the Book and the unopened software packet(s) to the place you obtained them for a full refund.

1. **License Grant.** IDGB grants to you (either an individual or entity) a nonexclusive license to use one copy of the enclosed software program(s) (collectively, the "Software") solely for your own personal or business purposes on a single computer (whether a standard computer or a workstation component of a multiuser network). The Software is in use on a computer when it is loaded into temporary memory (RAM) or installed into permanent memory (hard disk, CD-ROM, or other storage device). IDGB reserves all rights not expressly granted herein.

2. **Ownership.** IDGB is the owner of all right, title, and interest, including copyright, in and to the compilation of the Software recorded on the disk or CD-ROM ("Software Media"). Copyright to the individual programs recorded on the Software Media is owned by the author or other authorized copyright owner of each program. Ownership of the Software and all proprietary rights relating thereto remain with IDGB and its licensers.

3. **Restrictions on Use and Transfer.**

   (a) You may only (i) make one copy of the Software for backup or archival purposes, or (ii) transfer the Software to a single hard disk, provided that you keep the original for backup or archival purposes. You may not (i) rent or lease the Software, (ii) copy or reproduce the Software through a LAN or other network system or through any computer subscriber system or bulletin-board system, or (iii) modify, adapt, or create derivative works based on the Software.

   (b) You may not reverse engineer, decompile, or disassemble the Software. You may transfer the Software and user documentation on a permanent basis, provided that the transferee agrees to accept the terms and conditions of this Agreement and you retain no copies. If the Software is an update or has been updated, any transfer must include the most recent update and all prior versions.

4. **Restrictions on Use of Individual Programs.** You must follow the individual requirements and restrictions detailed for each individual program in the "What's on the CD?" section (Appendix B) of this Book. These limitations are also contained in the individual license agreements recorded on the Software Media. These limitations may include a requirement that after using the program for a specified period of time, the user must pay a registration fee or discontinue use. By opening the Software packet(s), you will be agreeing to abide by the licenses and restrictions for these individual programs that are detailed in the "What's on the CD?" section (Appendix B) and on the Software Media. None of the material on this Software Media or listed in this Book may ever be redistributed, in original or modified form, for commercial purposes.

5. **Limited Warranty.**

   (a) IDGB warrants that the Software and Software Media are free from defects in materials and workmanship under normal use for a period of sixty (60) days from the date of purchase of this Book. If IDGB receives notification within the warranty period of defects in materials or workmanship, IDGB will replace the defective Software Media.

   (b) IDGB AND THE AUTHOR OF THE BOOK DISCLAIM ALL OTHER WARRANTIES, EXPRESS OR IMPLIED, INCLUDING WITHOUT LIMITATION IMPLIED WARRANTIES OF MER-CHANTABILITY AND FITNESS FOR A PARTICULAR PURPOSE, WITH RESPECT TO THE SOFTWARE, THE PROGRAMS, THE SOURCE CODE CONTAINED THEREIN, AND/OR THE TECHNIQUES DESCRIBED IN THIS BOOK. IDGB DOES NOT WARRANT THAT THE FUNCTIONS CONTAINED IN THE SOFTWARE WILL MEET YOUR REQUIREMENTS OR THAT THE OPERATION OF THE SOFTWARE WILL BE ERROR FREE.

   (c) This limited warranty gives you specific legal rights, and you may have other rights that vary from jurisdiction to jurisdiction.

6. **Remedies.**

   (a) IDGB's entire liability and your exclusive remedy for defects in materials and workmanship shall be limited to replacement of the Software Media, which may be returned to IDGB with a copy of your receipt at the following address: Software Media Fulfillment Department, Attn.: *NetObjects Fusion 3 For Dummies,* IDG Books Worldwide, Inc., 7260 Shadeland Station, Ste. 100, Indianapolis, IN 46256, or call 800-762-2974. Please allow three to four weeks for delivery. This Limited Warranty is void if failure of the Software Media has resulted from accident, abuse, or misapplication. Any replacement Software Media will be warranted for the remainder of the original warranty period or thirty (30) days, whichever is longer.

   (b) In no event shall IDGB or the author be liable for any damages whatsoever (including without limitation damages for loss of business profits, business interruption, loss of business information, or any other pecuniary loss) arising from the use of or inability to use the Book or the Software, even if IDGB has been advised of the possibility of such damages.

   (c) Because some jurisdictions do not allow the exclusion or limitation of liability for conse-quential or incidental damages, the above limitation or exclusion may not apply to you.

7. **U.S. Government Restricted Rights.** Use, duplication, or disclosure of the Software by the U.S. Government is subject to restrictions stated in paragraph (c)(1)(ii) of the Rights in Technical Data and Computer Software clause of DFARS 252.227-7013, and in subparagraphs (a) through (d) of the Commercial Computer–Restricted Rights clause at FAR 52.227-19, and in similar clauses in the NASA FAR supplement, when applicable.

8. **General.** This Agreement constitutes the entire understanding of the parties and revokes and supersedes all prior agreements, oral or written, between them and may not be modified or amended except in a writing signed by both parties hereto that specifically refers to this Agreement. This Agreement shall take precedence over any other documents that may be in conflict herewith. If any one or more provisions contained in this Agreement are held by any court or tribunal to be invalid, illegal, or otherwise unenforceable, each and every other provision shall remain in full force and effect.

CD Installation Instructions

*T*o install the items from the CD to the hard drive of your Windows 95, 98, or NT PC, follow these steps:

1. **Insert the CD into your computer's CD-ROM drive.**

2. **Click Start⇨Run.**

3. **In the dialog box that appears, type** D:\SETUP.EXE.

   Replace *D* with the proper drive letter if your CD-ROM drive uses a different letter. (If you don't know the letter, see how your CD-ROM drive is listed under My Computer.)

4. **Click OK.**

   A license agreement window appears.

5. **Read through the license agreement, nod your head, and then click the Accept button if you want to use the CD — after you click Accept, you'll never be bothered by the License Agreement window again.**

   The CD interface Welcome screen appears. The interface is a little program that shows you what's on the CD and coordinates installing the programs and running the demos. The interface basically enables you to click a button or two to make things happen.

6. **Click anywhere on the Welcome screen to enter the interface.**

   Now you are getting to the action. This next screen lists categories for the software on the CD.

7. **To view the items within a category, just click the category's name.**

   A list of programs in the category appears.

8. **For more information about a program, click the program's name.**

   Be sure to read the information that appears. Sometimes a program has its own system requirements or requires you to do a few tricks on your computer before you can install or run the program, and this screen tells you what you might need to do, if necessary.

9. **To install a program, click the appropriate Install button.**

   The CD interface drops to the background while the CD installs the program you chose.

IDG BOOKS WORLDWIDE. BOOK REGISTRATION

We want to hear from you!

Visit **http://my2cents.dummies.com** to register this book and tell us how you liked it!

- ✔ Get entered in our monthly prize giveaway.

- ✔ Give us feedback about this book — tell us what you like best, what you like least, or maybe what you'd like to ask the author and us to change!

- ✔ Let us know any other *...For Dummies*® topics that interest you.

Your feedback helps us determine what books to publish, tells us what coverage to add as we revise our books, and lets us know whether we're meeting your needs as a *...For Dummies* reader. You're our most valuable resource, and what you have to say is important to us!

Not on the Web yet? It's easy to get started with *Dummies 101*®: *The Internet For Windows*® *95* or *The Internet For Dummies*, 5th Edition, at local retailers everywhere.

Or let us know what you think by sending us a letter at the following address:

...For Dummies Book Registration
Dummies Press
7260 Shadeland Station, Suite 100
Indianapolis, IN 46256-3945
Fax 317-596-5498

BUSINESS AND
GENERAL
REFERENCE
BOOK SERIES
FROM IDG

COMPUTER
BOOK SERIES
FROM IDG